beeline

beeline

What Spelling Bees Reveal About
Generation Z's New Path to Success

SHALINI SHANKAR

BASIC BOOKS
New York

Basic Books
Hachette Book Group
1290 Avenue of the Americas, New York, NY 10104
www.basicbooks.com

Printed in the United States of America
First Edition: April 2019

Published by Basic Books, an imprint of Perseus Books, LLC, a subsidiary of Hachette Book Group, Inc. The Basic Books name and logo is a trademark of the Hachette Book Group.

The Hachette Speakers Bureau provides a wide range of authors for speaking events. To find out more, go to www.hachettespeakersbureau.com or call (866) 376-6591.

The publisher is not responsible for websites (or their content) that are not owned by the publisher.

Print book interior design by Six Red Marbles Inc.

The Library of Congress has cataloged the hardcover edition as follows:
Names: Shankar, Shalini, 1972– author.
Title: Beeline : what spelling bees reveal about generation Z's new path to
    success / Shalini Shankar.
Description: First edition. | New York, NY : Basic Books, [2019] | Includes
    bibliographical references and index.
Identifiers: LCCN 2018043156 (print) | LCCN 2018044318 (ebook) |
    ISBN 9780465094530 (ebook) | ISBN 9780465094523 (hardcover)
Subjects: LCSH: Success in children. | Generation Z. | Spelling bees—Social
    aspects. | Performance in children. | Achievement motivation in children.
Classification: LCC BF723.S77 (ebook) | LCC BF723.S77 S53 2019 (print) |
    DDC 155.4/19—dc23
LC record available at https://lccn.loc.gov/2018043156

ISBNs: 978-0-465-09452-3 (hardcover), 978-0-465-09453-0 (ebook)

LSC-C

10 9 8 7 6 5 4 3 2 1

For Shyamala and Ratnaswamy Shankar,
who told me I could be whatever I wanted.

For Anisha and Roshan, my Generation Z loves.

Contents

Introduction

On a Thursday night in May of 2012, I sat in my living room folding laundry and watching the Scripps National Spelling Bee finals on ESPN.[1] Only 10 finalists had advanced from 278. If those odds sound bad, consider that those 278 emerged from over 11 million children. The kids I saw on-screen were confident, poised, and diverse, representing an amazing cross section of America.

The oldest spellers on that stage were fourteen; spellers as young as six had been eliminated earlier in the contest. Born after 1996, they were the first competitors of Generation Z, the generation following Millennials (born between 1981 and 1996) that still awaits an official name.

It had been a few years since I'd caught the contest live, and things looked different. Cosmetically, the kids were no longer all wearing standard-issue white shirts bearing the spelling bee logo. The backdrop was a gorgeous blue honeycomb that changed color to reflect the onstage action. The competition was fierce, more so than I remembered.

Despite the stakes, some spellers made funny quips when they came to the mic, while others greeted the pronouncer (the person who gives each speller their word and any information they request) in Latin, Hindi, or Spanish. Clearly, they were enjoying their moment in the spotlight. No one I went to middle school with had this kind of game, especially with ten cameras pointed at them as they performed an astonishing cognitive task. Who were these kids? I started to wonder why any young person would take this competition so seriously, what it meant to them, and how they managed to stay so effortlessly cool under pressure.

The producers had anticipated my questions and frequently cut to captivating human-interest feature stories. Some were shot in kids' homes and schools, capturing the hometown flavor of a speller's life. Not only were these kids orthographically advanced, but they were also dancers, magicians, model car racers, horse-back riders, and aspiring chefs. They spoke eloquently about these interests in scripted voiceovers. In other feature segments, spellers engagingly held up oversized cards comically explaining the rules of the Bee or otherwise had what looked like a fun time. Apparently, the kids had been there all week, making friends as they attended social events and presentations about the dictionary. They eagerly anticipated a banquet and dance party with lots of candy the following night.

Over the course of the broadcast, I got to know so many of these telegenic, camera-ready kids that I became conflicted about whom to cheer for. I wanted all of them to win, but which ones actually could? I realized I could answer this question if I listened more closely to the commentators as they analyzed each speller's turn, treating them like professional athletes. They knew each one's strengths and weaknesses, telling me about their favorite languages of origin and their foibles with the dreaded schwa (the unstressed vowel sound in the middle of many words). Spellers were ready to break down their strategy for sideline reporters who occasionally pulled them out of the lineup to comment on an especially tough word.

The spectacle called into question so much that I thought I understood about childhood and young people today. The kids at the spelling bee—with their intense approach to competition, their confident personalities, and their drive to succeed— embodied key characteristics about what it now means to be young in America. It foretold something about the future of my own children, then age six and two, who were blissfully asleep while I watched. Whether they would ever participate in a spelling bee was not important; this is what childhood had become, and this was their generation.

In the end, there were no participation trophies. Not even a runner-up trophy. Just one giant, shiny trophy that fourteen-year-old Snigdha Nandipati from San Diego, California, clenched and hoisted, beaming a smile too victorious for her mouthful of braces to diminish. For the next week she was ubiquitous on the media junket of morning shows, public relations appearances, and even *Jimmy Kimmel Live!* When the media buzz wore off, she could start to imagine what to do with her $30,000 in prize money.[2]

What started with my television viewing would develop into a major research project that extended far beyond spelling bees. Through the lens of the Bee, I began to explore the nascent shape of Generation Z. These kids' lives are filled with competitions, many of them brain sports like the spelling bee. More than just fun, the careers—and I do mean careers—that elite spellers develop open doorways to other aspects of Gen Z life, including greater participation in entrepreneurial activities and social media as children. Their parents—mostly US- or non-US-born Gen Xers who want their kids to thrive in a world they know is highly competitive—help them accomplish as children what previous generations may not have even attempted until adulthood.

I attended the National Spelling Bee every year from 2013 to 2018, plus twelve regional and minor-league bees. I interviewed past and present National Spelling Bee semifinalists and finalists, including seventeen champions, as well as parents and numerous adults whose livelihood is in some way connected to spelling bees. I visited ESPN in Bristol, Connecticut, and spent days in their studio at the Bee, watching speller features being filmed. I spent hundreds of hours observing, talking with, and getting to know elite spellers and their families over several years, seeing them once or multiple times a year at different competitions. The kids I met early on were in college by the time I finished my research.

Through the stories of these elite spellers, *Beeline* presents an understanding of the new childhood of Generation Z. It argues that this generation exemplifies a unique phase of childhood that is the product of heightened competition for kids, distinct US- and non-US-born parenting styles, and the affordances of social media. The book investigates several broad questions that parents face: What is the right balance for kids between competition, play, and preparing for professional life? Which parenting styles are best suited for childhood now? Can the contributions of immigrants mean something more impactful for Gen Z? And how is American society responding to these dramatic changes? Focusing on the intensity of kids' lives today, it draws on studies in anthropology, education, child-rearing, language, and culture, and my own experiences as a Gen Xer, child of immigrants, and parent of two Gen Z kids.

The chapters connect the rise of competition to shifts in generational characteristics and immigration and examine how childhood is becoming increasingly professionalized. Chapter 1, "Kids Today," lays out the basics of generation, childhood, and immigration. Chapter 2, "Brain Sports and Kid Competitions," and Chapter 3, "Spelling Bees," delve into the intricacies of the contests, looking at the rise of brain sports and how they are linked to human capital building, focusing in particular on spelling bees. Chapter 4, "Gen Z Kids," and Chapter 5, "Parents of Gen Z Kids," provide in-depth looks at what gives America's newest generational cohort its distinct character. Chapter 6, "Bee Week," Chapter 7, "Becoming Elite," and Chapter 8, "Making Spellebrities," together capture the training, performance, and media presence that make spelling bees today so intense and captivating. Chapter 9, "Professionalizing Childhoods," and my conclusion, "Gen Z Futures," look at how kids transition from elite spelling to becoming highly paid spelling coaches, giving TEDx Talks, attending incubators and founding start-up companies, and pursuing other things not usually done in high school.

Unless, of course, you are a Gen Z kid.

Chapter One

Kids Today

Thirteen-year-old Sai Chandrasekhar strode up to the mic during the semifinal round of the 2015 National Spelling Bee with the confidence of someone who had nothing to lose. This was not the case. Sai had spent three years preparing for this high-stakes competition. She was focused on surviving the two semifinal rounds and advancing into the coveted live finals on ESPN. Only a dozen or so kids make it each year. While she was grateful to be on the stage at the Gaylord National Resort and Convention Center in National Harbor, Maryland, just south of Washington, DC, she badly wanted to go further.

Ready to start, Sai paused when the competition director signaled her to wait. Auditorium lights dimmed and we turned our attention to the two giant screens flanking the stage. We watched Sai's speller feature while television audiences saw it on ESPN2. Sai loves this aspect of being in the Bee, she'd tell me later that summer. "It's so cool. It's the only way I'll be on ESPN!"

Sai's feature is captivating. It showcases her daily commute from Flushing, Queens, to the Upper East Side of Manhattan on the New York City subway. On a good day, it takes her forty-five minutes to get to Hunter College High School, where she attends middle school. On camera, Sai tells viewers that the building used to be a weapons armory and looks like a brick prison—no windows. Hunter is one of the most competitive public schools in New York City, with a gifted and talented program that she tested into in kindergarten. As she rides the 7 train, she gazes at the New York City skyline. She loves photography, telling viewers, "I probably have, like, a thousand pictures on my phone." She plays clarinet, is a midfielder on her school's lacrosse team, and likes to ice skate. She speaks Tamil and Spanish. Sai has long had a passion for language and has been an avid reader since she was a toddler.

The audience applauded enthusiastically when the feature concluded. If they had liked her before, they seemed especially impressed with her afterward.

All eyes were back on Sai as she stood onstage. She wore her thick hair in two plump braids with a middle part. Her striped cardigan was part of her signature look, along with a plaid shirt, jeans, and black Nikes with a white swoosh. Her casual style was a counterpoint to the clinical poise she demonstrated each turn at the mic. Unlike spellers who fidget, mumble, or wear anxiety on their faces, Sai remained calm.

Sai was not always such a cool competitor. She had to learn how to manage her excitement about her extensive word knowledge. She remembers misspelling *gingivitis* in a Manhattan bee in 2013 simply because she was so excited to recognize the word. Now when Sai gets a word onstage, she tries to visualize it in print. She writes the letters out on her palm and thinks about which version looks better based on what she is hearing. Sai has learned to go with her first instinct, even under the time constraints. "I'm fine with the time limit. It makes you think schematically, and I like that. I don't second-guess, I just spell it." Sai regards the Bee as a sport and thinks the mental strength and capacity needed to compete at this level should be celebrated.

Sai positioned herself at the microphone. She had some stage experience through her school debate team and playing the clarinet, but nothing quite like this. To handle it, she tells herself, "Don't focus on the cameras. Cameras are not there to hurt, just to document. Being distracted by them isn't what you're here for. You have to focus on the pronouncer and what you're doing." She smiled directly at Jacques Bailly, the 1980 National Spelling Bee champion and now pronouncer, and awaited her word.

Littoral, relating to the seashore. Sai's smile grew into a grin as she repeated it back.

Sai is extraordinary in many ways, but not unusual. At age thirteen, she has a public persona, has been the subject of several media features, has won national contests, and has participated in a staggering array of extracurricular activities. The opportunities available during childhood, as well as the number of activities young people choose to take on, has changed dramatically from past generations.

Now kids are doing in elementary and middle school what older Millennials were expected to do in high school and college. They have resumes, become Instagram and YouTube stars, establish corporations, and offer coaching services at pricey hourly rates. With the help of their parents, but driven by their own goals, they earn thousands of dollars, and in some cases, millions.

Many are interested in politics, current events, travel, and self-actualization. As I discovered over the course of my research, time management is something they learn to navigate early on in their heavily scheduled lives.

Like any national competition, the National Spelling Bee is the most challenging platform in the field of spelling. It has been dubbed the "orthographic Super Bowl" and has grown to fit that title.[1] The competition to get there intensifies each year. Since the 1990s, the size of the Bee has nearly doubled. Of the 11 million kids who participate in spelling bees annually, what used to be around 150 competitors has burgeoned to north of 500. Of those, no more than 50 advance past the preliminary rounds, and about a dozen are featured in the live championship finals broadcast during prime time on ESPN. The competitors I met during my research at the National Spelling Bee belong to Generation Z, born 1997 onward. They bring a distinctive approach to competition, self-presentation, and what it means to win.

Where does this drive come from, and how have children today learned to navigate the complicated path to success? Intense competition is now an openly acknowledged and routine part of childhood outside of the school day. Travel sports, televised contests, academic fairs, and game tournaments are standard fare for elementary school kids.

Even those who don't aspire to be national competitors still understand the playing field. My twelve-year-old son and eight-year-old daughter are like many middle-class children with a variety of extracurricular activities and interests. Like their peers, they are accustomed to thinking about time management, competition, and goals. Their friends compete in chess tournaments and science fairs, travel for soccer, and are on dance teams. On television, they see kids their age win cooking shows and face off against adults on *The Voice*. People don't tell them they are too young for anything because now there is a junior version of nearly every adult contest. They are not expected to just imagine their adult lives but to begin living them right away. The question has shifted from "What do you want to be when you grow up?" to simply "What do you want to be?"

As with any generation so new, few things are agreed upon about Generation Z. Two things are certain: they have had greater exposure to digital culture than any previous generation, and they are the most racially and ethnically diverse generation in US history. Marketers have taken the lead in sketching the contours of Generation Z, aiming to characterize their consumer and media tastes as young children, tweens, and teens. *Beeline* offers an anthropological counterpoint to those market-driven definitions. Parents, teachers, and anyone wishing to understand this generation can also do so by observing how it is a product of changes in childhood, the growing influence of immigrants, generationally distinct parenting styles, and kids defining themselves through social and broadcast media. Much can be learned from looking at National Spelling Bee participants, studying them closely as bellwethers of Generation Z.

Kate Miller entered the semifinal rounds of the 2014 National Spelling Bee with a powerful secret. The previous night, she'd received her score from the written test that spellers take to qualify for finals. After breezing through her preliminary-round words, *maelstrom* and *weevil*—child's play for a speller of Kate's caliber—she did well enough on the finals test to advance to the live prime-time competition if she could just make it through two onstage rounds of the semifinals. Kate had exceeded even her own expectations and had no intention of stopping. Just two words to spell correctly. She had spelled so many over her years of competition, what were two more?

Kate is from Abilene, a midsize town in West Texas. She is tall and slender, with wide, animated eyes and the long, smooth, straight hair of shampoo commercials. She had come a long way since she first became interested in spelling. When she was six, she watched her younger brother Jack playing with refrigerator magnets, making simple words. She decided it looked fun, and that she could do it better. Watching the National Spelling Bee on television that year piqued her curiosity further, and she became inspired by what she saw. Kate's mom explained to her that only the most accomplished, prepared spellers advance through regionals to the national bee. "I had no idea what it was like, but if the best spellers were there, I wanted to go. Early on, I developed a strong passion and that dream."

Kate won her first school spelling bee in second grade, when she was eight years old. Despite dominating her school bee again in the third and fourth grades, she had to wait until fifth grade to compete in regionals due to a minimum age requirement. Fifth grade came; Kate easily won her school and district bees and made it to the regional competition. She tied for fourth place. In sixth grade, she started to study word lists devotedly, determined to win at regionals and advance to nationals. That year, she made it to the National Spelling Bee. She was elated, but also didn't know what to expect. Each year, the National Spelling Bee modifies its format to suit the needs of that year's competition. In 2012, she would take a written spelling test before onstage competition, and a second if she was named a semifinalist. Between these tests she would spell onstage twice in preliminaries, and twice again in semifinals. If she spelled correctly onstage and had a high enough score, she would advance to the finals. Kate aced her two preliminary-round words, *fougade*, a type of land mine, and *trepak*, a Ukrainian folk dance. Her test score for semifinals was not high enough.[2]

Seventh grade was a big year for Kate. She handily won her regional bee and traveled to Washington. A new twist awaited. It was 2013, and the National Spelling Bee had just introduced vocabulary as part of the written tests. Like many of her 281 fellow competitors, Kate was less prepared for this aspect of the competition and missed semifinals by one point. She still managed to enjoy her time at the Bee, coming in contact with a world of word-lovers and connecting with one other speller in particular, Amber Born.

Amber is the first person Kate remembers meeting at her first Bee in 2012. They both returned to find each other in 2013. They had ample opportunity to socialize at Bee Week, the week of events that feels like a cross between summer camp and an orthography conference. When the three of us spoke on Skype in 2014, Kate reminded Amber, "We were nervous, and I thought you seemed smart, so I said you'd make it to semifinals and you did!" Amber progressed to finals, and Kate cheered her on. It solidified the bond that would make them BSFFs (best spelling friends forever).

Watching Amber advance, and realizing she had only one year left to compete, Kate completely gave herself over to training. As part of her practice, Kate participated in mock spelling bees on Facebook with other spellers. One person was the pronouncer and streamed a video of themselves saying the word, and the others spelled. They'd keep going until someone won, training together to hone their skills.

Kate's approach to spelling bees illustrates why they are considered brain sports, as one parent described them to me. They demand rigor and offer competition on a cerebral level, with great potential reward. As a brain sport, spelling bees offer an interesting window into childhood because they are age restricted. The oldest competitors are predominantly eighth graders, ages fourteen or fifteen.[3] The youngest are six. When you consider the kind of aspiration, discipline, and notoriety surrounding this activity, it is astounding that children take it on so early. What's more, spelling study at Kate's level can take over a kid's life, reorganizing the day-to-day rhythms of childhood. Those who become elite spellers manage and structure their time meticulously. As children do with other sports, young spellers build stamina and focus to become experts, often while taking on numerous other activities.

Until 2018, the only way to get to the National Spelling Bee was to win a regional contest and secure sponsorship from a newspaper or other business, organization, or institution. That changed in 2018 when Scripps introduced the RSVBee program that granted an additional 240 invitational spots, with spellers paying a participation fee and covering their own travel and lodging costs. Adding these wild-card spots has only increased the difficulty level of this competition, which has become much more challenging than a decade ago, when vocabulary was not assessed. The addition of vocabulary tests and several other rounds of written exams makes advancing through the contest dependent on test scores, not just spelling onstage. Many past and present spellers confirm that the difficulty of the competition continues to increase every year as the top competitors arrive better prepared and can thus handle more challenging words.

Gen Z spellers like Kate and Sai can be highly motivated without becoming ruthless in their pursuit of success. Their generation strives to be socially aware and admires those who add value to the world. They aim to make the world a better place and care about their public reputation as they do so. Like Millennials' childhoods, Gen Z's are highly organized. Millennials were the first to experience the hyper-scheduled childhood, with playdates and a packed slate of after-school and weekend activities. Taking this approach one step further, Gen Z kids are not only goal oriented and geared toward productivity, but can be intense competitors. They value success and acknowledge the challenges and sacrifices required. Participation trophies are meaningless, numerous kids told me. This is one of the key differences from Millennials, the "everybody gets a trophy" generation. I mean this not as a critique but as a fact: for Gen Z, winning, rather than effort, is acknowledged and rewarded.

As a sixth grader, Sai's focused preparation allowed her to accomplish in a few months what some spellers could not with years of study. Sixth grade is considered a late start in the world of elite spelling. By comparison, her fellow competitors may have started winning local bees as early as kindergarten or first grade. Without question, Sai is gifted. But she is also an innovative, self-directed problem solver. Part of her preparation involved charting a course toward her stated goal. The first year was about "testing it out, figuring out what competitive spelling is. I'd only learned there was a national bee a couple of months before it happened!" In a region as competitive as New York City, where Sai lived, making it to the Bee on one's first try after only preparing for a few months was astounding.

Sai was twelve when she arrived at her first National Spelling Bee in 2013. Wide-eyed and in unknown territory, Sai kept her composure and spelled correctly through the two preliminary rounds, withstanding a long first day of competition. She tested one point shy of semifinals and did not advance. "My loss drove me to tears," she admitted. But Sai was determined not to let her newly minted spelling career end in failure.

Sai and Kate, like so many of the kids I met, are more than simply hardworking. They have become great at what they do. And they persevere in the face of failure. What makes someone good at something, and why they stick with it, is a topic of some contention. Social psychologist Angela Duckworth has identified this as "grit."[4] It is what keeps people invested in succeeding at certain activities, even when they are not required to. For instance, there is no elementary education requirement for kids to learn the dictionary. Yet this is what some kids decide to do. Duckworth does not link grit to talent, as being talented at something does not necessarily make one persevere. Yet so many of the elite spellers I met wanted to do just that, and succeed.

How someone becomes an expert is also a relevant question to ask here. Journalist Malcolm Gladwell employs the concept of "deliberate practice" to suggest ten thousand hours of focused activity.[5] Others argue that some people are simply prodigies, and that hours alone won't matter if the person does not have an affinity and ability for the activity in question. In spelling competitions, practice undoubtedly does influence how far someone can progress and how they fare against others with greater talents.

It should come as no surprise that grit is required to do something as difficult and isolating as preparing for a national contest of any kind. Competitive spelling certainly calls for it. Answering a 2015 press conference question about what it takes to become a spelling champion, Scripps National Spelling Bee Executive Director Paige Kimble said that to become *the* champion takes "a lot of determination and an awful lot of hard work." She explained that all 285 kids that year were well-read and knowledgeable in word patterns, and that they were already champions of their regional contests. The elite spellers I met were willing to put in the hours over months and years to become a champion. They knew it might not be the final outcome, but it was their goal.

The most curious part of grit is what keeps people invested in an activity, especially in the face of failure. Psychology professor Carol Dweck addresses this matter through the concept of "growth mindset."[6] That is, the ability to learn is not fixed. Capabilities can grow in response to challenge. Failure, then, is not a permanent condition, as long as one is willing to get back into the game. This disposition toward failure is very reminiscent of what I observed in Silicon Valley in the late 1990s. During the dot-com bubble, there was no fear of failure at all. Failing at something—a start-up, a venture capital investment, or a career path—was seen as a learning experience. Sometimes it was even celebrated as a precursor for something better to come. Failing a few times could be a recipe for success. It was certainly not grounds for quitting.

Grit and growth mindset are part of what it takes to be an elite speller, as numerous kids demonstrated with their approach to studying and competing. Some of them made it to the National Spelling Bee each year only to fail to progress past the preliminary or semifinal rounds. Yet they didn't walk away from this activity. Sai's spelling philosophy, developed over her spelling career, captured this approach to competition: "Failure isn't not winning; it's not keeping it together, not being a good competitor. Winning is about keeping it together and being a good competitor as much as actually winning. People might tell you this, but it doesn't register until you do it. So that's been an important part of my growth." Playing hard, win or lose, is a very Gen Z concept.

Giving up never felt like an option for Sai. To prepare for the 2014 Bee, she spent the year working with her science teacher, who coached aspiring spellers. He had won an adult spelling bee that year, and she was one of three kids selected to go to his classroom each day at lunch for word lists and quizzes. Under his tutelage, Sai studied words and learned how to recognize word patterns. She came in first in her school, then in Manhattan, and then won the New York City regionals. When she took the written test for semifinals at the 2014 Bee, she received what she thought was a high score for that year. It turned out that her score was right at the cutoff. "I made it by the skin of my bones!" she exclaimed charmingly, adding that the minimum needed was so much higher than she expected. "It woke me up a little. Yeah, I made it to the national bee, but I still had to be on my toes." That year she spelled correctly in the semifinals but didn't score high enough to make it to finals.

I met Sai in 2014, when she had a year left in her spelling career. Like Kate, she was very warm and friendly, and her parents gave me their contact information. I planned to get in touch over the summer, since Bee Week is a time when kids are preoccupied with the contest while also focused on hanging out with their friends. This atmosphere was great to observe but didn't suit the lengthier interviews I hoped to conduct. When I contacted Mrs. Chandrasekhar, she warmly invited me to their home in Queens and said she would be happy to be interviewed as well. I drove to Flushing from Brooklyn on a sweltering Sunday morning in August. Finding parking was unusually easy, as many New York City families had fled the urban heat. As I walked from my car to Sai's building, I felt an eerie sense of familiarity. I had lived in this neighborhood for seven years when my family first moved to the United States from India in 1973.

I didn't realize until I approached her building on foot that we had resided in the very same apartment complex. As a child, I had memorized the address for my building on Colden Street, one of the two thoroughfares lining the complex. Sai's was on Kissena Boulevard, an address I had never learned. Kids skateboarded around me as I remembered playing in that same spot decades ago. The four large apartment buildings with a circular driveway, children's park, walking paths, and benches looked frozen in time. But from what I already knew of Sai and other spelling bee kids, along with my own experience as a parent, everything else about kids' lives had changed.

Sai's mom warmly welcomed me into their apartment, and I met Sai's younger sister and father on their way out to the park. We began our conversation about Sai's spelling career, the third and final year of which lay ahead.

Remarkably, it is becoming the norm to have a career, or even multiple careers, as a child. What kids in this world call a spelling career is analogous to how their peers approach chess meets, dance competitions, travel soccer, gourmet cooking, or whatever passion a previous generation might not have cultivated as early in life. Gen Z elite spellers I met are not only nationally ranked in spelling. They have also won the North American School Scrabble Championship, like 2016 National Spelling Bee finalist Cooper Komatsu.[7] The 2015 National Spelling Bee co-champion Vanya Shivashankar was also named the winner of the reality show *Child Genius* that year. After crowd favorite Shreyas Parab wrapped up his spelling career at fourteen, he became a nationally recognized entrepreneur by his sophomore year of high school.

Not so long ago, television shows featuring children could be summed up as "Kids say the darndest things!" In their innocence, they made endearing social mistakes and inserted themselves awkwardly into situations once associated with adulthood. Nowadays, media representations feature kids as preternaturally mature and poised, experts in their chosen field. Consider the slew of televised competitions that now have "junior" versions: *Top Chef*, *MasterChef*, and *Project Runway*, just to name a few. Contestants can be as young as eight, wielding professional kitchen tools and working with fire. Younger teenagers are regular contestants on *The Voice*. The show *Little Big Shots* features extraordinarily young children who bring their complex talents to a national audience. *Dancing with the Stars: Juniors* is a 2018 follower of this trend.

Gen Z kids are not just famous on television. Born into a digital, screen-filled world, they welcome the chance to use communicative platforms and experience notoriety outside their school and community. Certainly not all Gen Z kids have the same fluency with these interfaces, and not all of them will develop the skills to build a social media fandom. Yet many I met have recorded TEDx Talks and enjoy huge followings on Instagram, Twitter, Facebook, YouTube, and Google Groups.

Such focus on becoming an accomplished expert early in life poses questions about balance and time management. I suspect I am like many parents who grapple with how to handle their child's schedule. My son has played Little League every spring for the past five years. His coaches are wonderful, the parents supportive, and he is learning how to be a team player. His team won't make it to the Little League World Series, and their practice is focused but not deliberate. Every week of the season, he spends anywhere between five and ten hours on practices and games. When combined with school, homework, other after-school activities, and the good workout he gets by playing this sport, it definitely takes a toll. My husband and I had decided it was worthwhile because we value team sports and think the fresh air and exercise are good for him. Recently, though, I have begun to rethink what exactly he gets out of it. Especially when I watch him swelter on an eighty-degree day in swirls of dust, weighed down by a catcher's mask, leg guards, and a chest guard, I ask myself if this is really the best use of his time.

If I continue to emphasize balance and expose him and my daughter to a range of activities, do I miss the chance to develop their brains differently to become experts in something through deliberate practice? My parents seem to have avoided this existential dilemma. They emigrated from India to the United States in 1973. They are both well educated—my father has an Indian Institutes of Technology (IIT) Madras master's degree in engineering, and my mother studied journalism and worked for the *Times of India*. What's fascinating to me is that my immigrant father put my brother in Little League and never thought twice about it. Like most immigrant families, they were concerned with social and economic security. I also know that their children's success wasn't contingent on my brother or me becoming experts in anything by middle school. It was the 1980s, and things were simply not as competitive for us Gen Xers.

Young Gen Zers are becoming experts and developing childhood careers, but to what end? Considering this question across generations can be illustrative. In his book about Millennials, journalist and Millennial Malcolm Harris argues that his is the first generation raised for their human capital, or the expertise and skills people build that have market value.[8] From a young age, Millennials were told that doing internships and building one's skills in a number of areas were as important in childhood as learning basic algebra. This is consistent with broader shifts in the skilled job market. Over the decades since World War II, employers have invested less in developing new skills in their employees, both out of concern that their investment would not pay off if their employees left and because, increasingly, people entered the market with far better developed skill sets and more human capital. According to Harris, however, Millennials spent too much of their childhood developing human capital. Sectors of the job market became saturated with overqualified applicants, leading him to argue that his generation would have been better off enjoying childhood.

For better or worse, there is no turning back for Generation Z. Already a large cohort, they are accustomed to competing from a young age and watching their peers do the same. They work hard to become young social media influencers and entrepreneurs. They participate in incubators that hone their business skills and found corporations run only by the eighteen-and-under set.

For Gen Z elite spellers, the obvious next step after a successful spelling career is to become a spelling coach. These entrepreneurial fifteen- and sixteen-year-olds decide what to charge on a freelance basis—anywhere between $35 and $100 an hour—or work for tutoring companies that pay them even more while charging students over twice that amount. Some spellers, especially those who worked with a parent or teacher as a coach, express concern about the monetization of spelling coaching. Those who do it, however, see it as a natural application of their years of dedicated work and expertise.

There are certainly opponents to the notion that childhood should be productive. They tend to be adults—often Baby Boomers or older Gen Xers—who yearn for a simpler time, when being a successful young person meant lots of playtime, recreational sports, a modest array of extracurricular activities, and grades and SAT scores commensurate with their college aspirations. Admittedly, I am one of those people who sometimes wishes it all wasn't so intense and competitive for my children. In my day, kids competed in the spelling bee, but no one had spelling careers. There were no serialized child cooking shows offering major cash prizes. Being a "child genius" was not conferred by the eponymous reality show on the Lifetime network. Even the 1980s sitcom teenage doctor Doogie Howser, MD, looks like a slacker now, based on what many young people have accomplished before they get to high school. Being a slacker used to have some cachet, at least for those with a financial safety net. If I've learned one thing from researching and writing this book, it is that those days are completely over.

Another vital question in the human capital discussion is who is economically and socially positioned to build it? Many kids I met at the Bee have a great deal of support, nurture, and resources that bolster them as they compete at the national level. Even amid the striking racial and ethnic diversity of the hundreds of kids who compete in the Bee each year, economic diversity is sadly lacking. Spelling bees, like many high-powered extracurricular activities today, require significant investments of time and money.

To be an elite speller, having a coach is essential, whether that means hiring someone or having a stay-at-home parent devoted to filling that role. Despite Scripps engineering the fairest contest possible, the level of competition has become so intense that promising young people who do not have financial support may not realize their abilities or can't competitively develop their skills. The stakes are getting higher by every metric, including financial outlay, human capital, time, and energy.

Kate's time-management abilities rival any adult's, and she oversees her own packed slate of activities. Spelling, dance, sports, friends, and mentoring are just a few of her extracurriculars. She has made sacrifices in the name of spelling, including missing school dances, social events, and screen time to be an elite speller. Kate believes she can do it all. "You just have to use your time well, which I eventually learned to do," she said, responding graciously to my bewilderment about how she fits it all in. When I asked if she misses being out with friends, at the pool, at the mall, or doing nothing, she assured me with a smile, "Oh, I do some nothing. About an hour a month, I do some nothing."

Some outside observers might call Kate overscheduled. One could look at this picture of aspiration and competition and see a dark side: hyper-preparation, anxiety, and burnout. These are not new topics for those opposed to kid competitions. About a decade ago, critics were concerned about putting children on television. Writing in 2006, *New York Times* education reporter Tamar Lewin questioned whether we should be televising "America's children" in live broadcasts, in particular the National Spelling Bee.[9] The article echoed others of its time, critiquing kids' intense approach to competition and the unhealthy attitudes their parents may bring.

Like it or not, intense, often televised competition has become a fixture of childhood. The debate now is over how kids manage the expectations they place on themselves and what kind of toll it might take. Anxiety is frequently ranked as one of the most prevalent yet undertreated ailments in childhood today.[10] Considering how young elite spellers are and the numerous other interests they take on alongside spelling, this is not surprising. Spellers assured me that they have reasonable expectations for their performance. With the Bee having only one winner each year (or in rare instances, two), they are far more focused on pushing themselves to personally advance in the contest than they are stressed about winning it all. Some do get anxious, but they also seem to have strategies to manage their nerves throughout the contest.

The kids I met during my years attending spelling bees were thrilled to have made it to nationals. Some had been looking forward to the contest all year. Whether they were happy about everything they had to do to get there is less clear to me. For most, hours of studying and regional competitions are regarded with a mix of diligence, curiosity, amusement, frustration, tears, and satisfaction. They became ecstatic at the possibility of being on television and savor that experience. They thrive in this high-risk, high-reward culture.

They also greatly value the social aspects of the spelling bee world, including making friendships during Bee Week and staying connected via email and social media throughout the year. Kate is involved in a speller society called the Order of the Squushy Carrots. It had over one hundred members when she served as vice president, because "anyone in the Bee can be in it, they just have to ask." She was very particular in pointing out that they are not a clique, but rather a group of friends with much goodwill toward one another. For Gen Z kids, it is the norm to keep connected on social media, but in ways that are inclusive.

Onstage, Kate "air types." Much to the fascination of journalists, photographers, and ESPN on-air hosts, she moves her lithe fingers deliberately on an imaginary keyboard in front of her. Sometimes she air types while silently voicing letters before saying them aloud. The enthusiastic clicking of cameras eager to capture her in action simulate a keyboard soundtrack. When Kate is interviewed by ESPN hosts, it is the first thing they want to know about. How did she develop her strategy and what does it do for her? "I see the letters in my mind. It's like I have a screen in my mind, so I see the letters appearing."

Kate told them it was a study habit she cultivated in second grade and never stopped doing. "It's only natural I'd use it as a learning device, both to externalize my reckless energy as well as bring the word to me and order my thoughts." Momentarily stunned by her complex and articulate remark, the hosts scrambled to jot down the eloquent answer. Patiently waiting for the adults to catch up, Kate added, "But there is no backspace key. Once you say a letter you can't go back!" Precise and exacting, the technique would give her the best chance of correctly spelling the words she had painstakingly learned over several years. All the better if the cameras adored it.

At fourteen, Kate describes her love of language as an infatuation, using words she likes in her interactions and writing. "I like to slip my wacky words, and good words, into conversation." She demonstrates this quirky approach in her second ESPN feature, where she spells her favorite word, *absquatulate,* to hide. Kate jokingly suggests revising the name of the common childhood game to "absquatulate and seek." She likes watching people's expressions when she's suffering from a headache and tells people she has *cephalalgia.* "People would act like I had a terminal disease!" she exclaims gleefully. Using fancy synonyms and not saying *awesome* and *like* as much are her long-term pragmatic goals. Kate has more dictionaries in her private collection than her local library owns. "Eleven," she proudly states. "The library only has five."

Kate is homeschooled but also takes courses at a high school. She admits that she is more competitive with herself than she is with anyone else. After the 2013 Bee, she took her preparation to new heights. "I took a spelling book with me wherever I went," she told me. She described her mindset as "obsessed. I do school, exercise, sleep, and spelling," but not in that order. During her final year of eligibility, Kate designed a training regimen of sixteen hours a week in the fall, building up to twenty-five hours a week by spring. Kate researched and planned her course of study. She listened to interviews of advanced spellers for tips and tried to figure out which words were likely to appear in different rounds as the Bee increased in difficulty. "Last year I got out on vocab, and this year I made sure I knew the meaning of every word I could spell," she explained.

Like everyone else who had spent serious time on this activity, Kate wanted to figure out which words would be semifinal-level words, which were finals-worthy, and which might be reserved for the championship round, when there were three or fewer contestants remaining. But that was the hardest thing to decode. "Oh, I felt overwhelmed," Kate admitted readily. Homeschooling had left her less practiced at taking tests. She relied on the Scripps online practice test for preliminaries. She was determined to beat her previous finish and make it to semifinals. "I focused on semifinals. *My dream in life* was to make it to semifinals!"

Kate eventually just sat down with the dictionary. Recording her daily progress, she enlisted her mom to quiz her every two weeks. "I did most of my studying independently," she told me, but added, "It's a family effort." She won at regionals in 2014. When she got to the Bee, she felt confident that she knew all of the vocabulary questions—a first for her, and the result of assiduous and deliberate study. ESPN came to her hometown to do a feature on her. In it, she talks about her love of dance while twirling across a dance studio, gazing intently into the camera to punctuate each turn.

These features are a more recent innovation and were not part of cable sports network ESPN's first live broadcast of the Bee on June 2, 1994. Until 2005, ESPN broadcast the event exclusively during daytime hours. Beginning in 2006, the finals were shown on ABC in prime time, with ESPN covering earlier rounds in daytime. ESPN took over prime-time coverage in 2011, adding features and enhancing the broadcast each year.

Until 2010, the Bee was held at the Grand Hyatt in Washington, DC, conducted on a lower stage and in a small ballroom. Spellers lined up to spell, the littlest ones engulfed in the oversized Bee polos that participants were issued until 2007. Their matching shirts resembled a team uniform. In 2011, the Scripps National Spelling Bee moved to a significantly larger space, the Gaylord National Resort and Convention Center in National Harbor, Maryland. Scripps built a much larger stage set that lights up in different colors and is worthy of high-definition television. The pleasing color palette of the set's honeycomb design changes depending on the speller's progress. The calm blue morphs to orange and then red, akin to a game show, as the clock ticks down on each two-minute spelling bee turn. A fleet of television cameras cover the action from ten different angles, including a jib cam that offers sweeping views of the cavernous ballroom.

The Scripps National Spelling Bee has become more innovative in its branding of the event in recent years. Each year, Bee Week staff distribute swag to spellers in the form of T-shirts, sunglasses, watches, and other memorabilia. One year, it featured the word *spellebrity*, an amalgam of "spelling" and "celebrity." The allure of this word and its attendant fame remains strong. Kids hope to become spellebrities and get selected for a desirable ESPN feature, which the network began producing several years ago. Scripps provides ESPN with a list of noteworthy contenders—usually kids who have competed well in multiple Bees and younger siblings of elite spellers. Camera crews visit their hometowns, invite them to the ESPN studio at the Gaylord, or both. In the days leading up to the competition, the National Spelling Bee tweets out bios and fun facts about each speller.

The early onstage rounds are broadcast on ESPN3 and feature gaming graphics—usually multiple choice. The semifinals air on ESPN2 and the live finals on ESPN in prime time. During the competition, especially with its increasing size, the ballroom is fully packed.

Comedy writers are flown in to write humorous sentences for the pronouncer to offer, making the contest lively and entertaining. Given the high security of the word list, writers are asked to produce this content in real time, crafting sentences for words later in the round while the competition is in full swing. With thousands tweeting @scrippsbee and #spellingbee, it's a perfect storm for great television.

When Sai figured out that the hour her mother had earmarked for weekly spelling study needed to be more like six to ten hours, there were casualties. During my visit to their home in 2014, Mrs. Chandrasekhar told me, while looking directly at Sai, that she needed to start doing her prayers and other things that had been pushed aside during bee season, including clarinet and Carnatic music practice. The full list of activities Sai had tabled in favor of studying spelling included figure skating, piano, violin, and the Saturday science research program that conflicted with debate team.

Sai thinks she also could do well at other brain sports, but it is her love of language that draws her to this one. Sai sees language in her future, in at least a few forms: "Speaking, writing, policy, debate. I don't know if I'll be a hardcore linguist, but definitely something like that would be interesting to pursue." She had recently won a Scholastic contest for a humor essay on how men should try walking around in heels. The Onion is a favorite "newspaper." Years later in high school, she would become more interested in computer programming and biological research but stay invested in giving back to her community and amplifying youth voices. She would identify strongly as a young woman of color, be involved in several clubs, and join the New York City government's Youth Leadership Council. It's easy to see the roots of this bright future in her time as a young speller.

Facing her final year of competition before she aged out, Sai identified her drive as something that comes from within. "I really want to do it, I've realized I want to pursue it. It's important to me at this point in my life." Professional spelling bee coaching was financially out of the question for Sai's family, but her parents did all they could to support Sai's training. Mrs. Chandrasekhar recalled seeing coaches at the Bee: "Coaches flash the names of spellers that are learning from them and you see the kids on the stage. It's scary if you can't afford it, you don't get the material. If you don't get the materials, you need to have time to make them."

Sai's mother is a homemaker, and her father is an engineer. Mrs. Chandrasekhar told me she and her husband didn't have a lot of free time between helping Sai with school and activities and caring for Sai's little sister. She couldn't provide the expert coaching that some parents do, and yet she wanted to support her daughter's ambitions and was willing to put her own aspirations aside to do so. Sai voiced gratitude for her mother's support, in whatever form she was able to offer it. Even so, Sai did a lot of the hard work herself. Her family initially purchased some word lists but found the ongoing subscription too costly to maintain. She switched to studying the dictionary, in print and online. For her summer regimen, Sai studied twenty pages a day. There were two thousand pages in the dictionary that she wanted to cover, and she marked them up as she went along. She recorded herself saying words to become more conscious of their pronunciations.

In 2015, Sai sailed through her first onstage round of semifinals. She eagerly awaited the second round. When her turn came, she approached the mic with her characteristic aplomb. This time it was not in the cards. She misspelled *induciae*, a delay or pause in a legal proceeding. It was a definitive end to her National Spelling Bee career. The audience applauded heartily, as she was a crowd favorite. She was pleased with her performance and felt she had grown to a point of being better able to handle losing. She had accomplished her best finish, tying for eleventh place. She wasn't among the top ten heading to the finals, but she had come much further than millions of others. That night, she would watch two other children of immigrants, Vanya Shivashankar and Gokul Venkatachalam, each take home a 2015 trophy.

Children of immigrants comprise the largest minority group in Generation Z. While some of Generation Z's diversity is due to an increase in mixed-race children, the majority is due to immigration. If you have watched the National Spelling Bee in the last decade, it has become something of a cliché that an Indian American kid will win. Although they comprise only about 1 percent of the overall population, Indian American children are overrepresented in the finals and as champions for the past two decades. This dominance has also resulted in a racist backlash against Indian American spellers and their families, making this phenomenon impossible to ignore. Initially in the 1980s, there were two: Balu Natarajan in 1985, lauded as the first son of immigrants to win, and Rageshree Ramachandran in 1988. There were several in the 1990s, but none who shone like the 1999 champion Nupur Lala, whose win was captured in the documentary *Spellbound* (2002).[11] Countless spellers and families have been drawn to her energy and accomplishment as well as the excitement of competition portrayed in that film.

About a decade ago, I noticed what others had also observed, that Indian American kids had started to win every year. In the United States, no immigrant community has embraced spelling as completely as South Asian Americans. The two largest bees for children of South Asian parentage, the North South Foundation (NSF) spelling bee and the South Asian Spelling Bee, draw several thousand spellers a year. The 2018 documentary film *Breaking the Bee* captures this trend and chronicles the Indian American winning streak.[12] Each time an Indian American wins the National Spelling Bee, some attribute their win to this ethnic group being "naturally" gifted in spelling. Yet, there is nothing natural about spelling, for any human. Spelling is a completely arbitrary representational system, learned through focused study of etymology, grammar, and some memorization.

The Indian American winning streak is a result of the efforts of highly skilled immigrants who arrived in the early 1990s, a time when Baby Boomers and Gen Xers did not meet the growing demand for workers in STEM—science, technology, engineering, and math. They settled into an existing infrastructure of immigrant neighborhoods, community organizations, and retail stores. They made use of the experiences of friends and family to navigate the educational system. Many of these individuals were trained in the IITs and other extraordinarily competitive colleges and universities. These immigrants not only value education but prioritize academic enrichment over all else. They forego their own leisure and position educational accomplishment as the focal point of their children's lives.

Rather than regarding the winning streak as an isolated phenomenon of Indian American kids excelling at spelling, I am interested in how this brain sport offers a window into how immigrants are having larger effects on American society. Social scientists run the risk of relying too heavily on the narrative of assimilation, so prevalent throughout American history, when it comes to describing the effect of immigrants in America. When their social contributions are considered, they are largely acknowledged only within their communities, not as having an effect on the mainstream. Yet immigrant parents, who now exist in far larger numbers than when my family immigrated in 1973, are enacting parenting practices that have broader impacts on American society.

We consider assimilation to be about merging imperceptibly into a mainstream, but rarely do we interrogate what "mainstream" means beyond a white majority. Gen Z will be America's last generation with a white majority. Depending on the start date, estimates for Gen Z size range from 69 to 73 million, with approximately 52 percent white, 25 percent Hispanic, 14 percent African American, 5 percent Asian American, and 5 percent other.[13] By comparison, 72 percent of Boomers are white.[14] With the steady rise in immigration, the "second generation," or children born of immigrants, has increased as well. For instance, in 1970, only 274,000 children had immigrant parents. By

2014, that number had more than tripled, amounting to about 901,000. Coinciding with this, the annual number of births to US-born women dropped by 11 percent, from 3.46 million in 1970 to 3.10 million in 2014.[15]

Generation Z not only contains the most children of immigrants, but it is also the most diverse in history. Immigrants have always been a part of the American narrative, and they are featured centrally in this book as members of Generation Z, rather than as an isolated group. The Indian American "Bee Parents" who devote their adulthood to cultivating their children's spelling careers have transformed the contest for all 11 million children who participate. The way they have professionalized this particular childhood activity complements the parenting styles of US-born Gen X parents but also extends it. Bee Parents' emphasis on extracurricular education, combined with today's competitive culture, makes their impact visible beyond the spelling bee to other brain sports and academic achievement for Generation Z.

Inside the National Spelling Bee ballroom, parents vie for a good spot from which to photograph and videotape their speller. Some parents frequently appear on camera, cheering and waving. Sai's mother refuses to enter the ballroom. She attends all of her daughter's other activities with adoration, including drama, dance, and music. But she won't watch the contest in person, preferring to view it instead from her hotel room, in the very same building where the event is unfolding. Sai's mother does not consider spelling bees to be fun. "I feel like I'm sending her to God. Even if she were winning first prize, every other child loses, and it breaks my heart." It is difficult for her to see kids losing, and to see the way the media stands at the ready to document tears if smiles are not available. She has watched her daughter stay up late studying for the competition for months on end and can't decide if it's worthwhile.

Sai's mother had not heard of the National Spelling Bee before her daughter qualified in sixth grade. Once Sai started progressing further in spelling contests, she described the level of words and the competitiveness as a "blast in the face." She recalls her first visit to the Bee, when her family sat with other Indian American families at the closing banquet. It was there that she learned that other children had been competing since second or third grade. She was astonished to learn that there are bees open only to kids of South Asian heritage, where there is no minimum age. She found these families to be well versed in the world of spelling bees, and closely connected to one another. She recalled, "They were speaking about how French words were pronounced. They were speaking about that *in their native language.*" Some even attended nearby bees as spectators to gain an advantage in their upcoming contest. "They knew everything! They knew the tricks of the trade. I had no clue," Sai's mother exclaimed. "I think it's all about knowing."

When Mrs. Chandrasekhar talks about spelling bees with her friends, she finds many are not receptive. While Indian American kids have done very well at the Bee, it is only a small number of families that dedicate themselves to producing elite spellers. Mrs. Chandrasekhar's friends don't understand Sai's dedication. "They tell me, 'Sai is smart, she should do math instead of wasting her time on spelling!'" Their remarks echo the widely held South Asian view that STEM is more prestigious than the language arts. STEM is what allowed her family to immigrate, so its value is proven in the community.

The professional qualifications of Indian Americans and the high value they put on education make them very focused on their children and grooming them for successful futures. While they share these characteristics with US-born Generation X parents, Bee Parents bring an intensity to parenting that rivals, if not exceeds, their US-born peers. Most Bee Parents I met seemed perfectly fine spending their social and leisure time on their children's extracurricular study and travel for competitions. They devoted financial resources and extensive support, which very often included a stay-at-home parent. Some families are limited in what they can afford but nonetheless emphasize their children over individual gratification. Few bemoan it as sacrifice.

Over the six years I went to the Bee, I watched my own young children grow up with only a nominal interest in spelling bees. My son was seven when I started and my daughter three; they are now in seventh and third grade, respectively. Every year when I go to Bee Week and meet dozens of bright, motivated, young orthographic experts, I return home a bit anxious. Watching how accomplished these kids are, and how involved their parents are, I wonder if I should be doing more. As I got to know parents of spellers, they sometimes asked where *my* kids were and why I was not grooming them for the Bee. It was a great question, and it really stumped me the first few times I was asked.

Over time, I realized how hard it is to do what Bee Parents do. My husband and I are often flattened by the logistical rigor of our working-parent lives. Our children are tired after being in school all week. They are not overly enraptured by their classroom spelling activities, and while they enjoy reading, spending hours each day and time on weekends and holidays on spelling seemed unappealing to them. And to all of us, really. Perhaps I am too unimaginative to make it fun, as some are able to do for their kids. But this is my internal dialogue. I simply told the Bee Parents that we were exploring the possibility.

These discussions led me to better understand that I am a successful child of immigrants, who valued education enough to get my PhD and become a university professor but not enough to steer my kids toward brain sports like spelling bees. I have become comfortable with the irony of this situation, where I think highly enough of this activity to study it academically but not participate in it. Even so, as a Gen Xer, I understand the playing field has changed and do what I can to get my kids ready for the changing realities of their generation.

Demographers theorize that US-born Generation X parents watched the teeming population of Millennials in their rearview and realized something major had changed in America. Consequently, they developed a different parenting style than Baby Boomers. Other members of Gen X learned the importance of being successful from their non-US-born parents. Gen Z kids seem aware of the obstacles that Millennials face with their large cohort size, noting how competitive college admissions and job searching has become. As they enter the job market, which will begin over the next five years, Generation Z kids will have to compete with Millennials, Gen Xers, and even some of the youngest Baby Boomers. They are predicted to become the largest of the four cohorts and are coming into adulthood in a quantifiably more competitive environment.

Kate took the stage at her final National Spelling Bee in 2014. In the first semifinal round, she was almost eliminated. She had never heard of her word, *duello*, an Italian variant of *duel*, but stayed calm and managed to piece it together. Later on, Amber would compliment her, commenting, "It's a great feeling to get a word right you didn't know by figuring it out." Kate concurred, saying, "That's a shaky euphoria right there." Her second semifinals word, *brachypterous*, short-winged, posed no challenge. Kate had to wait for the formal announcement but already knew she had made it to the prime-time finals. With a finalist medal around her neck, she was swarmed by journalists, including someone from her hometown newspaper, the *Abilene Reporter News*. It was already midafternoon, and Bee officials ushered her through an hour-by-hour schedule that included more interview time with ESPN hosts and another visit to the ESPN studio to record her finals introduction. She and her family were invited to a catered meal along with Bee officials and Scripps staff. She waited in the wings with the other eleven finalists to be led onstage—a much more dramatic entrance than the daytime rounds, when spellers simply use the stairs on either side of the stage to shuffle on and off.

After the national anthem, introductory remarks, and a pause for the ESPN commentators to welcome the television audience, the prime-time finals began. Kate felt the nerves onstage but knew how important it was to keep them in check. "Although you're tense, full of adrenaline, you make small talk because if you showed how freaked out you were, you would lose all your composure." Kate calls this an exercise in self-control, finding ways to appear calm and collected when "inside you feel like butterflies erupting." She has built up this discipline over several years. Like many of her fellow elite spellers, Kate draws on her stage experience from theater, debate, and dance. The most grounding part is seeing her people in the audience. "You look out and see your friends and family rooting for you. It feels amazing to be that supported, to be lifted up there. Then you have to push that aside and just focus on the word. The pragmatism kicks in."

Kate stepped up to the mic to receive her word. *Osteochondrous*, relating to or composed of bone and cartilage. She repeated it and asked for the definition, part of speech, other contextual information, and the word used in a sentence. She found the sentence amusing and smiled. Kate got to work on her imaginary keyboard and the cameras started clicking. Unlike the kid before her, she didn't risk losing her concentration by attempting a joke or banter. Director Kimble has advised against this, in case competitors get distracted and misspell. Kate thinks this is good advice. But, she adds, "Amber pulls that off. Amber is superhuman; I don't know how she does it." Kate spelled her word correctly and high-fived several spellers as she made her way back to her seat. She sees this as a unique bonding experience, where spellers cheer each other on and chat during commercial breaks.

"We all want the same goal, but we wouldn't knock each other out to get it." When I suggested that's exactly what they would need to do to win, she smiled and shared a phrase that I had heard from other spellers. "We compete against the dictionary, not each other. It's individual." I initially regarded this sentiment to be sweet but ridiculous, and inaccurate. It turns out I was wrong (except for the sweet part). Any elite speller will tell you that there is some amount of chance involved with knowing the word they get. Even champions have admitted that they were unsure about some of their fellow spellers' words and were relieved that they got the words they did. In six cases, two kids have beaten the dictionary together to be named cochampions. The winner truly is the last speller not felled by the dictionary.

In 2014, that last speller was not Kate. She received *exochorion*, the outer layers of an insect egg, and was one letter off. "The dreaded bell awaited me after I left out the *h*," Kate told me. It was the end of an excellent run. At the close of her spelling career in 2014, Kate shared her concerns about "the void of high school without spelling." The thought of life without competitive spelling filled her with melancholy. Kate has written about her spelling career, journaling about her experience on a blog that Scripps subsequently picked up and published as a three-part series. She planned to transition her love of words into debate, which would allow her to continue to be "competitive and verbal."

Kate turned her attention to her younger brother Jack, who had come in second to her in several regional bees. She saw great potential in him but warned, "He's only eleven so we can't expect him to devote his life to the cause just yet!" Like Kate, Jack would take up that pursuit and make several trips to the Bee himself. Kate concluded, "The Bee has shaped and changed my life. I think about it multiple times a day. It was life changing. It will carry on throughout my life. I'll have the memories, the friends, and the work ethic."

To be sure, every generation can boast precociously successful individuals. Yet what kids today have to do to cross the same hurdles that professions-bound individuals did in past generations is far more extreme. Perhaps this is why values such as efficiency, time management, networking, and other features we might associate with corporate culture have trickled down into kids' everyday lives. Young people are goal oriented beyond the

moment, seeing the value of networking and building relationships. Their motivation to follow paths that are intense, consum-
ing, and professionally oriented can begin in elementary school.
Gen Z kids seem to know that everything they do won't be a
success, but that the discipline and experience of the activity has
its own long-term benefits. The extraordinary kids who attempt
an elite spelling career today don't just speak for their generation,
they stand for it.

Chapter Two

Brain Sports and Kid Competitions

Only Gokul Venkatachalam and two others remained in the finals of the 2015 National Spelling Bee. Maybe he was channeling basketball champion LeBron James by wearing his jersey under the blue oxford his mother made him put on. Maybe he was just tired of losing to the dictionary. Either way, he was on the precipice of becoming a champion. Gokul had effortlessly sailed into the championship round while eight of the other finalists had been eliminated. Gokul spelled his first word, *zygoneure*, a connecting neuron, quickly and confidently. Subsequent words gave him slight pause and he asked multiple questions. None stumped him. *Acritarch*, a fossil one-celled marine planktonic organism, felled Cole Shafer-Ray, who placed third. Just Gokul and Vanya Shivashankar remained.

Seasoned spellers, especially past champions, can differentiate between when a speller onstage knows a word and is asking for information to confirm it and when they are hoping the information they glean allows them to make a correct attempt. The latter can certainly lead to success, but the former is a sure thing, according to the two past champions I sat next to. Sameer Mishra, 2008 champion, and Anamika Veeramani, 2010 champion, were present as members of the Bee Week staff and sat at the media table tweeting and Snapchatting. They acted as my play-by-play commentators while they clacked away on their laptops. They were confident that Gokul knew every word he was given—*caudillismo*, dictatorship, *scytale*, a method of cipher writing, and *filicite,* a fossil fern, were no match for him. Gokul would later tell me he knew all of his opponents' words too, something that most spellers can't say. Usually there is a bit of luck involved, and elite spellers readily admit the words they didn't know, relieved that they avoided them. Not that year for Gokul. Gokul knew, and Dr. Bailly confirmed, that if he could spell correctly until they exhausted their list of championship words, he would become a champion.

Before the finals, Gokul met with ESPN on-air hosts Paul Loeffler and Chris McKendry. He had made it to the 2013 finals, so he knew the drill. They wanted to gather interesting tidbits about him to use for color commentary during the live broadcast. Gokul told them that he likes listening to rap and alternative music, watching movies, and reading books. Photography is a hobby. He was highly specific about words he does not like, which include words from Russian, words about minerals, and people's names. "You've either seen it or you haven't. The unknown is amazingly large," he told them matter-of-factly. The hosts asked if he would compare his spelling game to LeBron's. Gokul shied away from that comparison. He did not concede to being like NBA player Chris Paul either, but finally did to Ray Allen. "Be

Ray Allen tonight," Loeffler encouraged as Gokul nodded. The non-NBA fans in the room, including his parents, smiled politely.

The biggest thing Gokul had learned from his years of competition is "don't give up." He didn't. Gokul and Vanya exhausted the entire championship list, not missing a single word. In the final round, Vanya correctly spelled *scherenschnitte*, the decorative art of paper cutting, and was named a champion. Would she stand alone or become part of the fifth set of cochampions? Having spelled nearly a dozen championship words correctly, it all came down to one final word for Gokul: *nunatak*, a hill or mountain surrounded by glacial ice.

The championship round of the National Spelling Bee is one of the fiercest arenas in any competition. The national level of any contest is intense, but the scale of this one makes it even more so, as it involves over 11 million kids from all over the United States and several other countries. As far as kid contests go, nothing matches its scale. Child-centered contests have long been part of the American childhood but have transformed significantly over the last few decades. Today's preparation techniques and conditions of competition are far more elaborate and intense than decades past. More than just raw talent is required here. Kids cultivate expertise and high degrees of proficiency to become contenders. Through ongoing participation, they develop preprofessional skills. This may be the case with a number of kid activities but is especially so with brain sports.

This chapter looks at brain sports as a kind of competition that is linked to building human capital—skills, experiences, and expertise that can be valuable in the job market. Beginning to build human capital in elementary and middle school can influence activities undertaken in high school, college admissions, and entry into the workforce. Some Gen Z kids are already working as coaches, entrepreneurs, and social media influencers. The lines between play, education, and professionalism have become blurred. This confluence is a point of critical debate as well as a lived reality for many of today's young people.

Televised kid competitions are proliferating in every category. New shows debut each season, like *Little Big Shots* hosted by Steve Harvey. In this catchall talent show, contestants as young as preschool and elementary-school age perform their mind-boggling talents. These can include song, dance, comedy, memory tricks, spelling, martial arts, juggling, and anything else that has the potential to astound a prime-time audience. Precocious Akash Vukoti from San Angelo, Texas, who made his National Spelling Bee debut as 2016's youngest competitor at age six, easily felled Harvey in a spelling contest staged for this show. In October 2018, Akash starred in a new reality competition, *Dancing with the Stars: Juniors*. While older shows like *Star Search* in the 1980s allowed teens to compete against other young people, some shows today allow younger contestants to compete against adults. Recent seasons of the singing competition show *The Voice* have featured participants as young as thirteen for the "blind" auditions, in which judges can only hear, but not see, a potential singer they may wish to coach.

Other competition formats require great discipline, skill, and expertise, in addition to raw talent. *MasterChef Junior* is an American cooking competition modeled after the popular *MasterChef*. In each season, twenty-four children ranging in age from eight to thirteen audition on television, with twelve selected to compete.

Two are eliminated per episode, and the series winner receives $100,000. The perseverance and stamina to last one competitive round after the next is challenging for adults and extraordinary for kids. In a faster-paced format, *Chopped Junior*, another reality-based cooking show, is contained to an hour. Four young contestants transform mystery ingredients into dishes for judges to evaluate. In each of the appetizer, entrée, and dessert rounds, one chef is "chopped" and does not advance. The winner of each episode receives $10,000.

Anyone who has watched these shows might be as amazed as I am at the knife skills of nine-year-olds and their improvisational creativity to take random, mismatched ingredients and create something that is aesthetically pleasing and tastes amazing. Can you imagine making an appetizer that incorporates pork belly, wasabi paste, peaches, and rainbow bagels, and have it plated in under thirty minutes for celebrity chefs to judge? What both of these shows require are not just basic cooking skills, but vast culinary knowledge and deep self-confidence. Perhaps the most fascinating part is the presentation. The plating of each creation is greatly enhanced by the narration that accompanies it. "Chefs, today I have prepared for you..." is usually followed by highly specialized terms from the foodie register, like *chiffonade* and *sous vide*. An equally impressive aspect of the kids' performance is how they receive criticism. The judges can be scathing, but young chefs accept it and express gratitude. These kids are not simply displaying raw talent that will one day allow them to become accomplished adults. Rather, they are showcasing well-developed skills that make them experts as kids.

This range of competition was simply not available to kids in generations past, at least not on this scale. Consider the difference between a 1990s kid who liked fashion and one today. In the 1990s, that kid might have a flair for style, make some of their own clothes in high school, and apply to design school or colleges that offer coursework in this area. Today, that aspiring twelve-year-old might aim to be a contestant on *Project Runway Junior*, the fashion design show where contestants perform in tailoring and styling challenges. When a kid takes on a contest as complex and multifaceted as this, they have to show up with more than just a flair for fashion. They have to be goal oriented, manage their time, promote themselves, and market their creative work.

Critics point out the dangers of contests that encourage people to consider it normal to put in an enormous amount of labor for "free" when only one or two are rewarded. This is consistent with broader critiques about human capital and how the costs of building it measure against the potential payoff. For some kids, the skills they build certainly require sacrifice, but also seem to be valued as part of their broader development. Especially in the case of spelling bees, the social aspects are a major draw.

Kids go to great lengths to stay connected even with no guarantee of seeing each other the following year. Speller groups on Facebook, Google, Instagram, and other social media platforms make it easier to keep in touch. Over the years, spellers make many friends at the Bee and have reunions there, even after they age out. "Everyone lives for those," Amber Born told me. She met her best friend, Kate Miller, at the Bee. Amber explained that making friends can happen faster during Bee Week because kids are less self-conscious; everyone knows they are going home at the end of the week.

"I write jokes and I do school" is how Amber described herself to me the very first time we spoke on Skype in 2014. She began our interview by telling me exactly how many minutes I had to ask her questions. This no-nonsense approach would take Amber far in spelling bees and in the world beyond them. Amber first became interested in spelling when she read the book *Akeelah and the Bee*. "I found out it was an actual thing you could do, so I thought, 'I should do that,'" she told me.

Amber didn't make it past the regional level as a third or fourth grader. As a fifth grader in 2010, Amber triumphed over the previous year's winner when he spelled *chagrin* too quickly and botched it. The irony was not lost on her, nor was the lesson of taking her time and not making mistakes by rushing. In Amber's region, there is no minimum age to compete, but only the first-place winner advances to the Bee. Getting to Washington, DC, as a fifth grader was a tremendous accomplishment.

Amber had followed the Bee closely on television in 2009. Being there herself was like making it to the Oscars of spelling, finally seeing your favorite and venerated screen talents in the flesh instead of on television like everyone else. She trembled with delight to share elevators with famous spellers. As a first-timer and an eleven-year-old, Amber was too nervous to talk to them. "I thought people would be mean and intense, but everyone was nice, and I appreciated that." She was pleasantly surprised by the warm and friendly vibe of the competition, with its numerous social events. "You meet a lot of like-minded people. It's all precocious and cool people that have similar interests as you," she told me. *Precocious* and *cool* were two words I had never heard used together in a sentence. Yet when she said it, I was immediately convinced. She continued, "They're academically focused, and they're doing competitive spelling with their life, so they're kind of automatically your friend."

In the book (and the 2006 film of the same name on which it's based), Akeelah wins the Bee in her first year, Amber explained, so she assumed that she would too. That didn't happen. She spelled correctly onstage during both of the preliminary rounds but was six points away from semifinals. In retrospect, she conceded that she was naïve about her expectations for her first national appearance. "I didn't know how to do it coming in. It was way harder than I expected, and I didn't know how to study." Even so, this did not deter her. "From the beginning, I considered myself to be a serious competitor," she said. In 2011, despite steadily improving her spelling prowess, she missed semifinals again, but this time only by one point. "It was so annoying!" she exclaimed.

In 2012, on her third trip to the National Spelling Bee, Amber got exactly the score she needed to make it to semifinals. Finally, she was going to get past the preliminary rounds. She took her place onstage with about fifty other remaining contestants. Despite being confident and prepared, she misspelled the first word she was given. Her quick elimination was unlucky, as she knew most of the other words in that round. Though frustrated with her early outings at the Bee, Amber was not ready to walk away from spelling.

Intense competition like the kind Amber and Gokul seek out is part of childhood in the United States, as it is in numerous other societies worldwide. But unlike many other places, K–12 schooling is available to all in America. By design, it is free for all children, and deliberately noncompetitive. Admissions tests are only required for the most elite public schools, if you choose to test into charter or magnet schools, or pay to attend private schools. Outside of gifted and talented programs, differences in student abilities are kept private in public schools. This is a sharp contrast from other regions of the world, such as most of Asia, where school is fee based, test scores are publicly announced, and student ranks are known. In America, K–12 students are not privy to the scores of their peers. It is only toward the end of high school that a valedictorian and salutatorian are announced.

This is the case because the United States takes a deliberately inclusive approach to education. The Elementary and Secondary Education Act (ESEA), passed in 1965, ensured all children a public education. Its successor, the No Child Left Behind Act (NCLB), likewise emphasized equality in schooling as a way to draw in and retain students of all levels. As of 2015, this initiative took the form of the Every Student Succeeds Act (ESSA). The goal of American K–12 education remains the same: for all students to succeed as a way of leveling inequality. Fostering competition by publicly ranking students would be at cross-purposes with these programs.

Commendably, the United States has sought to maintain an inclusive education system and encourage those of all achievement levels to complete high school. At the same time, it has become highly reliant on immigrant labor for its economic growth, particularly in the STEM arena. Many of the best and brightest kids in India, for instance, go into STEM fields. They tend to have the best scores and rankings and are often the very people whom the United States solicits in the category of highly skilled labor. The kind of competition that the US education system tends to downplay is precisely what other countries emphasize to groom talent. While the US education system has prioritized inclusion over allowing some to get ahead at the cost of others being left behind, other kinds of intense competition have begun to fill this gap.

American children's competitive activities have evolved significantly from the turn of the twentieth century to the present. Organized competition for kids heightened after World War II, and today a competitive childhood is increasingly accepted by families, whether they like it or not. Compulsory education, the self-esteem movement that sought to downplay competition within classrooms, and highly competitive college admissions are contributors to this change.[1] Activities from Little League to science fairs became the competitive field that the school could no longer be. In the last decade, extracurricular competition has expanded in previously unseen ways, including brain sports. Outside of spelling, they include debate, science fairs, math bowls, and numerous other academic contests.

I t's a sport now. It's not athletic, obviously. But it requires the same amount of dedication, passion, work. You have to really, really want it in order to come close. It requires sportsmanship," Kate remarked about the National Spelling Bee when she, her fellow speller Amber, and I Skyped together in 2014. Like other kid contests, the intensity of the Bee had increased even over the years Kate and Amber competed. The addition of vocabulary and other changes to the contest structure attest to this. None of it made the Bee any less attractive to them. They can remember the words that knocked out many top spellers, just like people remember sports statistics. "This is our thing. It's something we follow and remember," said Kate. Amber recalled a commencement speech in which a speaker said: "Why would people spend hours learning to spell?...Why do people spend hours kicking a ball into a net? It's the same thing." Kate agreed and added, "It is on ESPN, and therefore it is a sport!"

From an elite speller's standpoint, the spelling bee is more than an educational contest, the traditional category into which it falls. Rather, it's a brain sport. The use of the word *sport* draws attention to the intensive practice and coaching contestants undergo, as well as the spectator value of this contest. I first heard this term from Roopa Hathwar, mother of two National Spelling Bee champions. We spoke in 2014, at the South Asian Spelling Bee finals in New Jersey where her son, 2013 SASB champion Sriram, was performing a role in the opening ceremony. Dr. Hathwar and her husband, Dr. Jagadeesh Hathwar, are physicians in a small upstate New York town near Corning. Sriram joined our conversation, but his father and younger brother, Jairam, were traveling to a North South Foundation bee. Sriram competed in the Bee five times overall and was very active in the minor-league circuit open to Indian American spellers.

As Sriram's stature as a speller grew, his parents found themselves being asked by colleagues and friends why their family spent so much time and effort on spelling. His mother drew an analogy between her family's approach to spelling and the copious amount of time she observed other families spending on physical team sports. She offered the example of travel soccer, where a parent and child, or sometimes the entire family, travel significant distances for matches over weekends and summers. They know that their child will likely not become a professional player, but they see the intrinsic value of it for their child's development and enjoyment.

For Sriram's mother, the travel, time spent on evenings and weekends, and parental effort were quite similar between spelling and travel soccer. This is how she and her husband prioritized spending time with their boys, driving to regional contests and flying to national ones, sometimes at their own cost, in order to compete at the highest levels of the sport. She explained, "Some families spend so much time on those kinds of sports. This is our mental sport, our *brain sport* that we encourage. That's how we try to analogize it."

Elite spellers train hard to excel at this brain sport. As a term, "brain sports" captures the elevated nature of the spelling bee today, illustrating how these competitions are about so much more than simply learning content. The National Spelling Bee will always be about orthographic and etymological knowledge, but it is also about onstage performance, written test skills, and finding a way to remain grounded and focused under very bright lights and dozens of cameras. Being a neuro-athlete, a term I introduced in an op-ed I wrote for the *Boston Globe*, has legitimacy, especially when there is a competition in place, prizes to be won, and public, as well as broadcast, interest.[2] Neuro-athletes are concerned with training, performance, perseverance, and public presentation.

With a brain sport as intense as spelling, moving on after an elite career can be challenging. Kate and Amber identified "disorders" that elite spellers could develop as they exited this world. Even though their graduation from spelling could mean pursuing other competitions more fully—like debate, science fairs, or anything else—there seemed to be a special fondness for this world that made them reluctant to leave. Amber referred to it as "postorthographical competition inefficiency disorder," a clinical term for "when you study so hard for the Bee you can't do anything afterwards. You're just limp and your academics dip." Kate credited the acronym POCID to 2014 cochampion Sriram Hathwar. Both referenced the affliction of not being able to truly leave this activity and the spelling bee world behind. I believe them. They call *Webster's* third edition, the dictionary they studied, MW3 or "our beloved Webby." "Actually, that is the seventh edition published, but it's named the third. The soon-to-be-released fourth edition will retire the dictionary that was the authority of so many of our young years," Kate explained. Webby was on its way to becoming a collector's item.

Even after aging out of their spelling careers, Amber and Kate remain active in one society in particular, the Order of the Squushy Carrots. *Squushy* is a lesser-known alternate spelling for *squishy*. I learned more when Amber and Kate invited me to have coffee at the 2015 Bee. Kate was there to accompany her brother Jack, while Amber came to cheer on spellers and see Kate and other friends. Kate and Amber wanted to get all the semifinalists and finalists to join the society. "If they're not a carrot, we'll make them a carrot!" exclaimed Kate. In 2015, Kate hadn't initiated anyone but had seen others do it. Amber knew of at least one person who'd been initiated the previous night—someone's brother. As they told me about how the society had been growing, Amber and Kate abruptly turned to address each other in hushed tones. They debated whether they could initiate "an adult." They decided that they could, since some past spellers in the society are no longer in high school.

They invited me to join. I was honored but didn't think I qualified due to my middling spelling skills. After further deliberation, they decided that my research qualified me as worthy of an exception. We started the initiation. "Do you have feelings?" Yes. Hearing my affirmative response, Amber barreled forward with more questions. I wondered what the questions sounded like to a young person, as they did not quite make sense to me. For each, I looked to Kate for hints on how to respond. "Are you forever alone?" I was stumped, but eventually Kate prompted me to say yes, so I did. Amber told Kate, "I feel like she's lying." I admitted I didn't understand the question. Besides, having two kids makes me not forever alone. They decided I could be "forever alone together, her and the two kids."

Once that was resolved, they queried whether I like my carrots "squushy" or crunchy. Squushy. "This is a vital question in the initiation," Kate affirmed. "That's it!" Amber exclaimed. We were suddenly done. Next, they demonstrated a multipart handshake that I struggled to replicate. Finally, Kate delivered a "ding" on my forehead that was harder than I expected it to be. I noticed that she hesitated before releasing the middle finger cocked against her thumb onto my face; I think it was a more delicate ding than she would have delivered to a peer. Amber asked if I felt different, and I confirmed that I did. That was no lie. We commemorated by taking a *spellfie*, a speller selfie. It was quickly established that Kate had the longest arms and would take the picture. Once I was initiated, they continued to describe the nitty-gritty of post-spelling-bee life.

B rain sports may be a recent term, but only some extracurricular academic competitions are new. For instance, the National Geographic GeoBee is a newer, growing contest, limited to fourth through eighth graders. Longer-running contests include the US Academic Decathlon and the National Ocean Sciences Bowl, both team-based contests. Education and social science researchers have attempted to assess the immediate and long-term benefits of academic competitions like these and their effects on students who participate in them.[3] They claim a variety of motivations for engaging in these events.

In one study, students saw the value of these activities as learning new content.[4] Science Olympiad students enjoyed being part of a team and felt their experience prepared them for the future, while science fair students felt rewarded by learning the scientific process. Student participation in the former tended to be voluntary, as many students in the survey-based study were required to enter a science fair. Both were deemed rewarding, despite their competitive formats.

Researchers found that academic contests such as science fairs and Olympiads benefit students in multiple ways.[5] By comparison, the researchers found nonacademic competition to have several physical and emotional benefits but concluded that they are not significantly related to academic achievement.[6] Brain sports motivate kids to study and work diligently. They teach kids to cope and develop intellectual maturity through managing emotionally difficult moments. They can also teach children to manage subjective judgment and disappointment.[7]

The most intriguing and intense brain sport for older kids are science fairs. The Intel International Science and Engineering Fair is a highly competitive event that displays the work of 1,500 high school students from around the world. It can be a recruiting ground for university and industry programs seeking to find the youngest and brightest minds in science.[8] With thousands of dollars of prize money on the line, the fame and recognition can catapult an aspiring scientist into early stardom. Many kids who have excelled at spelling bees also gravitate toward science fairs, even though the competition is very differently structured.

Still, some are critical of science fairs and other brain sports, especially as they pertain to younger children. Naysayers contend that elementary-school science fairs tend to be more for "over-involved adults" who do more than give their kids a winning edge; they actually do the work of winning.[9] In some cases, the guidelines of the competition are not achievable by most of the young children who are eligible to compete. For older kids, however, science fairs are intended to foster innovation and identify scientifically gifted students, especially those from lower socio-economic areas that may not otherwise be identified. Like the spelling bee, these contests can be a coveted opportunity to shine.

Several spellers I've followed have participated at the local levels of these contests, and some have made it to the national level. One very talented science fair participant, Pranav Sivakumar, came in second at the 2013 National Spelling Bee. In 2016, he was named an individual winner of the Siemens Competition national semifinals (a STEM-based competition), having already been named a Google Science Fair global finalist twice and winning the 2015 Virgin Galactic Pioneer Award. He even received a shout-out from President Obama on White House Astronomy Night for his research on dark matter.

These competitions tend to draw some media coverage, but not a steady television presence. On the other hand, one long-running televised brain sport is *Jeopardy! Teen Tournament*. Anurag Kashyap, the 2005 National Spelling Bee champion, also won this tournament. *Jeopardy!* began holding a yearly teen tournament in 1987, featuring students age thirteen through seventeen.

Contestants compete in five quarterfinal games and advance to the semifinals and wild-card matches, with finalists competing in a two-game championship series. The show has since created a contest for younger children called *Jeopardy! Kids Week*. During most seasons since 1999, children age ten through twelve are invited to compete.

A newer televised brain sport comes in a reality show format. *Child Genius* aired on Lifetime in 2015 and 2016. Vanya Shivashankar was named the first winner in 2015, the same year she became cochampion of the National Spelling Bee. The show was developed by and orchestrated in collaboration with American Mensa. Based on a UK program of the same name, the show presented twenty children age ten to fourteen who competed for a $100,000 college fund and the title of Child Genius. The children were selected from across the country and faced off in challenges on a variety of subjects, including math, spelling, vocabulary, current events, geography, the human body, US presidents, zoology, astronomy, language arts, earth science, logic, and others. By elimination, one was chosen for the title.

For Generation Z kids, regarding cerebral contests as brain sports can alleviate the stigma of being labeled as nerdy or geeky. Liking language and being good at spelling is not automatically uncool, especially when it's broadcast by ESPN. Even so, the "sport" aspect of the term is not one that all spellers I met agreed with, some arguing that spelling did not fit their definition. A sport had to have more movement, a ball, and possibly teammates. When I asked ESPN staff for their opinion, Dave Miller, who then worked on the broadcast of the National Spelling Bee, told me that they televised competitions including traditional "stick and ball" sports as well as other tournaments like poker. Since their acronym stands for Entertainment and Sports Programming Network, the National Spelling Bee certainly qualifies. Most agree that elite spellers require the same kind of discipline and training that is a hallmark of any athlete striving to become great in their field. Brain sports encompass the route that young competitors take to become highly accomplished spellers.

"Before a game, LeBron James uses his focus and doesn't worry about other things. That's the same thing I do when I prepare for a spelling bee," Gokul says in one of his ESPN features. At the end of the feature, Gokul echoes James's announcement to join the Miami Heat, saying, "I'm taking my talents to the National Spelling Bee." Growing up in St. Louis, Gokul became a huge LeBron fan and plays basketball himself. It was the one other activity he retained while studying for his final year of the Bee. During the height of his training, Gokul went to school, had a snack, studied spelling, then took a small break to go to the gym, followed by more spelling, dinner, and homework. "Sleep and repeat," he told me. Gokul draws a distinction between what he calls "smart hard work" and "pure hard work." The first relies on efficiency and strategy. In his calculus, "smart hard work" involves not memorizing every word, in favor of spending hours studying roots and memorizing only some key words. "Pure hard work," which Gokul thinks is less efficient, would be studying and memorizing pages of the dictionary at a time.

Gokul learned that "you have to put in smart hard work and need to be efficient, because pure hard work won't get you anywhere if you're not doing it smart at the same time." He is appreciative of the work ethic and time management he culti-vated over his spelling career. "I go through about six hundred words in about ten minutes," he reported. When I asked him to elaborate, he explained, "Sometimes I could play on my phone, web surf, and read an article, and I'd forget that I was even spell-ing." At the spelling bee mic, Gokul is all business. Unlike Am-ber and other spellers who attempt banter or greet Dr. Bailly in a language other than English, he simply gets down to spelling. So steely is his composure that he barely smiled when he received the word *smellfungus*, a faultfinder, in the 2013 semifinals, re-maining stoic while the audience erupted in awkward laughter.

Gokul's final Bee turn was so short that it stunned the judges and the audience. *Nunatak*. He said the word but didn't wait for confirmation about whether he heard the correct word, or ask for a definition, sentence, or language of origin. He blurted it out a second time before letting the letters tumble out of his mouth so quickly it was a wonder the judges heard them. Confetti began to rain down on him. "My brain just went into that mode, just like, say it right back." It was a bold and risky move, given the cham-pionship was on the line. "Yeah, I mean, I just knew the word. My original style is that words I memorize, I can easily spit them out so fast," he later told me.

Onstage, Gokul didn't hesitate, he explained, because "there's no point in that. Like, I still had a long night ahead of me with tons of media." Very few kids would be so close to the finals but also so relaxed as to think more about an imminent media junket than methodically completing his turn. But Gen Z kids like Gokul are competitors. The media attention is part of the achievement. One of the highlights of Gokul's tour was to go to ESPN LA and see the NBA finals and *SportsCenter* studios. But the biggest thrill of all? Getting an autographed pair of sneakers from King James himself. LeBron sent him signed high tops with a video message of congratulations.

Gokul's engagement with the Bee extends far beyond what his peers consider usual for an extracurricular activity. But what is normal for childhood today? The first two decades of the twenty-first century have accelerated some changes for children while dramatically ushering in new ones. The most striking shift is how white middle-class childhood transitioned from being focused on play, exploration, and some competition to becoming highly scheduled, activity driven, and extremely competitive. This shift is the latest in a long line of transformations.

Scholars who study patterns of child-rearing in America identify several distinct periods. Focusing on white settlers and not considering parenting among slaves and Native Americans, they include the Colonial Child (1620–1770) and the Republican Child (1770–1830); continuing their focus on the white middle-class, they offer the Victorian Child (1830–1900) and the Modern Child (1900–present). Historian Karin Calvert argues that these periods represent moments when a significant portion of white middle-class families had adopted a new method of raising children.[10]

At the turn of the twentieth century, these parents encouraged their children to be more independent and self-assertive, and they sought environments that would stimulate and channel youthful energy. Historian Peter Stearns argues that childhood emerged as a defined entity during this period, giving shape to the role of the child in family, school, and society.[11] This, in turn, produced new anxieties among adults and thus new efforts at parental control and expert advice, resulting in the rise of organized activities and family involvement in the development of the child.

The idea that children *should* play developed in the late 1800s and early 1900s and became enshrined as our postwar ideal of a carefree childhood.[12] In the second half of the twentieth century, after World War II, white middle-class American childhood balanced academics, play, and unstructured time. Until very recently, this concept seemed impossible to change. Even in the 1970s, anthropologist Helen Schwartzman identified play as vital to childhood as a distinct stage of American social development.[13] Some place a high value on play as integral to learning as well. Continuing today, play-based learning is a model that many progressive preschools follow for early education.

This version of childhood became enshrined as the ideal. The population of the country grew, but so too did industry, higher education, and infrastructure. Still, being a kid was about play and experience, rather than highly structured activities measured by productivity and accomplishment. These middle-class values are largely those of white families in the United States for several generations, with accumulated or inherited wealth. For the privileged, childhood could be carefree because the prospect of adulthood was not yet one of shortage and competition.

Importantly, this is not a uniform set of values, and economically disadvantaged families and those entrenched in structural racism did not, and still don't, have the luxury of a carefree childhood. Moreover, play is not universal. There is great variation in how childhood is perceived around the world. Children may have to work inside or outside the home, caring for siblings and contributing to household income. Parents may emphasize academic accomplishment far more than unstructured playtime. From these possibilities, a trend is emerging: childhood is moving toward more structured activities.

Since the early 1980s, scholars have argued for the "normal-ization" of childhood, that is, creating a childhood governed by greater systemization, efficacy, and predictability.[14] Sociologist Giovanni Sgritta argued that normalizing childhood involved the imposition of a whole new set of rules created to restructure society. Childhood became a realm governed by an overwhelming multitude of prescriptions and controls exerted over a child's time and energy by those entrusted to care for them (parents, extended family, new categories of professionals, etc.). Meanwhile, the family moved more toward disciplining, protecting, controlling, and privatizing child development.

By the early 1990s, there was already evidence of regulated, career-building after-school activities. One 1994 study looked at the rise of the "institutionalized 'afterschool' period" to understand the impact of adult-organized activities on high school kids.[15] Rather than simply being left to play or devise their own amusement, these children were groomed to develop an "extracurricular career." When performance criteria were introduced, children became more involved and focused. The authors conclude that this kind of skill building readies high school students for the corporate world. Nowadays, this same pattern can be seen with students in elementary and middle school, when they are beginning to build these careers.

US-born Baby Boomers (born 1946–1964) are arguably the most invested in the idea of childhood remaining about play and exploration. This viewpoint is understandable in some ways. As ten-year-old children, Boomers were not practicing their culinary knife skills and strategies to plate gourmet meals. That was simply not something kids did in their day.

While Boomers bemoan the death of play, some began to prepare their Millennial children for the modern marketplace. In a 2006 article about the National Spelling Bee, Dr. Harold Koplewicz, director of the New York University Child Study Center, commented: "Among the Baby Boomers, and I am one, expectations for our children are very high. Baby Boomers prepare their children for all kinds of bizarre things, as if their children are extensions of themselves. These are kids who have résumés by the time they apply to college. As a society, unfortunately, we have changed focus so we value our children for their achievements, not because they're our children."[16]

This is the crux of the human capital debate, that investment in people amounts to what can be cultivated for the marketplace. It is rooted in the economic ideology of neoliberalism. Neoliberalism reconceptualizes labor from simple work for pay to a set of skills that enable an individual to earn an income. Neoliberalism emphasizes self-sufficiency, expertise, and entrepreneurial drive to far greater extremes than prior economic models. Being productive, developing expert skills, being self-directed and innovative are engrained societal values that have not only trickled down into childhood, but have established a presence there. Once reserved for the adult workplace, these concepts have become a foundational part of kids' extracurricular activities.

Neoliberal values shaped the course of younger Millennial childhoods, especially those of high achievers. We see this in a study published in 2000, in which educational researchers analyzed competition essays written by over one hundred Presidential Scholars (a Department of Education program that annually honors 161 graduating high school seniors in Washington, DC) and interviewed nineteen of them.[17] Researchers sought to uncover and document the cultural values and individual characteristics that the American K–12 educational system rewarded in its students—that is, what did students consider to be the "ideal self"? Students identified being hardworking, competent, and ambitious as core prescriptions for the ideal self. They also valued morality, authenticity, and uniqueness within traditional education and career paths, suggesting that Generation Z's emphasis on entrepreneurial innovation and self-presentation was already in development among Millennials.

We find ourselves in the period of the neoliberal childhood, one that focuses relentlessly on kids accumulating human capital. The proliferation of kid competitions and brain sports is one trend that confirms this emphasis. Even though competition and organized sports increased after World War II, only in the last twenty years has the emphasis on human capital grown from a parental preoccupation to a childhood occupation. According to journalist Malcolm Harris, Millennials are the first generation to be raised as investments of human capital.[18] Harris explores the complicated nature of this shift, and how Baby Boomer parents have implemented this approach but also critiqued the impact it seems to have on their Millennial children. US-born Gen X parents may have observed these changes in Millennials, with younger Gen Xers beginning to experience preprofessional aspects of childhood. Compared to Baby Boomers, Gen Xers are more pragmatic about raising children who know the kinds of internships and extracurricular activities needed to gain admission to competitive colleges and universities.

Notably, Harris doesn't approve of this trend, declaring, "Competition is ruining childhood. The kids should fight back."[19] He cites statistics about how the rise in education and human capital is not translating into well-paying jobs for Millennials; if anything, it is leaving employers with more people to choose from and the option to pay them less. Harris sees this as kids getting conned and recommends that students protest and advocate for slowing down the race for human capital. Collective organization has certainly brought attention to some aspects of this problem, like crushing debt from student loans.

As promising as this idea is, it seems highly unlikely that young people will collectively discredit the importance of human capital. If these values formed over the course of Millennial childhoods, they have become far more engrained for Generation Z kids. Hilary Friedman's ethnographic research explores aspects of competition for white middle-class kids.[20] Looking at dance, chess, and travel soccer, she identifies the ways adult-organized, competitive extracurricular activities can be connected to children's success later in life. The privilege of these activities is available primarily to those who can dedicate time and money toward cultivating this aspect of their children's upbringing.

One takeaway that emerges from these studies is that modern childhood prepares kids for increasingly challenging adulthoods. Perhaps a more relevant question for today is not why kids build human capital, but how kids regard these activities. Amber would have studied nonstop for the Bee if her mom did not intervene. "She made sure I did my homework, chores, and called my grandma before I could do Bee stuff." She thinks these breaks helped her absorb what she was studying better. Spelling was a motivation to get through some of those other things.

For her final year of Bee competition, Amber willingly ramped up her preparation. Investing far more time and effort, she sought help with root words from her Latin and Greek teachers. Going through the whole dictionary was not a viable study method for Amber. Instead, she used various lists and books, and pored over word patterns. She acquired numerous spelling tricks of each language to "hack open" words she didn't know. Not only did she enjoy learning all of it, but it imparted "a feeling of power" to have a "whole arsenal at your disposal." Her mother gave her words and quizzed her for practice.

In 2013, her fourth straight appearance at the Bee, Amber clung to her final year of eligibility. It all had to happen this year; there wouldn't be another chance. Onstage, Amber's approach was "go slow, ask questions," to ensure that she heard the correct word. Misspelling a known word out of carelessness is "the worst way to go," as Amber put it. "I didn't want to get eliminated unnecessarily." She never focused on the cameras because she was most concerned with "trying hard to not be eliminated." She paid no mind to people taking photos.

After trying every year since the third grade, Amber made it to the live nighttime finals. She sailed through the first five rounds, offering witty remarks at her discretion. During one turn, she watched a montage of her finishes from 2010, 2011, and 2012 and declared, "I guess I beat those records. That is cause for panic!" In round six, she opened with "please give me something I know" and covered her face with her name tag as she ruminated on her word. *Hallali,* a huntsman's bugle call, eliminated her that night and burns in her memory.

Spellers like Amber value the broader benefits of competition in their lives, especially the disciplined habits brain sports demand. Amber maintains that kids who win do so because they have worked really hard. She should know. She finished in fourth place at the 2013 Bee, a monumental accomplishment by any standards. She knows it too, and once described herself in her Twitter bio as "excellent speller," followed by "future POTUS."

Chapter Three

Spelling Bees

Jacques Bailly's voice is synonymous with American spelling. It is so iconic that movie production firm Lionsgate cast him to play himself as the pronouncer in the spelling bee film *Akeelah and the Bee*. Dr. Bailly, as spellers call this University of Vermont classics professor, is possibly the most popular person at the National Spelling Bee. Soft-spoken and calm, he offers the most difficult words in a clear, gentle voice. This is his personality, but also conveys his empathy for kids doing tough things. He should know—he is the 1980 National Spelling Bee champion. Bailly's spelling career began in third grade. He became intrigued with lexicon when his teacher pointed out that English words have roots, histories, and are made up of words from other languages. I had seen Dr. Bailly at the Bee for years, first on television and then in person. I introduced myself in 2014 and we spoke later that summer on Skype.

As Bailly recalls, his love of language grew over his elementary school years. A sixth-grade teacher at his Catholic elementary school, Sister Eileen, was also a spelling coach. She invited Jacques to be on the spelling team. To prepare, he studied a list called "Words of the Champions" that was updated annually.[1] "If you memorized them, you could go far," he explained. Additionally, he studied lists of words from past bees, though those were more difficult to obtain. "People treasured their lists and didn't just give them out," he noted. Even so, the study materials spellers coveted during this pre-Internet era were shorter than the "ten-thousand-word list" that became popular among spellers who followed him. As a Denver native, Jacques Bailly participated in a regional bee sponsored by the *Rocky Mountain News* that included portions of Colorado and Wyoming. It was quite competitive. With his late start, it took him three attempts to advance to the National Spelling Bee. He finally arrived as an eighth grader, in his final year of eligibility. Jacques had no idea whether he would do well at the national level.

The spelling bee today is a contest celebrating American English, with one dictionary as its arbiter. This chapter traces the development of early spelling contests into the regional and national prime-time events we see today. The spelling bee has transformed from a classroom learning exercise to a major national competition. In recent years, the proliferation of bees for adults, kids of South Asian heritage, Native Americans, and those conducted in Spanish attest to their ongoing popularity.

Since 1957, the Scripps National Spelling Bee has used the *Merriam-Webster* dictionary as an authoritative source. *Webster's* and *Funk & Wagnalls's* unabridged dictionaries were the final authorities from 1951 through 1958 according to the national contest rules. Prior to 1951, an official source was not listed in the rules—it was simply stated that "the judges are in complete control of the Bee. Their decision shall be final on all questions." According to records, the Bee began a relationship with Merriam-Webster in 1957. It was not until 1959 that the Bee chose one official dictionary, which was *Webster's New International Dictionary, Second Edition*.[2]

The Merriam publishing company printed its first dictionary in 1847, based on Noah Webster's 1828 edition of his dictionary of American English. As a lexicographer, Webster sought to authoritatively establish a word list of American English. Webster had previously created and circulated multiple dictionaries himself, the first in 1806. Merriam bought Webster's last printing of it, dated 1841. It is considered to be Webster's masterwork and is the culmination of his decades of labor.

Most controversial was its division of syllables to an American standard, which, English scholar Rachel McArthur argues, "became one of the major sites for specifically nationalistic linguistic posturing."[3] Syllabification was emphasized, as was mastering rules of pronunciation *and* orthography. As lexicographer Kory Stamper writes, *Merriam-Webster Unabridged* (www.unabridged.merriam-webster.com), based on *Webster's Third New International Dictionary, Unabridged,* is true to these early roots but also includes the myriad words that have found their way into English via other European languages, languages spoken in British and American colonies and settlements, and lexical innovations necessary for a changing society and world.[4]

The hardcover dictionary is too big for younger spellers to lift unassisted, even though every regional winner in the National

Spelling Bee receives one. The book creates common ground among spellers. One contestant at the National Spelling Bee told me, "You can talk with more people if you have the same interests, and spelling is a big one. For example, if you're talking about a new word being added to the dictionary, spellers know about it and are interested and would talk about it. Whereas conversation with an average person at your school would just die off."

Curiosity about this weighty volume peaks during Bee Week, when Merriam-Webster editor Peter Sokolowski gives an annual lecture. When I attended in 2014, National Spelling Bee director Paige Kimble announced his talk the evening before and cautioned interested parties to arrive early because the room would fill up quickly. I dutifully arrived at 7:45 a.m. the next morning to find the auditorium jam-packed with spellers and their families. I found one of the few remaining seats before it became standing room only. Kimble had taken great care to emphasize that Sokolowski knew nothing about the word-list creation process or which words would appear in the upcoming competition. Perhaps audiences in past years had pressed him on that point; the questions that would follow the talk that day were far less instrumentalist, ranging from fascinating to downright erudite. As I waited for the lecture to start, I reflected on just how much time these people had spent with the tome that was to be the featured topic in mere moments.

For the next forty-five minutes, the room hummed with dictionary love. Sokolowski began by welcoming the true believers into his world. "How many of you *read* the dictionary?" he asked, calling for a show of hands. "You're all my friends. You are among the tiniest percentage of people." Sokolowski offered a well-sketched portrait of how the dictionary came to be in the

United States. He described how Noah Webster changed some spellings for American English to make it distinctive from other varieties. The schwa received extra attention, as a single sound from German via Hebrew that can be spelled in many ways. Making a play on a pop song, he quipped, "I fought the schwa and the schwa won." Parents chuckled and spellers stared with blank expressions, wondering why the adults were laughing.

Highlighting online use, Sokolowski discussed how certain words "trend" and "spike" in conjunction with world events and holidays. *Rubble, triage, terrorism, jingoism, succumb,* and *surreal* spiked after 9/11, in that order, while some sought to understand *cortege* when Princess Diana passed away (it means a funeral procession). On Valentine's Day, people look up *love*. Sokolowski thinks that this is about individuals turning to the dictionary for psychological reasons, to learn about what love is and how long it lasts. Moving on to other terms, he remarked that speakers would do well to learn proper usage for *epic*, which is too often used for things not epic, or *literally*, which suffers even greater abuse, as in "I *literally* laughed to death." Unlikely. The figurative use of *literally* must be used with care and clarity. From their phones, users look up *qi* around 11 p.m.—presumably for their Words with Friends games. The audience laughed appreciatively.

The talk concluded with a question. "Why did Webster change the spelling of some words? He believed America should have its own words. He believed politically in this new country, and that it deserved a dictionary of American English." Applause rang through the room and hands shot up with questions. Most pertained to how words get into the dictionary and how others are removed. The short answer is by an ongoing process in which media is read and common usage tabulated. There are also routine online updates, many of which are for social media terms like *unfriend, blogging,* and so on.

By the time I next attended the lecture, it had become a far larger event. In 2018, Sokolowski's talk was held in the Maryland Ballroom, the auditorium where the Bee itself is staged. Despite the much larger space, he more than held the audience's attention. Families sat rapt, murmuring in admiration when bits of dictionary ephemera appeared on the massive screens flanking the stage. They laughed in unison, as if on cue, in response to the dictionary humor peppered throughout the talk. Some parents took notes. Sokolowski explored why some words are included in the dictionary and who gets to decide what they mean. It is a time-intensive, continuous, research-based process by the editorial staff. Even with an oversized authority like *Merriam-Webster's Unabridged*, there are still variants that people want acknowledged. Consider when 2013 National Spelling Bee champion Arvind Mahankali correctly spelled *knaidel,* matzo ball, to win. The Internet exploded with alternative spellings of the word. According to linguist Sarah Benor, this is in part because each Jewish ethnic group has a distinctive linguistic repertoire consisting of different grammatical constructions and pronunciations from Yiddish, Hebrew, Aramaic, and other sources, including New York regional speech, that influence the English of American Jews.[5]

To this audience, these were more than academic questions; they shaped the day-to-day reality of the hundreds of spellers in the room. Sokolowski certainly gave them a lot to think about. Following the talk, spellers were invited to take a small, red "word nerd" button. They eagerly queued up to do so. Some mothers asked to take an extra button; those who reached in to take a handful were gently admonished by the Scripps staff member who told them to just take one. Spellers swarmed Sokolowski, a true dictionary celebrity, hoping to get a picture.

"I love sports and I love words," former speller and current ESPN copy editor Amy Goldstein told me. Her job is a perfect marriage of her two favorite things. I met Amy in 2015, when she reached out to me via Twitter to introduce herself after reading an op-ed I had published. We met later that summer at ESPN. I visited her during a sweltering August morning on the network's sprawling campus in Bristol, Connecticut. We sat at a picnic table facing a meticulously manicured grassy courtyard.

Amy's spelling career began in second grade, in 1992, during a show-and-tell-with-words activity. Amy brought in the word *skink* but her teacher insisted she meant *skunk* until she later turned to the dictionary to confirm its validity. The next day she told Amy she was going to make it to the National Spelling Bee. Amy had not heard of the contest and became the first in her observant Jewish household to gravitate toward spelling. The road to the national finals via Long Island, New York, was grueling, as competitors needed to win their school and district bee to move on to regionals, where the winners of eighteen districts competed. After finishing as a district alternate in 1997, she won and advanced as a fourteen-year-old with *Newsday* as her sponsor.

When Amy participated in the 1998 National Spelling Bee, it was held at the Grand Hyatt in Washington, DC, with 249 participants. The contest had only been televised for three years, and there was no vocabulary portion yet. She recalled that it was the year before the *Spellbound* movie crew filmed at the Bee. She would see them the following year when she went to cheer on several friends she had made. Amy was speller 143, the eighteenth speller in the afternoon round. Amy's goal was to make it to the fourth round of the competition. She remembers it being "a killer bee," in which an unusually large number of spellers misspelled in the early rounds. "Whole states were eliminated all at once!" she exclaimed, recalling that rounds three, four, five, and six were all "lawnmower rounds." Each of them knocked out more than half of the remaining spellers.

Amy made it past round four, all the way to the finals. ESPN was not making speller features in that era, but she had caught their attention. They took photos of her, and she was shuttled around to interviews, speaking to reporters. "I got lost in it all." At the time, she didn't realize that she had been tapped as a favorite to win. Ultimately, she finished fourth. Jody-Anne Maxwell from Jamaica took the top spot, remaining to this day the only international winner. After the Bee, Amy patiently waited for friends and neighbors to send her the VHS recordings they had made so her family could watch her performance on videotape.

Amy's siblings kept the Goldstein family's spelling legacy going. This remains fairly common today; some families count as many as five kids who have, at one point in their lives, competed in the National Spelling Bee. Two of Amy's siblings were drawn to the Bee, and she encouraged their interest, telling them, "The Bee was the best week of my life. A formative week of my life. My Bee memories are all positive." In 2000, her sister JJ finished seventh nationally. "She didn't study much," Amy remarked casually, adding that she would study a lot more after her older brother, Ari, defeated her in a heated battle at their 2001 regional bee. He placed sixteenth nationally. Not done yet, JJ went back two more times in seventh and eighth grade, finishing third nationally in 2002 and 2003. "All spellers are destined to do great things one day," Amy declared optimistically. In addition to the accomplishment of arriving at a national competition, "the overachievers around you inspire you."

Spelling bees developed as a result of many factors linked to a freshly emerging United States after the Revolutionary War. A newly formed nation needed a language of its own, with uniform rules. The US Spelling Reform Association was assembled for the explicit purpose of creating spellings that differed from British English. Not all spellings were changed, but enough were, and with some consistency. For instance, when we see *colour,* we identify it as a British English spelling, and *color* as the American English spelling. The two words are otherwise indistinguishable with regard to meaning, but their pronunciation and spelling indicate which country they belong to—a distinctly political act. Linguistic anthropologists Bambi Schieffelin and Kathryn Woolard have identified such standardization as linked to nationalism and nation building.[6] The "language ideologies" or systematic beliefs about a language, including phonology, or what it should sound like, and orthography, or what it should look like in written form, help to create a distinct national identity.

Without question, American English was standardized as a national language to the detriment of other American languages, especially Native American tongues. These languages rarely had a written record, making their preservation solely reliant on speakers passing them on to subsequent generations. The widespread genocide of Native Americans and relocation of remaining tribes to reserved lands only severed their place-based relationships to their mother tongues. In some states, such as Hawaii, American missionaries purposefully Anglicized names of places and cultural concepts.[7]

In other regions, anthropologists and other researchers hired by the US government were sent to catalog and make records of Native American languages. This early-twentieth-century activity was popularized by the eminent anthropologist Franz Boas, who trained students to do the same. However, due to limited transcription techniques and partial knowledge of the sound system, or phonology, of these languages, it became very difficult to preserve them alongside the rise of American English.

Linguist Mark Sebba writes that orthographic choices can be used to construct identity, mark boundaries, and display opposition to the mainstream.[8] In a new nation with various European and Native American languages, deliberately elevating one language variety and standardizing it was critical to nation building. Yet in a vast geographic space with no centralized educational policies, how a particular variety of English would be selected and standardized posed a major challenge. Even more confounding was how to be sure children learned that variety rather than some other one. Enter the dictionary.

At the heart of the matter are the phonological principles of orthography, which translate spoken sound into written form, and the semantic principles of orthography, in which meaning is represented through specific letter combinations, such as "their" versus "there." The ultimate arbiter is the dictionary. Even for the American English that emerged as our national language, however, a "standard" language is an impossibility. Language is a dynamic communicative medium that changes as people use it. Innovation that occurs in speech is slower to take hold in writing and may not change how a word is represented in written form or recorded in the dictionary.

In every spelling competition, the dictionary is the authority. Pronunciation is meticulously represented through an elaborate guide designed to eliminate any ambiguity. Reading the dictionary the way elite spellers do requires a thorough understanding of the pronunciation guide and the diacritical markings used to represent sound. Even when words have an alternative pronunciation, their standard pronunciation appears first and most authoritatively. It ensures that American English speakers will always choose *tuh-MAY-toe* over the British English *toh-MAH-toe*. In rare instances outside the United States, spelling bees have been staged to challenge, rather than uphold, a national standard.[9] For example, one such bee is held in Corsica, where regional Corsican spellings are valued over their French standardized versions as an expression of political protest in this multilingual region. Analogous dissent has not been documented in response to American English.

Silent letters, variably pronounced consonants, and the confounding schwa are what make American English spelling competitions so fascinating and challenging. Recall that highly entertaining moment of the 1992 presidential campaign when then vice president Dan Quayle went head-to-head with elementary school children. In Trenton, New Jersey, Quayle obliged a campaign-trail request to conduct a classroom spelling bee for about twenty-five students. A gaggle of reporters had gathered to chronicle his visit. While Quayle handled the first word, *president,* with ease (as one would hope), the second word proved to be more challenging. When he asked a student to write the word *potato* on the board, a boy named William wrote out the dictionary spelling. Eager to make this a teachable moment, Quayle sprang up to offer his corrective to what he erroneously believed to be William's misspelling. "Phonetically," Quayle asserted, William was correct, but he had failed to add the *e* at the end. The former veep had inverted the relationship between sound and representation: *potato* is spelled phonetically, as it sounds, whereas *potatoe* is not.

Quayle's mistake highlights the complexities of learning English spelling, which stymies even educated adults. Spelling expertly is a badge of high scholarly competence, which is what makes young elite spellers so remarkable.

"During Jacques's era, the rules of the Bee were different than they are today. The contest ended when one of the last two remaining spellers misspelled a word and the other person spelled that same word, as well as an additional word, correctly. In the end, it was just Jacques and a speller from El Paso, Texas, named Paige Pipkin. After several tense rounds, Paige received the word *glitch*. She spelled it G-L-I-T-S-C-H. In a pre-computer era, Paige had never heard of the now commonplace word. Bailly remarked, "It is a good way to spell a German word, but it was wrong." He made what he called an "obvious" guess and spelled it without the *s*. He went on to win by spelling *elucubrate*, to work out or express by studious effort, correctly and was named champion.

Bailly remarked that the correction of a misspelling was not the best route to naming a winner. Even though the rule had benefited him tremendously, it gave the second speller an unfair advantage. "So many words are binary, in that they only have one area that is a 'problem,'" he explained. Bee officials would later amend this rule to have the second person spell an altogether different word, plus one in the following round, to win.

At that time, it didn't help Paige Pipkin, who only had one remaining year of eligibility. Pipkin's married name, Kimble, would become well known to generations of spellers when she became the director of the Scripps National Spelling Bee. Young Paige was not deterred by her second-place finish. Paige first became interested in spelling bees when she was nine and came across a taped broadcast of the 1977 Bee on PBS. That fall, she obtained a word list and learned every entry on it. But extreme shyness combined with nerves led her to switch the order of letters in *mango* at her school bee. "I had a vision of going to Washington and I knew that it wasn't going to happen," she told me when we spoke on the phone in February 2018.

After the *mango* debacle, a family acquaintance studying hypnotherapy offered to use it to help Paige with her concentration. He was eager to see if his nascent hypnotherapy skills were effective, and Paige wanted her studying to pay off. It did. "History tells the rest. Coming out of that experience, I was always very calm, centered, focused, methodical when I went to spell. There was no chance I was going to transpose my letters or lose track of my thoughts." On her second trip to the Bee, she was named the 1981 champion.

The National Spelling Bee that Paige and Jacques participated in, which seems so old-fashioned compared to the Bee today, is itself barely recognizable compared to early spelling competitions. Spelling bees have been part of America's history for at least a few centuries. They are both curious vestiges of past educational urgencies and legitimate competitions in their own right, commanding community-level, regional, and national audiences. Underpinning spelling bees, especially those of America's early years, is the objective of standardizing language as part of a nation-building project. This project, emergent in the eighteenth- and nineteenth-century United States, became fully actualized in the twentieth century.

How the term *spelling bee* came about remains a topic of speculation. McArthur has written about the etymological and cultural development of spelling bees. She argues that this term developed through an American usage of the term *bee* to form compounds with verbal nouns such as *quilting bee*, *reading bee*, and so on.[10] Another theory she explores is based on the word *bean*, drawn from New England town life, itself based on English customs. In England, on Yorkshire bean-days, farmers could be called on to assist other villagers in large projects. *Bean* was transformed into *bee*. There is little consensus about which is correct.

Cultural Studies scholar Sam Whitsitt links the spelling bee to Puritan scripture, magic, ritualism, and Americana.[11] Focusing on the "arbitrary character" of spelling in America, Whitsitt argues that through spelling, Americans found a way to execute control and closure over greater, random forces that seemed to structure the larger Puritan world. In other words, spelling bees offered a methodical contest free from supernatural forces. Whitsitt asserts that anyone with the dictionary, from anywhere in America or the world, can compete against anyone else and win.

What is widely agreed upon is that in early American society, spelling was more than a way of standardizing language; it was also a socially relevant and prestigious activity. Allen Walker Read's account of the first American spelling bees, published in 1941, offers one of the earliest histories of the competition.[12] Read wrote about how "spelling matches" became a well-established practice in American schools during the latter half of the eighteenth century.

The antecedents of the spelling bee can be found in the practices of Elizabethan schools. In 1596, Edmund Coote, schoolmaster at Bury St. Edmunds, recorded his method of "how the teacher shall direct his schollers to oppose one another" in a spelling contest. By the mid-eighteenth century, Benjamin Franklin had advanced the study of the vernacular, or American English, and began to create the basis for a standard. By the latter half of the eighteenth century, spelling matches became a well-established practice in American schools.

In these early years of nation building, the mastery of conventional spelling was a status marker, and some welcomed the activity as conferring prestige. They were highly popular in New England especially. Read writes, "Neighboring districts would send their champions for the combat, and the rest of the community would join in.... They became, naturally enough, a social event, although the name 'spelling school,' which clung to them, salved the Puritan conscience." They waned in popularity in New England during the middle of the nineteenth century, but conversely grew in interest in other regions of the country.

Over time, spelling bees had become too established an activity to ever be completely replaced by rote memory drills. Public spelling bees were held for Illinois school children in the 1850s, while in Iowa they provided community entertainment. The expansion of this activity westward followed other kinds of settlement and development. Bees were staged for diversion in California mining camps. By the Civil War, their entertainment value began to fade on the frontier as well. Nonetheless, the positive effects of the contests could be noted in the overall popular knowledge of American English.

The first "national" spelling bee was held in 1925 and was organized by the *Courier-Journal* in Louisville, Kentucky. The newspaper initially conducted a statewide contest to find the best spellers in Kentucky and then invited other newspapers around the United States to choose champions to participate in a national competition in Washington, DC. The "national" part was more a feature of its location in the nation's capital than actual representation of every state in the union. For this spelling bee, more than two million schoolchildren competed at the local and state level, with nine advancing to Washington. They met with President Calvin Coolidge before the contest. Frank Neuhauser won for spelling *gladiolus* and received $500 and a gold medal.[13]

Newspapers, community organizations, universities, sports commissions, and even an NFL team (the Tennessee Titans) continue to sponsor regional contests and their winning spellers today. They do the work of promoting the spelling bee and increasing its visibility in their region. The Bee in turn publicizes sponsors and links them to this enriching contest. With such explicit ties to newspapers, it seems fitting that the E. W. Scripps Company (then known as Scripps-Howard Newspapers) took over the competition in 1941. The company held numerous newspapers and eventually also television, radio, and digital properties.

Until 2018, all competitors were sponsored by a newspaper or other organization. The Bee has also partnered with major corporate sponsors. As part of its 2014 sponsorship, Microsoft distributed Surface tablets to every speller, eliciting squeals of delight from a stage full of kids. Other partnerships have included Zynga (Words with Friends) and Amazon Kindle. Despite commercial sponsorship, the concept of education remains centrally important to the Bee's mythology. In its mission statement, the Bee assigns itself a pedagogical function. In the face of this claim, the contest is, at best, a para-pedagogical event. Although Scripps works *with* schools at the regional, qualifying level, it is not itself affiliated with any educational institution nor does it espouse any specific curriculum.

Therefore, it is up to spellers to invent their own pedagogy and devise their own methods of studying and learning. George Thampy, champion of the 2000 National Spelling Bee, figured this out along the way. As a small, bespectacled boy who spoke with a lisp, he is shown as a fierce competitor in *Spellbound* at the 1999 Bee. Despite his diminutive stance, he commanded attention through the authority with which he spelled. He uttered each letter distinctly and was unflinching even in error. When George was two years old, he watched 1988 National Spelling Bee champion Rageshree Ramachandran hoist the trophy on television. By age five, he decided he wanted to participate in spelling bees.

George and I first met in 2013 at the National Spelling Bee, where he serves as a judge. We spoke at length in 2016 about his spelling career and the years that followed. He described his study method, which seemed technically savvy for his time. George reminded me that there were no "modern Google chat groups" when he was a speller. He was on his own. He read through the dictionary twenty pages at a time, collecting the words he did not know and entering them into a Corel WordPerfect document. He printed out the pages he had accumulated containing several thousand words. "I just really drilled my notes," he told me.

George's parents quizzed him from his lists but were unfamiliar with the pronunciation guide and approximated how to say some of the words. In his fourth-grade bee, he did not recognize a word he knew how to spell because his mother had pronounced it differently in their practice. This was an oversight that he subsequently corrected by creating phonetic pronunciations for her. "I can't ever blame her! I'm very grateful that she spent a lot of time with me," he said. The setback only seemed to motivate George further.

George grew up in St. Louis, where his Christian parents moved after they emigrated from Kerala, India. His father trained to be a physician at Saint Louis University, while his mother homeschooled him and his six siblings. George could understand his parent's native language of Malayalam but could not read the script or follow traditional Malayalee services. Rather than drilling him in Malayalam, George's parents encouraged his pursuit of English at the Bee. They thought it would make him fully American, in a way that they as immigrants were not always acknowledged to be. George agrees that the Bee encouraged his mastery of the English language and helped him find some sense of belonging in America. He was twelve when he won by spelling *demarche*, maneuver, making him one of the youngest-ever champions.

B ee official Paige Kimble is asked annually whether Scripps intends to expand the contest. The response given when I first began attending the Bee in 2013 was that it's already grown tremendously, from around 110 spellers in the 1980s to over 275 this decade. Every year, spellers and families reportedly tell Scripps that those in intensely competitive areas are at a disadvantage. While strong competitors can come from urban as well as less populated areas, some strong spellers never make it to nationals from talent-rich regions like New York City, Houston, or Silicon Valley. Sometimes one speller keeps a stronghold on a smaller region throughout their competition years, only allowing others a chance when they age out or retire. Ostensibly this can mean another very qualified aspiring speller never makes it to the Bee. In response, some regions send two spellers, as became the case in Houston. Parents petitioned the sponsor, Houston PBS, arguing that a region that houses NASA and numerous technology companies and universities has far too much brainpower to send only a single contender.

In the spelling bee world, regional competition of this caliber can be too much for families to handle. Relocating based on a child's promising spelling talent is not out of the question. Parents of kids in a number of activities—from soccer to equestrian sports—upend their lives and move to reside in a location or work with a coach that they believe will allow their child to become the very best.[14] Parents with disposable income and flexible jobs that allow for travel are best able to manage these moves. In many cases, they are done to be closer to academies and facilities that will allow their child to train. In spelling, relocating can improve spellers' odds of advancing to nationals by entering a less competitive regional bee.

In 2018, Scripps offered a fix for this predicament with a new program called RSVBee, intended to address glaring disparities between regional bee programs. While some kids participate in regional bees with about twenty-five other spellers, others go up against hundreds of school bee champions. Many highly talented spellers were not advancing to the Bee due to the tremendous volume of competitors in their region. In the RSVBee program's pilot year, 855 kids applied for an invitation to pay a participation fee and fund their own travel and lodging. RSVBee applicants must be a school spelling bee champion or a former national finalist. They are ranked according to a points system, with priority given to eighth graders and prior national finalists. In 2018, spellers in Georgia, Alabama, Arizona, Arkansas, and Wisconsin; in Dallas, Houston, and Denver; and those in regions without a sponsor stood to benefit most. Ultimately, 238 additional spellers were selected to join 277 sponsored spellers, bringing the competitor total to 515. Kimble justified the growth by stating, "When kids aspire to achieve through our program, we have a responsibility to provide opportunities and experiences commensurate to their efforts."

Kimble herself would have benefited from RSVBee, as she nearly became ineligible to participate. Between her sixth and seventh grade, her father took a job in a Texas town that was six hundred miles away from her hometown of El Paso. He was unsuccessful in petitioning the new town to start a spelling bee program, despite trying to convince them that they had the next national champion on their hands. "So my parents made a huge sacrifice and decided they would keep their residence in El Paso so I could continue with my teacher/coach at the junior high school, and we would have split households. My father took the job and rented a room in a home. We would connect as a family every six to eight weeks." This kind of sacrifice is uncommon, but certainly not unheard of. Today, as a second-place finisher in her sixth-grade regional Bee, Paige would have qualified for RSVBee, making it unnecessary for her family to maintain two residences for her spelling career.

RSVBee spellers I spoke with were thrilled at the chance to compete. "Oh man, it's great!" exclaimed Georgia eighth grader Garv Gaur about his first national finals appearance. "I thought I was done when I finished fourth at state," he added. In 2018, the expanded pool of competitors required Dr. Jacques Bailly and judges to cycle through hundreds more words than past years. Anticipating fatigue, Scripps instituted a "swing protocol," allowing officials to signal for a replacement if they need a break. For the first time, the backup pronouncer, Dr. Brian Sietsema, had a chance to pronounce the Bee.

In the end, the winner of the 2018 Bee was an RSVBee invitee. Champion Karthik Nemmani's school paid his $750 participation fee, while his parents bore the cost of their travel, lodging, and food. For spelling bee families—as with chess, geography, Scrabble, and other brain sports—it is a small price to pay. Some families will make any sacrifice to give their child an opportunity. Eighth-grade Wisconsin speller Ronald Walters's mother is a native of Lima, Peru. She learned about the spelling bee when Ronald made it to regionals last year. The price seemed reasonable to her: "For some families maybe it's difficult, but for us it is also a gift." RSVBee underscores the continued growth of children's competitions and what families are willing to do to give their kid a shot.

Sukanya Roy is a former elite speller whose family was involved in the South Asian American spelling bee community. Growing up, she participated annually in two bees for children of South Asian heritage: the North South Foundation spelling bee and the South Asian Spelling Bee. Her first NSF contest was in third grade, and she kept returning and progressing to the national level. There, she learned that many NSF kids go to Scripps, and that it was a possibility for her. When she found herself age-eligible, she decided to try for the national stage.

Sukanya advanced to Scripps three consecutive times, beginning in sixth grade, when she was twelve. When asked if she had increasingly better finishes, she explained, "No, actually. It's very common for rankings to bounce around. Once you get past a certain skill or training level, so much of it is luck. It's about being able to feel out the roots of the word or guess or correctly discern, even if you either haven't seen it before or can't recall it perfectly." Her first year she placed twelfth, but then dropped to twentieth in seventh grade, getting eliminated in the semifinals.

Sukanya did not believe she had a chance of winning until she saw Nupur Lala become a champion in *Spellbound*. She also realized that one of the girls profiled in the documentary, April DeGideo, was from her region. "I remember thinking if someone from this area is capable of coming to the Bee, maybe I am too." While she was inspired by Nupur, she did not want to get ahead of herself, reflecting, "It's always dangerous to think that you can win in the lead-up to the Bee, and I definitely did not want to be overconfident. If you've been preparing all year, you know that you might be capable of winning, but after that it is a question of luck. Is the word you get one that you can recall, one that you can piece together from roots, one that you have seen enough times that you will not stumble on it somehow?" She did not stumble. At her third National Spelling Bee, Sukanya wasn't even nervous; as she describes it, "I just went into a trance state." She was so focused that the most nerve-wracking part became waiting for her next turn. She heard the bell ding for everyone's misspellings but her own. She was named the 2011 champion for spelling *cymotrichous*, having wavy hair.

Over her spelling career, Sukanya's family drew heavily on the broader community of Scripps, NSF, and SASB spellers. "Just knowing other people who had come to Scripps and being able to ask them for tips was so helpful. That is something that I've prioritized since I won. Whenever anyone wants to ask for pointers or anything, I'm ready to help." I had already witnessed this by walking down the main hallway outside the auditorium with her. Several parents approached her for her email address, with some instructing their children to pose for a photograph if she was willing. She gracefully obliged each time. Parents seemed to want some of a champion's luck to rub off on their child as much as they sought her advice. Those pictures would be hung in speller bedrooms as inspiration.

Communities across the United States and the world are creating thriving spelling competitions. According to participants I spoke with, the North American Spelling Champion Challenge is held in Maryland and California each summer as a sleepaway camp. It offers a cultural-exchange environment with aspiring spellers from China, in which all participants train together and ultimately compete for a title. Spelling bees in different languages are also growing in popularity worldwide. The National Spanish Spelling Bee, in which participants need to also include diacritical markings like accents and diaereses, is held annually in multiple states. For adults, there are numerous options. For several years until 2014, a monthly spelling bee at Pete's Candy Store, a bar in the New York City neighborhood of Williamsburg, Brooklyn, was held on the first Monday of the month.[15] Participants signed up at 7 p.m., and spots filled up quickly. The grand prize was a Scrabble coffee mug. Contestants sipped beer and watch their fellow adults dazzle and fizzle. Among the senior set, the AARP conducted spelling bees for a time, and the National Senior Spelling Bee remains popular.

Scripps has franchised the National Spelling Bee competition to seven other countries, including the Bahamas, Canada, Ghana, Jamaica, Japan, and South Korea (China previously participated), all of which send spellers to the national finals. Other countries—including Australia, Belize, Germany, Japan, South Africa, and the United Kingdom—all hold spelling bees in English. The African Spelling Bee is a continent-wide contest with seventeen nations participating. The winner receives a full undergraduate scholarship. India hosts the Wiz National Spell Bee, which increased from 2,200 contestants to over 2 million in just eight years.[16] As of 2017, they shortlist 2,000 contestants, versus only 150 in 2003.

The spelling bee also continues to thrive in the American public imagination. *The 25th Annual Putnam County Spelling Bee* is a musical that has been staged to great acclaim in several cities across the United States. The 2002 Oscar-winning documentary *Spellbound* and 2006 crowd favorite *Akeelah and the Bee* are still watched by aspiring spellers.[17] In 2018, the documentary film *Bee Nation* about Saskatchewan spellers was released.[18] It chronicles the Canadian First Nations Provincial Spelling Bee and its role in promoting education and community pride.

These values also underpin the two most prominent and established minor-league bees, the North South Foundation bee and South Asian Spelling Bee. The NSF emerged from a charitable organization founded to help meritorious kids who live in abject poverty in India go to college. Its founder, Ratnam Chitturi, is from Andhra Pradesh, India. The Immigration and Nationality Act of 1965 had just set new quotas for immigration based on broader national origins, and solicited skilled professionals. Chitturi, a mechanical engineer, answered the call. He immigrated to the United States in 1965 to pursue higher studies, including MS and PhD degrees, and settled in the Chicago area in 1984.

Seeking to do more than live a comfortable life and raise a family, Chitturi augmented his career as a vice president of a bank by founding the NSF. The name, which refers to the wealthier nations of the northern hemisphere and their struggling southern-hemisphere counterparts, is intended to draw attention to the success enjoyed by immigrants like Chitturi and the rampant illiteracy and poverty that much of India and other countries faced in the 1980s, and still do.

In 1993, Chitturi established educational contests for children of the Indian diaspora, beginning with a spelling bee. He was inspired by Balu Natarajan, the first Indian American spelling champion in 1985, followed by Rageshree Ramachandran in 1988. Community interest was solid, and it proved to be a good way to fundraise for Indian education. In the ensuing decades, through volunteer labor, small regional contests grew and culminated in a national-level final. As interest burgeoned, so too did the number of regional bees and participants. This growth was also in keeping with the size of the Indian American population over the decades. Whereas there were only about 12,000 Indian immigrants in the United States in 1960, by 2015 there were 3.1 million.[19]

According to Chitturi, NSF activities are "an Indian American community endeavor to help its children. The fruits are there to see." Aside from the junior spelling competition for children in kindergarten through third grade and the well-known senior spelling competition for those from fourth through eighth grade, NSF also holds contests in geography, science, math, the anatomy of the brain, essay writing, and public speaking. All of the contests continue to be run by volunteers, who also generate content such as word lists. About three thousand volunteers conduct the contests and also offer online and on-site workshops and coaching. Nearly four thousand children avail themselves of the online coaching provided by some two hundred volunteer coaches. Each volunteer devotes two hours per week over fifteen weeks—an extraordinarily generous time commitment when spelling coaching pays top dollar. Current and past elite spellers travel annually to help run the regional bees and the national finals. Chitturi believes these returning spellers act as role models for new generations of spellers.[20]

Today NSF enrolls more than sixteen thousand contestants annually, ranging from kindergarten through twelfth grade. Their ninety-two chapters were founded through word of mouth with no marketing or publicity—evidence of how this immigrant community shares information and knowledge about academic enrichment activities. The top prize today is $1,000 in scholarship money, a fraction of the $40,000 disbursed by Scripps. Moreover, competitors fund their own travel expenses to compete in the national finals. Still, the prestige of winning this long-standing contest and the draw of community service has made it a fond favorite in the South Asian American spelling world.

NSF gave speller Sanjana Malla her start in spelling bees in first grade, when she competed in one of their regional contests. Sanjana lives in Haverstraw, New York, about an hour north of New York City. Her father admitted that he had never heard of spelling bees but learned about them when they visited friends in Connecticut. "They took us to watch an NSF bee and the next year we put her in. She did well even without preparation." The following year she placed second at NSF regionals and went to nationals. "It didn't go well!" Sanjana laughed. It nonetheless launched her spelling career. During the years when there was no regional sponsor for Scripps in her area, she continued to compete in the South Asian American circuit while her father continuously petitioned. Eventually, in 2011, a regional bee was established. Sanjana was in sixth grade and made it to the National Spelling Bee that same year.

Sanjana's family relied heavily on other South Asian American families to learn what to do. Her father told me, "It's not a laid-out path. You come from another country, you have to take care of jobs, housing, and so on. You don't know how to do this additional work." He continued, "We started watching Kavya [Shivashankar] on TV. We saw her in NSF bees as a small kid, so when we saw her on the TV we thought we could follow that path." With two working parents, it left limited time to intensively prepare for the Bee. Her father said, "During Bee season, I tell [Sanjana] to be ready for spelling by the time I get home— eat dinner, practice violin, finish homework and Kumon—so we can have time for it." Sanjana's mother described spelling as their family's activity. She told me, "I was happy to spend quality time with the kids instead of socializing. We made it fun. If you like something, obviously you make time for it." Part of her enjoyment is seeing a community of speller families at these bees each year.

In the final summer of her spelling career, Sanjana's parents suggested that she ease up on spelling prep and enjoy some free time. She countered that it was her very last year of competition and insisted on going to the South Asian Spelling Bee. Produced by the marketing and public relations firm Touchdown Media, the South Asian Spelling Bee is a newer contest modeled more closely on the National Spelling Bee. Its founder, Rahul Walia, operates it under a different philosophy than the NSF bee, and the South Asian Spelling Bee aims to be a high-profile event. In recent years, nearly every South Asian American speller who has won the National Spelling Bee has also won or placed competitively in the South Asian Spelling Bee. In fact, Walia insists that it is even more competitive than the National Spelling Bee.

I first learned about it when I was visiting ad agencies for a research project on advertising to Asian American consumers. I met Walia in Metuchen, New Jersey, in 2012, where Touchdown Media is based. He emigrated from India in 1995 with a marketing degree and has worked with South Asian brands in the United States as well as global corporations wishing to reach South Asian immigrants. Walia saw an opportunity for furthering this immigrant population's involvement in competitive spelling. He likes to ask, "What can we do that is relevant for the South Asian community, that is not Bollywood related?"

The contest emerged from a brainstorm for events that would draw South Asian American consumers. State Farm and, later, MetLife have each served as title sponsors. He asserts that there is an emotional connection that people form with spelling bees, and that they also enjoy the sport and competition of a good bee. It constitutes what he calls "the trifecta: it is education focused, family focused, and reaches a market that is serious about their life planning." Emphasizing the power of education to make his client's brand "look like a king," he recited the tagline he had developed for MetLife's South Asian American campaign: *"Apki zindagi main apke sath"* ["With you throughout your whole life"].

Each year since 2008, SASB has held regional spelling competitions in areas of the country with sizable South Asian populations. Walia runs each of the regional contests and the national finals with his sister, public relations executive Daisy Walia, and production director Rupam Kavi. These culminate in a national competition with the winner and runner-up from each region. The South Asian Spelling Bee is not just another tournament that helps spellers prepare for Scripps, but a prestige event in its own right. Walia analogizes the South Asian American spelling circuit to Grand Slam tennis tournaments. Participating in a circuit can only improve one's game, he explained. The professional lexicographers, judges, and pronouncers Walia hires have created a winning formula. The television exposure and prize money for this contest similarly aim big. The SASB is broadcast on Sony Entertainment Television, with speller interviews and biographical details—a scaled-down version of ESPN's production model. Likewise, the $10,000 prize is not Scripps-size, but is respectably large for a middle school student. ESPN commentators now routinely mention elite spellers' finishes in the South Asian Spelling Bee, noting the pipeline effect.

At the Houston 2014 South Asian Spelling Bee, siblings Shobha and Shourav Dasari went head-to-head for so many rounds that Walia stepped in and declared they could no longer request sentences. Such unorthodox moves are not uncommon in his administering of regional bees, especially when there are only two spellers left and both are guaranteed a spot in the SASB nationals. The remaining question of who would be champion and runner-up seemed unresolvable until Shobha finally misspelled and Shourav won. The third-place contestant, like the rest of the room, was in awe, and leagues behind their level of prowess.

I interviewed Shobha and Shourav, along with their parents, Usha and Ganesh, after this bee. We planned the conversation after we met at the 2014 National Spelling Bee, where Shobha finished as a semifinalist. Neither speller seemed the slightest bit tired after their intense competitive exertion. As we settled into sofas in the community-center lobby, the third-place winner's family came over to congratulate the Dasaris. They also asked for advice and recommendations on how to study. Between the two of them, the Dasari siblings had several years of competition left. The Dasaris wanted to be collegial and supportive while not revealing their entire strategy. Whatever they were doing to win had to be guarded to some degree. They kindly spoke to the other family, suggesting several approaches that would prepare their speller for different levels of competition. The family seemed a bit overwhelmed by the information but was nonetheless very grateful. They took their leave and the Dasaris and I settled in to talk. We sat in a semicircle while people wandered in and out. The remaining SASB attendees and staff waved to the Dasaris as they exited the building.

For over a decade, Mr. and Mrs. Dasari have lived and breathed competitive spelling. Mrs. Dasari identifies what she calls the South Asian "spelling community" through which she has gotten to know other parents and their spellers. In the Houston region, this is how she came to learn about the South Asian Spelling Bee, study materials, and other resources to start developing practice materials for her children. The interaction between the parents tends to be friendly and collaborative, especially when the spellers in their family have aged out of competition. This was especially helpful as Mrs. Dasari worked with her own children. About those families, she exclaimed, "They are like an open book! They tell you exactly what they studied and did." The recruitment of new kids seems to happen organically, with parents seeing others and thinking, "Hey, my kids might want to do that!" as Mr. Dasari put it. He believes interest in spelling spreads via ripple effect.

He is right. Recently, the South Asian American spelling community has received increased media attention. A 2017 *Harper's* magazine article titled "Bee-Brained: Inside the Competitive Indian-American Spelling Community" by journalist Vauhini Vara offers an overview of this alternate circuit.[21] As a former competitor, she brings her insights from her forty-fourth-place finish at the 1994 National Spelling Bee to bear on the current state of South Asian American competitive spelling. She contrasts her outing to the Bee, during the very first year of ESPN's broadcast, with the scale, visibility, and public engagement of the 2016 Bee. In her day, this minor-league spelling circuit had not yet been established, but would be a major game-changer for spellers like her in the decades to come. In 2018, filmmakers Sam Rega and Chris Weller released *Breaking the Bee*, a documentary focused on Indian American spellers in the Bee.[22] It follows the progress of several top competitors, including Shourav Dasari, at NSF, SASB, and the National Spelling Bee, exploring from a number of perspectives how this community has mobilized around this activity.

Despite the deep community investment, there is skepticism of this activity's value among the broader South Asian American population. Some of the Malla family's friends cannot understand their passion for this brain sport and why it is worthwhile to invest this kind of time. "Lots of people ask me how it helps," said Sanjana's father. He views it as an actual investment and expects spending copious time on this activity to have some kind of payoff. He tells them that it increases vocabulary, knowledge of root words and languages of origin, and exposure to multiple languages. Some are still not convinced, so he goes on to say that it gives spellers an intimate knowledge of terms in science, medicine, reading, and so on. One of the major benefits is that "it gives their brains exercise from childhood onward. Working the brain as a muscle is important."

Sanjana competed in the National Spelling Bee three times, qualifying for semifinals twice. Once she aged out, the family turned their attention fully to her younger brother Sravanth's spelling career. They already had the lists they'd created for Sanjana and now had far more time to go through the dictionary, which they admitted never completing in Sanjana's day. They are expanding on the categories they initially created and have over 250, for the kinds of terms they see emerging in bees—geographical locations, animal species, trademarks, and so on. Every word counts. They look at what was asked in previous bees and identify difficult words they think will have a higher likelihood to reappear. In the ensuing years, Sravanth Malla competed in the Bee three times as well. In 2018, he made it to the finals handily, getting one of the four perfect scores on the written exam.

The camaraderie spelling families find is rooted in their philosophy that one's performance at a bee is about their own preparation and a bit of luck about the word they are given. "So it's technically not competing," added Mrs. Malla. It seems easier for families to see spelling bees as a cutthroat competition against the dictionary rather than among kids. This is the very philosophy that Scripps adheres to and is also true to the historical roots of the contest. As the spelling bee is a language arts exercise promoting American English, it is only fitting that kids and communities continue to find enjoyment in this competition.

Chapter Four

Gen Z Kids

Vanya Shivashankar's on-screen life started well before her spelling career. She first appeared on the National Spelling Bee stage in 2009, as a seven-year-old. For those finals, families watched from one side of the stage to add drama to the live broadcast. Still, she sat with the focus and intent of a competitor, next to her parents who wore the tense expressions of people trying to look relaxed. Her older sister, Kavya, was making her fourth appearance at the National Spelling Bee. When Kavya was named the 2009 champion, Vanya sprang up to hug her sister, who was quickly enveloped by her parents and a swarm of reporters amid a deluge of confetti. The cameras love this family, especially charismatic, adorably young Vanya, and had followed her closely during her sister's years of competition.

Vanya had to wait until Kavya won or aged out to make it to the Bee, as their region only sponsored one speller. She was ready for the moment when it came. In 2010, eight-year-old

Vanya began appearing in local news footage as a competitor.[1] The media rarely gets excited about first-time spellers, but Vanya was newsworthy on two counts. In addition to being the sister of the reigning champion, she was also the youngest speller in that year's Bee. Commentators like to reference the "legacy spellers" who have successful older siblings. It had been several years since the last legacy speller, Akshay Buddiga, followed in his older brother Pratyush's footsteps. Akshay made it deep into the finals during his competition year but did not win. Until 2015, the Bee had yet to see two siblings both win the national competition. It was up to Generation Z.

Vanya made it to the Bee every year except 2011. In 2013, she advanced to the finals, but in 2014 was stunned to not be included based on her written test. For a speller so accomplished, this was a major disappointment. It only motivated her further. Vanya is camera-friendly and articulate, continuing to exude the poise she possessed as a six-year-old talking about becoming a speller like her older sister. In her numerous appearances, she is exuberant and self-assured. In one of her ESPN features, she describes herself as *debonair*, "easygoing and pleasant in disposition." This pairs well with the shot of her riding a roller coaster. She draws an analogy between the ride and the ups and downs of her Bee experience, reminding viewers she has been attending since she was four. The Bee audience uttered a collective "aww" at her flashback image.

At the 2015 Bee, Vanya easily advanced through the semifinal rounds. Backstage before the Bee, the camera followed her as she stood with her fellow finalists. Vanya commented that she wanted to emulate her sister Kavya's "calm composure" as a way to manage her own enthusiasm about her success.[2] She must have found a way. Vanya spelled *scherenschnitte*, an infrequently used German word describing the art of decorative paper cutting, correctly to be named cochampion. This time it was Kavya's turn to deliver the onstage hug to Vanya.

Vanya embodies the emerging hallmarks of Generation Z, in that she is camera-ready, organized, driven, and goal oriented. Rather than accepting an "everyone gets a trophy" approach to competition, winning was Vanya's goal, even though she would take defeat in stride. Vanya and others born after 1996 belong to America's youngest generation. The nascent characteristics outlined here will only become more defined in the coming decades. Two things are of primary interest: the emerging features of Gen Z, based partly on our understanding of Millennials, and the significance of the diversity of Gen Z, especially that it includes the most children of immigrants of any American generation. Of secondary interest is their digital literacy, Gen Z's use of social media in particular.

Generational groupings have been a useful analytic in demographic research since at least the post–World War II era, but this concept is not without its shortcomings. Scholars have argued that the distance between generations is somewhat artificial and cannot be regarded as empirically precise.[3] There may also be considerable overlap, for instance, between the last birth years of one generation and the first few of the next. Rather than viewing the qualities of a generation as hard-and-fast truths, I consider them a collection of traits, several of which may be present in any individual. To be sure, members of generational cohorts do share numerous absolute facts, even if they experience them differently. They come of age during distinct presidential eras such as those of Reagan, Clinton, Bush, and Obama. They witness major calamities—such as the terrorist attacks of September 11,

2001, or the Great Recession—that formatively and indelibly mark their youth. They also come to take certain social and economic conditions ranging from civil rights to digital culture as the norm.

Even so, some critics argue that the evidence regarding generational characteristics is lacking, and that the size of these cohorts complicates broader generalizations.[4] One of the issues I've identified in reading this vast body of literature is its focus on white middle-class families. At the center of most theories of generation are US-born whites who regard themselves to be middle class and either single or in heterosexual nuclear families. US-born minorities such as African Americans and children of immigrants are not acknowledged but lumped into white middle-class norms. This creates very narrow definitions of generations, especially as cohorts grow in racial and ethnic diversity.

My aim is to decenter the whiteness of these major demographic cohorts. I consider the impact of children of immigrants as part of Gen Z, rather than a separate case study. If Gen Z is the most diverse generation to date, then understanding that diversity, rather than continuing to only focus on white middle-class kids, is essential. How anyone experiences being part of a generation varies greatly depending on their race, gender, sexuality, and economic background. Generational identities are rarely considered in this intersectional way, but doing so is crucial to forming a complex picture of this cohort.

The experiences of kids of color and immigrants are vital to Generation Z. The group I predominantly focus on—South Asian American spellers—offers a case study to understand immigrant impact on Generation Z. This small but highly visible community's transformation of competitive spelling offers a window into how Gen Z kids approach extracurricular careers and other activities during childhood.

"It's like you're the CEO of your own life, right?" fourteen-year-old Shreyas Parab declared the first time we met. He was standing in line to be interviewed on camera at a South Asian Spelling Bee regional competition in Washington, DC, in June 2014. I had first seen him onstage a month earlier at the National Spelling Bee, when he had been given a role at one of the opening assemblies at Bee Week. Confident and charismatic, he was called upon by name to explain the rules of the contest to fellow spellers, including how they should conduct themselves onstage during their turn. Shreyas enjoyed the limelight and the reporters. "It's fun to talk about how much work you put into it."

Shreyas welcomed the opportunity to be interviewed and pulled out his smartphone to show me videos of his recent media interviews and appearances—CNN and a TED junior talk being just two of an impressive collection. Shreyas told me to look out for his next TEDx Talk. His friend Sriram Hathwar, co-champion of the 2014 National Spelling Bee, had offered Shreyas helpful advice based on his own experience of delivering a TEDx Talk. Shreyas felt confident after a run-through at school in front of about four hundred peers. "I held notes for emphasis, when I wanted to make gestures," he explained. Shreyas's talk focused on education reform and he discussed spelling as his inspiration.

Shreyas is one of those middle school kids who appears natural in a necktie because he projects something believable about the look. So believable, in fact, that in high school he founded his own necktie company called NovelTie. Putting his neoliberal life-management strategy into practice, he became the CEO of his own life and company. Along with three other teenage boys who serve as the director of sales, director of technology, and senior sales associate, Shreyas sells ties that are handmade in Delaware by an African American seamstress. He was named Philadelphia's Young Entrepreneur of the Year and one of America's top six young entrepreneurs by the US Chamber of Commerce.

We can consider Shreyas a bellwether of Generation Z, looking at his approach to childhood as marking potential contours and directions. To understand the emerging trends Shreyas and his spelling peers might reveal about their larger cohort, it's important to think about what a "generation" means. The concept of generation can elucidate the kinds of commonalities a group of people might share based on the year and place of their birth. Major world events and societal challenges can create a shared way of experiencing life. This perspective was originally introduced by the sociologist Karl Mannheim in the mid-twentieth century.

For Mannheim, generations are multidimensional social groups that take shape within the flow of history. The concept can be useful for understanding the priorities of a group, as well as how a group might make sense of itself and others. The impetus to name generation and assign attributes to the tens of millions of people born during a fixed span of time was popularized by demographers William Strauss and Neil Howe. Their 1991 book *Generations* circulated the idea that people in an age group share a distinct set of beliefs, attitudes, values, and behaviors because they all grow up and come of age during the same period in history.

The Pew Research Center's approach to generation involves tracking the same group of people over time on a range of issues, characteristics, attitudes, and behaviors. Generation may also be informed by historical events, popular culture, demographics, and academic consensus. Pew cautions that the lines it places around generations should be thought of as guidelines rather than hard-and-fast distinctions between groups. Three main effects produce differences in attitudes between age groups: *life cycle effects* (sometimes called age effects), which emerge between older and younger people depending on their life stage; *period effects*, when large-scale events and broader social forces impact everyone, regardless of age; and the *cohort effect*, which identifies the unique historical and social circumstances that shape the group's view of society and the world.

The intended audience of a generational study dramatically shapes its focus and content. Much of what we know about generations, especially Gen Z, has emerged from market research, as a way to create more effective branding and increase consumer consumption. Marketers and advertisers are often the first to try to define a cohort, emphasizing their media tastes, spending priorities, and anything they can glean about their overall mindset. Other players in this conversation are organizational management professionals who aim to demystify new age cohorts as they enter college or the workplace. They promise college administrators and corporate executives of earlier generations an inside view into what makes young people tick. These observations are not to discredit the insights of these studies, but rather to consider the agendas by which findings are offered.

The limitations of generation as a concept are most pronounced when the category is applied too broadly. Some comparisons are helpful, but others can obscure more than they reveal. For instance, scholars have pushed to identify simultaneous generational formations in different parts of the world. Sociologists June Edmunds and Bryan Turner advocate for "global generations" shaped by the evolution of communication technologies, offering a first-world focus that looks at Western Europe, Canada, the United States, and Australia.[5] Discrepancies of technology and infrastructure between these regions and differential dynamics of access within them make this comparison tricky. Moreover, this concept of "global" does not include Africa, Asia, and Latin America. There are also differences in how these societies view childhood, what can be accomplished during this time, and when kids are expected to become adults. Given the difficulties of talking about a "global" cohort, for the purposes of this book I focus on American generations while also considering the cultural differences that immigrants bring to bear on them.

When Kavya Shivashankar first made it to the National Spelling Bee in 2006, she was an excited fifth grader. As a ten-year-old, she had tempered expectations. Kavya advanced to finals during that first appearance in the National Spelling Bee— something most spellers never accomplish. Kavya was the youngest competitor in finals that year and was in awe of the much older eighth graders onstage. Kavya started studying for spelling bees in second grade by memorizing a local competition list. After a few years she realized she couldn't only memorize words, especially since she sometimes learned them with pronunciations that differed from the dictionary. Instead, she focused on understanding the languages that make up English, which helped her figure out what to do with unfamiliar words during competition. She remarked, "I could put together words I didn't know, so that helped."

For example, at the 2009 Bee, she received the word *ergasia*, organismic behavior, in the semifinals and did not know it. For onlookers it looks like an easy word, she explained, "but when you're onstage, what could the *er* sound be? *So* many questions running through your head." She asked all the allowed follow-up questions and recognized the Greek root *ergon*. The rest was how it sounded, so she went for it. "It doesn't always work out, but you definitely make your best guess." Kavya recalled being "so involved" in onstage competition that she focused only on Dr. Bailly and blocked out everything else. Kavya's last word at the 2009 spelling bee was *Laodicean*, lukewarm or indifferent to religion or politics. She spelled it correctly and was named champion.

Kavya came away with many lessons from her years of spelling. She reflected that she developed "discipline, focus, and life skills that the Bee teaches, along with composure onstage and public speaking." When she studied for the Bee, she would set goals depending on the activities of that day, especially during seventh and eighth grade. She made it to finals every year, and consistently managed to finish better than the year before. She placed tenth in 2006, eighth in 2007, and tied for fourth in 2008. When I marveled at this stellar performance, she modestly added, "Any word at any point can get you out, so I was lucky." Alongside the benefits of developing poise and time management, the Greek and Latin roots Kavya studied would resurface repeatedly in the years to come, especially as a neuroscience and premed major at Columbia, and afterward as a med student.

Kavya was thrilled to learn that her younger sister, Vanya, wanted to compete in the Bee. She was also excited to go back for Bee Week and accompanied Vanya every time. At the Bee, she helped manage spellers onstage and escorted them offstage when they were eliminated. She waited with them on what spellers call the "comfort couch" at stage left until their parents could make their way through the giant ballroom to retrieve them. We spoke in 2014, when she was in college and unable to help Vanya prepare throughout the year. During Bee Week she offered mental support and helped her sister review face-to-face. She knew Vanya was in good hands with their dad as coach. She remarked, "He loves it. All of us, as a family, the Bee is a big part of our lives. We love coming back to Bee Week, it's our favorite week of the year."

As one of the last Millennial champions, Kavya shared a lot in common with her Gen Z sister. The two are also united by a shared upbringing as the children of non-US-born parents. As I noted earlier, Generation Z contains the greatest number of children of immigrants as well as mixed-race kids, making them the most racially and ethnically diverse generation in history. More than half (56 percent) of minorities in America in 2015 were Millennials or Gen Z. America's growing minority population is young and concentrated into Generations Y and Z.

To consider immigrant impact on these generations, we can look at how Vanya's and Kavya's dedication to and focus on spelling is a product of their own drive as well as the support and training their parents have offered. Mirle Shivashankar, their father, has been consistently involved in helping them prepare and study for the numerous spelling competitions they have each entered. Like his wife, Sandhya, he is a software engineer. The two live and work full-time in Olathe, Kansas, while also investing tremendous time and energy in their daughters' spelling careers. Kavya was born in Boca Raton, Florida, and relocated with the family to Kansas when she was four. Vanya was born and raised in Olathe, where the family moved for work opportunities.

Mr. Shivashankar nicknamed himself "the BeeFather." He has authored a blog by the same title, in which he's chronicled the experiences and approaches he has taken in nurturing the spelling careers of his daughters. He initially acted as Kavya's coach and helped to prepare study materials. She made it to the National Spelling Bee as a fifth grader in 2006. "That's how it began," he stated for one televised interview. In the family's many media appearances, Mr. Shivashankar can be heard delivering a consistent message about the spelling bee: Vanya should set goals and try to meet them before the Bee. At the Bee, she should just have fun, the outcome does not matter. Mr. Shivashankar has spoken on camera about the importance of the other families who come to the Bee. The Shivashankars can talk to them and relate to them in ways that non-spelling families might not be able to. Enjoying Bee Week together has been a beloved tradition for their family. When Bee Week concludes on Saturday morning, the family goes to the Washington, DC, Grand Hyatt where Kavya won so that the family can relive past Bee Week experiences and take in the sights.

Mr. Shivashankar has remarked that Vanya has "grown with the Bee" over her nine years of attending and later competing. Mrs. Shivashankar added that her husband chose to prioritize his daughters' spelling interests over his own career growth. The family likes to "watch tape" of old spelling bees, like athletes who want to improve from reviewing recordings of their past performances. Vanya and her father relaxed on their couch, watching her spell at a past Bee. "See how loose you are on this word?" he asked. Poring over previous appearances, they deliberate about what might work best for her next competition. "It helps me strategize," remarked Vanya.

Immediately following the declaration of Vanya as co-champion, Mr. Shivashankar donned a yellow T-shirt bearing his nickname in a graphic fashioned after *The Godfather* film's logo. Twitter declared the shirt a winner along with his daughter, and #BeeFather trended. One media outlet named them "the first family of spelling" for their multiple successes. Although all National Spelling Bee winners are invited to meet the president at the White House, for the Shivashankars, like other immigrants, it can also be viewed as a legitimization of racial belonging. The picture of the family visiting President Obama at the White House after Kavya's win is emblematic of where America is moving, even if detractors are resistant to this powerful image of diversity. An African American president hosting an Indian American family whose child won America's most iconic educational contest epitomizes the combination of Generation Z drive and immigrant drive.

To understand the impact of immigrants on Gen Z, we can look back a generation to Millennials to see how these demographic changes began to take shape. Immigration is expected to grow Millennials' numbers more than any other official generation, and this cohort is predicted to peak at 81.1 million in 2036.[6] Alongside new immigrants, US-born children of immigrants will make up a growing share of working-age Millennial adults: 13 percent in 2035, compared with 6 percent in 2015. For the whole country, census projections indicate that 17.6 million new immigrants will be added to the working-age population by 2035, offsetting the aging or death of other working-age immigrants.[7] This shift also means that the number of US-born working-age adults with US-born parents will become a smaller share of the working-age population: 66 percent in 2035, compared with 74 percent in 2015.

While mostly projections, these numbers provide some specific ways that diversity in this cohort will increasingly matter. Gen Z kids like the ones in this book will comprise the majority of the 2035 workforce. What they are doing now, as children, can have a major impact on not only their positioning within this future workforce, but also on its very character. This is why assimilation is no longer a viable way to understand what immigrants are doing in the United States today. Attending to, rather than downplaying, certain cultural and social traits of different kinds of childhood can be far more revealing. This is a familiar idea to anthropologists, and a long-standing one at that.

The numerous anthropologists who study children and youth today owe a debt of gratitude to the prescient Margaret Mead. When Mead set sail to study rites of passage on the South Pacific island of Ta'u, part of American Samoa, in the 1920s, she observed a society that stood in stark contrast to the cultural norms of Western Europe and North America. Her book *Coming of Age in Samoa*, published in 1928, demonstrated that looking at youth and children could be as productive and insightful as studying adult society. There was value in understanding young people.

This idea was reiterated decades later when Mead built her stature as a public intellectual. From 1963 through 1979, Mead published a column in *Redbook* magazine in which she responded to queries about society and culture. She used her years of field research and anthropological knowledge to offer broader insights about her own culture. The range of topics was vast and impressive. At times, it stretched the limits of what any one person could claim as expertise but nonetheless offered a voice of cultural relativism at a time when far less reasoned approaches to cultural, ethnic, and racial differences prevailed.

Mead wrote about many of the same issues we still ponder, including how the United States is changing; how to make sense of the differences between generations; where immigrants and other minorities fit into the changing US demographic amid broader economic, social, and political shifts; and what impact this has on the American childhood. She focused on the post–World War II era, especially in the 1950s and 1960s, when the United States underwent tremendous transformations. Everything was changing, including social structure through desegregation, civil rights for minorities and women, an influx of immigration beginning in the mid-1960s, and antiwar protests. It was, in essence, the period in which the categories of "youth" and "childhood" took shape as being something in their own right, as part of public culture.

In one column from 1967, Mead responded to a query that elaborates on this point: *Of all the societies of which you have first-hand knowledge, which has the most effective means of disciplining its children and which has the least? What are those methods?* Even though Mead likely had her own opinion as a mother, she confirmed that the most appropriate means would be those suited to that society. She offered contrasting examples of New Guinea people who were frequently warring and trained their children to be self-reliant and tough, and those that were peaceful and nurturing even if their children misbehaved. She wisely concluded, "There is, in fact, no single answer to the problem of childhood discipline. But there is always the central question: For what future?"

Mead reminds us that childhood has always looked different across cultures, and that it has always been goal oriented. While the most pressing goal of childhood is to become a competent member of one's society, and of one's generation, American childhood is changing in reaction to the influx of immigrants from different cultures. As these growing numbers of immigrants bring their own ideas of childhood with them, we can expect that not only will day-to-day upbringings and priorities look different, but also the central ideas that comprise these children's futures.

Shreyas's spelling career began while watching Kavya Shivashankar win the 2009 Bee. Her victory inspired him to work to make it to the national stage. Shreyas was born in Wisconsin but lived in India for a few years, where he was a fluent Hindi and Marathi speaker. He transitioned back to English when his family returned to the greater DC area. Shreyas first won a bee when he was in grade school but did not begin competing seriously until middle school. "I took the extra step and studied a list," he explained, and won his class and school bees easily. Over the years, Shreyas worked with his older brother, his mother, and his English teacher. Shreyas's brother enjoyed helping him study. "He loves language, so he likes helping me. When we study, we also throw around a ball, joke around, hit each other, and have fun." He is proud of the skills he has acquired over the course of his spelling career, including an expanded vocabulary. "When you know more words, you're a more interesting person to talk to."

Shreyas did not spend his childhood studying the dictionary, but he studied enough to make it to nationals in 2013 and 2014. At the Bee, he did not advance to semifinals either time but wasn't concerned about it. "It was fine because I had a lot of fun over the years and learned more words than I could have imagined." He additionally logged in four trips to the North South Foundation finals and three to the South Asian Spelling Bee finals. He knows that friends have more elaborate strategies for spelling bee preparation.

Shreyas reminded me that over 11 million kids compete each year, and that he was among the 285 spellers at the 2014 national finals. "That meant we were the 0.000011 percent to make it. I remember that stat because I like to repeat it." For Shreyas, the most challenging aspect of the Bee is also the most exciting: "Everyone here is good at everything!" He loves the social aspect of Bee Week, including meeting other spellers and going to dinner and social events with them. Shreyas celebrates the friendships he has made through spelling, including kids competing from Africa and Asia who he keeps in touch with through email and social media.

Like other Gen Z spellers I met, Shreyas relished his onstage turns at the mic. He enjoyed the attention and welcomed the multiple cameras clicking in his direction. The camera followed his celebrations, like high- or low-fiving everyone in his row and exchanging fist bumps with people around him. He found it deeply satisfying to get a word right after hours of studying on nights and weekends. "When you get it right, it's hard to describe the happiness. When you go back to your seat it's like a victory lap. You get to take your time and go back and sit down."

To date, Shreyas's cohort does not have an official name, though I, and others, refer to them as Gen Z. The Pew Research Center and the US Census Bureau, from which I draw most of my demographic data, only refer to them as the "post-Millennial" cohort. A 2018 Pew study on generations research notes that those born after 1996 are unaffiliated to a specific generation.[8]

The authors report, "It will take several years before enough post-Millennials have reached adulthood to allow for meaningful statements about the next adult generation."[9] The moniker "Generation Z" is simply a placeholder. It is the sequel to Generation Y (Millennials), which followed Generation X.

The year 1996 is just one possible cutoff date, as demographers and marketers have offered alternatives. Howe, for instance, sets the end date of Millennials around 2005–2006, asserting that eighteen to twenty-four years is an ideal window of time to mark the emergence of the next generation after the previous one. He argues, "Generational boundaries are also typically drawn 2 to 4 years before abrupt changes in the national mood."[10] Using 2005 as a start date means that these kids will have known nothing before Obama's presidency and the Great Recession, with these two events strongly marking their early childhood. I have chosen to follow the Pew and US Census date range, but it's more than likely that those dates will change over time.

The contentious process of deciding age range indicates how invested different constituencies have become in defining generational cohorts, present company included. Even less certain is what to call this generation. As with Millennials, there is a scramble to name Gen Z. Unlike other generations whose names have come from novelists, demographers, and cultural commentators, suggestions for Gen Z names have been crowdsourced via online surveys or offered by pundits. None has received a particularly warm reception.

Demographer Neil Howe, one half of the duo who popularized "Millennials," offered the "Homeland Generation," generated by an online contest for his readers. Critics dismissed this moniker for its namesake in a post-9/11 government agency.

Another possibility is the "Founder Generation," derived from an MTV survey administered online of over one thousand high school students in 2015. Mixed responses from major cultural publications such as the *New Yorker*, the *Atlantic*, and the *Huffington Post* have given it little traction. Likewise, "Generation Wii" has fallen flat, as have names generated by public relations and marketing firms. These include "New Realists," the "Pluralist Generation," and the "iGeneration."[11]

The most recent contest I followed was administered by *New York Times* reporter Jonah Bromwich in 2018. After crowdsourcing names for a week, his article "What to Call Post-Millennials? Maybe None of the Above" confirmed that there is still no consensus, only many competing ideas. When the call for names appeared, my then twelve-year-old son Roshan offered "Generation Meme." He was one of several Gen Z kids interviewed, and remarked, "I think it goes with how our generation goes through life. We go through life fast. And just like that, memes spread fast."

Generation Meme does draw attention to this cohort's digital savviness and captures something fundamental about their mindset. Their sophisticated understanding of social media and viral circulation makes them as much creators of content as consumers of it. It has my vote. All this attention is a sign of how pervasive these categories have become in young people's lives and how their motivations and views are often filtered through the lens of generation.

What people do agree upon is that children are growing up engulfed by digital culture. Generation Z came into a world filled with cell phones, screens, and social media. Even though smartphones, Facebook, and Twitter came into popularity in the mid-to late 2000s, they are still a major part of Gen Z childhood.

John Palfrey and Urs Gasser discuss the rise of "digital natives," which they define as those born after 1980 who came of age with online social and networked digital technologies.[12] Various technologies are driving forces for social life, and younger kids experience this extensively.

Still, the idea of Gen Z consisting of "100% digital natives," as some contend, is an oversimplification.[13] Social psychologist Sonia Livingstone counters the myth of the digital native by drawing attention to the inconsistent ways that kids have access to and engage with the Internet.[14] She also notes that their media literacy of what to believe on the Internet and how to interact with other users further complicates this idea.

Most agree that this newest generation uses the Internet and digital technologies from a very young age. Generation Z reportedly does much of their social networking and interaction on social media platforms including GroupMe, Snapchat, Periscope, and Instagram.[15] YouTube and Instagram remain the main platforms for Gen Z bloggers and social media influencers. These are the fashion-forward young people who snap and post selfies in outfits that set trends. The youngest Gen Z style influencers are preliterate. They have their parents photograph, curate, caption, and hashtag their photos. Parents start by buying clothes, and successful kids have designers send outfits to them. They are very camera-ready and know how to strike a pose. Some are siblings clad in designer threads. Preternaturally beautiful and photogenic, they post regularly on Instagram or their own websites, run by their parents. Some seek a digital following, while others use it as an avenue into child acting and modeling.

For the most part, Gen Z kids are just excited to share their ideas. They take to the Internet and try to shape literary tastes, like the blog *Childtasticbooks: Great Books for Great Readers,* in which kids post critical reviews of books they have read.[16] They write travelogues, like *Hagan's World of Awesome,* in which the seven-year-old blogger from Iowa writes about his day-to-day as well as global adventures.[17] Kids record podcasts for one another, ranging from adventure stories to explorations into the natural world.[18] Gen Z kids are as much producers of media content as they are consumers of it. Brand researchers call them "culture creators" as well as heavy consumers who are "catalysts of a burgeoning cultural revolution."[19] Many seem to share a fundamental ease with media of various kinds.

Millennials, also called Generation Y, are the last generation to be named by the Pew Research Center and the US Census Bureau. Millennials were born between 1981 and 1996. Strauss and Howe mention them in several of their writings and devoted an entire book to them in 2000, when they published *Millennials Rising.*[20] US-born Millennials are the children of Boomers and older Gen Xers. Like Boomers, they are outsized due to a large surge in birth rates during the 1980s and 1990s. According to population estimates from the US Census Bureau, Millennials officially surpassed the Baby Boomers as America's largest generation in 2015. That year, Millennials numbered 75.4 million, as compared to 74.9 million Boomers.[21]

By and large, public depictions of Millennials are not flattering and are somewhat contentious. Millennials are the best-educated cohort of young adults in American history. Media accounts often call them narcissistic, self-absorbed, and entitled. Psychologist Jean Twenge argues that these traits run deeper in

Millennials, which she calls "Generation Me," than in other generations. Personality tests and surveys administered among those in their teens and twenties show a big difference in self-interest between Millennials and other age cohorts.[22]

Like most studies of generations, these characterizations of Millennials are steeped in white middle-class cultural norms. Their parents, Baby Boomers, are among the least diverse cohorts alive today. Even so, there are hundreds of thousands of non-US-born, as well as African American and Native American, Baby Boomers whose parenting styles are not accounted for; likewise, their children tend not to be central to how Millennials are characterized. These caveats are important to remember when discussing Millennials.

Researcher Paul Taylor and the Pew Research Center call Millennials "America's most stubborn optimists. They have a self-confidence born of coddling parents and everyone-gets-a-trophy coaches."[23] Taylor contends that Millennials focus on themselves due to their upbringing as "special snowflakes" who deserve to be recognized for achievements small and large. They publicly share everything. They remain optimistic and self-confident in the face of economic adversity. As a result, the argument goes, Millennials became overconfident in themselves while pushing adulthood milestones later and later.

In *Millennials Go to College*, written with college administrators and marketers in mind, Howe and Strauss further their portrait of this group by focusing on their transition into higher education and changing parental cohorts.[24] They elaborate on what they see as the seven core traits of Millennials: special, sheltered, confident, team-oriented, conventional, pressured, and achieving. According to 2014 Pew data, Millennials have higher levels of student loan debt, poverty, and unemployment and

lower levels of wealth and personal income than their two immediate predecessor generations had at the same stage of their life
cycles. They have struggled to find steady careers, which makes
them less inclined to marry at younger ages as Boomers and
Gen Xers did.[25] The share of young adults living in their parents'
home reached a historic high in 2012.[26]

Some Millennials are leaning into aspects of this characteri-
zation. Consider Jeffrey Jensen Arnett, who in 2010 told the *New
York Times* about his movement to identify the twenties as a distinct life stage, which he calls "emerging adulthood." During this
time, people could feel "more self-focused than at any other time
of life, less certain about the future and yet also more optimistic,
no matter what their economic background."[27] Others counter
with evidence that Millennials actually are hardworking. For instance, youth studies scholar Peter Kelly argues that this cohort
has mobilized "new work ethics" suited to the globalized yet pre-
carious labor markets of the twenty-first century.[28]

Offering another counterpoint to negative characterizations,
Malcolm Harris paints a very different picture.[29] As a Millennial,
he refutes the stereotypes of his generation being entitled and in
need of praise. Rather, he focuses on their hard work and efforts
to enter an unforgiving job market. The rise of intern culture, as
he notes, has become normalized for middle- and upper-middle-
class Millennials. "Working for free" in the form of internships
and even homework was beneficial and a privilege. According to
Harris, being averse to hard work is not their issue; it is being in
a job market already flooded with human capital. Millennials
found college admissions to be vastly more competitive than it
was for their Gen X predecessors. In 2015, they surpassed Gen
Xers as the largest generation in the labor force.[30]

To provide a point of contrast, consider my own experience of growing up in New York City and its suburbs in the 1970s and '80s. My brother and I were the children of immigrants in a time when there were far fewer of us. As Gen Xers, we belong to a small generation sandwiched between two outsized ones. The suburb where I went to high school was not nearly as filled with Asian immigrants as it would be a mere decade later. Most of the families in my area were Irish, Italian, or Jewish. I studied reasonably hard to get into my pick of colleges, but the intensity of academic competition was nothing compared to what it would become. Anecdotally, I've learned that many of my Generation X peers had similar experiences in high school and they too found the college admissions process to have been far less cutthroat. Watching each other's highly qualified children apply to college supports this idea.

Some of the trends noted with Millennials have strengthened for Gen Z, especially the idea of beginning professional work early. By middle school and high school, kids do internships in labs, offices, and programs designed for them—start-up incubators that train kids to raise capital and establish and run their own corporations. More than any other before it, Millennials experienced the pressure to fashion themselves in ways that meet the demands and expectations of entrepreneurship. The call for reinvention is an ongoing, never-ending enterprise. Gen Z seems to be aware of this from the get-go.

"I retired my placard," Shreyas told me via email about the end of his spelling career. He was ready for his second act: an entrepreneurial career. He was accepted into the Young Entrepreneurs Academy (YEA!), a training course offered by a nonprofit serving the greater Philadelphia area and funded by corporate sponsors. During ninth grade, Shreyas completed a thirty-week course and learned how to create a business plan, pitch a concept, register a business, and network. This is essentially what friends of mine paid top dollar for in their MBA programs. Shreyas lives by the program's motto: "Make a Job—Don't Just Take a Job!" When Shreyas decided to start his own necktie company, he raised capital for his business idea and represented his region in a national competition. Ultimately, he was recognized as one of the top six young entrepreneurs in the country. He pitched his idea to Walmart executives. As of 2017, NovelTie had made over $15,000 and is featured at major retail outlets such as Sam's Club. This success makes Shreyas one of the youngest people to supply goods to a Fortune 500 company.

If entrepreneurism is not enough to keep him busy, Shreyas has his hands full with being president of the student council, captain of the science Olympiad team, and captain of the reading Olympics team, plus playing soccer for his school as well as an outside team. He also plays lacrosse and swims, "just for fun," on a swim team at the local pool. "It's hard to balance it out with school and the extracurriculars, and then spelling." The way he sees it, "it's a lot of stress, but the stress pushes you to become better." His parents routinely tell him to take breaks, balance how he spends his time, and manage his stress. "I push the limits of myself sometimes. But it's a healthy balance. Whenever I feel like it's too much, my parents have to cut me off and say that I have to sleep." Finding time for sleep might be the most challenging part of Shreyas's multiple careers.

Shreyas's generation sees Silicon Valley and the apps it creates as a foundation on which to build. The *New York Times* notes that, as largely career-focused individuals, many Generation Z members will value safe jobs and steady careers but also seek new opportunities in start-ups and as entrepreneurs. This is confirmed by market research firms like Magid, which has contended that the recession has forced this generation to be more entrepreneurial, more conservative, and more pragmatic about financial issues compared to Millennials. Sparks & Honey, in its 2014 report on Generation Z, claims that this cohort places heavy emphasis on being "mature and in control."[31] Shreyas embodies these Gen Z characteristics. For his next venture, he collaborated with Sriram Hathwar to create a spelling app called *Spell for Success*. The two won $8,000 in seed money for the project in a University of Delaware competition called the Diamond Challenge for high school entrepreneurs.

Gen Z is a cohort that values entrepreneurial innovation and creativity. They are surpassing their Millennial predecessors by cycling through activities at record speed and pushing themselves to master new, complex areas as children. At fourteen, Vanya plays the tuba and knows she wants to be a cardiologist. She is an avid international traveler who has dabbled in paragliding and skeet shooting. She loves acting and enjoys being onstage in front of a live audience. She also likes swimming, biking, piano, and drama. Heading into the 2015 Bee, Vanya already had one televised contest win under her belt. Earlier that spring, she had been named the champion of the multiweek reality television contest *Child Genius*, featuring twenty children between the ages of ten and fourteen. She competed weekly in various mental challenges and won the grand prize of a $100,000 college fund.

As the focus of media attention during most of her life, Vanya is remarkably at ease sharing her hopes and goals on camera. One feature shows Vanya as a driven competitor who draws inspiration from another great, Michael Jordan. A whiteboard in her room displays a quote attributed to him: "Some want it to happen. Others wish it would happen. A few make it happen." After she aged out, ESPN producers would take note of her camera-readiness and invite her to join the Bee Week production crew. In 2016, she would tape a feature on the National Mall, seeing which passersby could spell *misspell* correctly. In 2017, she would appear on *SportsCenter* with host Kevin Negandhi.

Vanya is special, but she is no special snowflake. She, like her fellow Gen Z elite spellers, has worked exceedingly hard for what she has accomplished. The spelling bee kids I met scoffed at participation trophies, regarding them as the useless landfill that they are. This differs from Millennials, who came to expect this kind of recognition. Several other differences emerge between Millennials and Gen Z. Unlike Millennials, who began in a time of optimism and then watched the War on Terror and the Great Recession set in, Gen Z was born into these realities.

Gen Z kids are skeptical of economic prospects and traditional paths for education and careers, making entrepreneurship that much more attractive. Consider, for instance, this 2016 *Huffington Post* blog entry titled "5 Ways That Gen Z Is Changing the World," authored by a seventeen-year-old named Grace Masback.[32] She writes that her generation consists of "culture creators" who are highly focused on being entrepreneurs. When she was not selected to write for her high school paper, she instead started her own news website.

For pop culture, they prefer the clever, lilting social critiques of the singer Lorde and the zeitgeist of the musical *Hamilton* over the flash and excess of Lady Gaga or reality TV celebrities like the Kardashians. If Millennials valorize the self-absorption of Hannah Horvath from HBO's *Girls*, Gen Z aligns with Alex Dunphy from *Modern Family*.[33] The former is lost in her own world of indulgent self-exploration and puts her dream career ahead of her financial stability. By contrast, the latter is hard-working, highly organized, and planning for her future.

Socially, Gen Z is the generation most exposed to LGBTQ issues. They are least likely to believe in the "American Dream," similar to their Gen X parents.[34] Also coloring their view of society is the aftermath of the terrorist events of September 11, 2001, and ensuing War on Terror, the Great Recession (2007–2009), climate change, increased school shootings, and now the most xenophobic president in recent history. That's the bad news. The good news is that they are very likely to take on the struggle for social justice—several studies identify Malala Yousafzai, who won the Nobel Peace Prize at seventeen, as their role model for activism.

Commitment to community and a focus on service are common denominators across Gen Z. Gen Z blogger Masback believes her cohort could be the "greatest giving generation." Wanting to make an impact on the world, they are cautiously optimistic. She writes, "Unlike our pathetically pessimistic Millennial friends," Gen Z will leave their "community and the planet better places than we found them."[35]

This was certainly demonstrated in 2018 as Gen Z continued to contend with school shootings on a scale unlike any before it. Gen Z kids at Marjory Stoneman Douglas High School in Parkland, Florida, used every tool at their disposal to draw attention to the mass shooting that happened on February 14, 2018. Students took to Twitter and organized the highly successful March for Our Lives in over eight hundred cities across the United States. They distributed press kits and spoke to hundreds of thousands of adults. In the face of tragedy, they demonstrated their social conscience, social media prowess, and the urgency with which they want to see change happen.

While there is considerable overlap between the youngest Millennials and the oldest of Generation Z, there is an equally clear divide between what these two generations believe in and care about. This is true even for children of immigrants who competed in the Bee a decade ago. The 2008 National Spelling Bee champion Sameer Mishra captures a major difference between his experience and the kids who compete today. He observes a rise in the intensity of every competition, not just the spelling bee. When we spoke at the Bee in 2017, he remarked, "Now there are kids in science fairs who have almost cured cancer. Kids feel they can change the world more than we did ten years ago. It's more on their minds than ten years ago. It has definitely gotten more competitive to get into college."

Explaining that today's young people have to distinguish and differentiate themselves at an early age, Sameer believes they are much more focused than he had to be. "That's why we see more entrepreneurial kids doing all these cool things. They are more aware about what you need to do to get into college. They work hard to do that. It's pretty inspiring." Generation Z is a cohort about which we have little conclusive data, but it is already clear that this group of kids is quite different from Millennials and preceding generations. Looking more closely at their parents, and the varied styles they bring to child-rearing, offers deeper perspective on their approach to competition and success.

Chapter Five

Parents of Gen Z Kids

Shayley Martin knew she could spell well before she knew whether she could do it in a contest format. While Shayley was in elementary school, she became very interested in spelling, especially attempting complex words backward. "Forwards must have been too easy," her mother, Lydeana, mused. *Chrysanthemum* was her favorite. Shayley's grandmother taught her to read when she was a young toddler, making three- and four-letter sight words (commonly used words that young readers are asked to memorize whole) with refrigerator magnets. Shayley's mother, however, did not realize that her daughter could already read until well after she turned three. By that time, Shayley was reading works of poetry and anything else she could find. "Not kid books, but serious things," Shayley clarified. Mrs. Martin is part of the first generation in her family to graduate from high school and is a first-generation college graduate. She credits her mother for valuing education, even though she did not advance far in her own studies.

Shayley is tall and slender with long, light brown hair. Bespectacled and somewhat taciturn, she is an only child. Shayley's entrée into the Bee came with little pressure or expectation in fifth grade. Then people started paying attention. "After you win once," her mother began, but Shayley completed her thought, "*Everyone* expects you to win." Shayley is the first person from her West Virginia town to win her region's bee and advance to the National Spelling Bee four times. Shayley's mother describes her as a "mini-celebrity," with townspeople recognizing her as their regional winner. Her love of language sets her apart from most of her friends, who tell her to not speak languages other than English to them. This local disinterest in language helped Shayley repeatedly make it to the regional bee with relatively little preparation. Even though this contest includes spellers from seventeen counties, it does not cause Shayley concern. Each year, she kept an eye on the competition. Depending on the other entrants, she would work with her mother to study. Together, they would decide how intensively she would have to prepare to win.

Generation Z kids like Shayley are shaped by the world around them but are also deeply influenced by their parents. In Chapter 4, I explored Generation Z's hallmark traits of being competitive, entrepreneurial, digitally savvy, and media-ready. This chapter more fully examines the way Generation X and Baby Boomer parenting styles contribute to overlaps and differences between Gen Z and Millennials, respectively. It also examines areas of similarity and divergence between US- and non-US-born parents. Professional immigrants who came to the United States under the Immigration Act of 1990 with STEM and other advanced qualifications have their own parenting priorities. If we consider what shapes the character of Gen Z, looking at this range of parenting styles can provide timely insights.

Like any cohort, there are many parenting approaches enveloped in Gen X. Researchers credit Gen Xers with "stealth-fighter parenting," in which parents don't hover like Baby Boomer "helicopter parents" but do surveil from a distance and intervene when needed.[1] While I don't favor the military analogy, I'll use these terms for sake of illustration. Compared to helicopter parents, stealth-fighter parents give kids more space to navigate their own challenges while still advocating for them. Distinctions between these two styles can be helpful in understanding why Millennials may expect recognition and praise while Gen Z is more focused on winning.

The way Gen Xers parent also varies considerably based on whether they are US-born or non-US-born. A third parenting style is relevant to this conversation, that brought by Asian immigrant parents. A version of this parenting style is most sensationally known in author Amy Chua's *Battle Hymn of the Tiger Mother*.[2] A far more tempered, moderate version of this model, which I refer to as Bee Parenting, emphasizes how immigrant parents value educational achievement and set goals for their children, without the abuse.

Helicopter, stealth-fighter, and Bee Parenting are of course limited in what they can explain. Anyone who has children knows that parenting is a complex, emotionally charged daily balance of individual personalities and needs; it is shaped by time and resource constraints as much as it is by idealized values. Still, if stealth-fighter and Bee Parenting help explain how Gen Z is being raised and how these approaches differ from the helicopter parenting Millennials experienced, we can piece together a much clearer understanding of what drives Gen Z to compete, succeed, and shine in the spotlight.

The US Census Bureau defines Generation X as those born between 1965 and 1980. Gen Xers were born during a period when Americans were having fewer children than previous and later decades, averaging around 3.4 million per year compared with the 3.9 million annual rate during the 1980s and 1990s when Millennials were born. The term "Generation X" had been used as far back as the 1950s, by World War II photographer Robert Capa in a photo-essay describing the alienation and disaffection of young adults. With the release of Canadian author Douglas Coupland's 1991 novel, *Generation X: Tales for an Accelerated Culture*, the name stuck. The popularity of *X* as referring to an unknown variable and a desire not to be defined had strong pop-cultural resonance.

Early descriptions of Generation X focused primarily on its small size. Older members of the cohort started their professional careers at a time when pensions began disappearing, jobs were drifting overseas, and the 1987 stock market crash set off a recession. These conditions led to initial descriptions of Gen Xers by the press and marketers as angry, cynical, and profoundly insecure.[3] Demographers William Strauss and Neil Howe were among the first to highlight these characteristics in a 1993 study on the "13th Generation." They collected newspaper stories, research studies, and a variety of reports published in the 1980s and early 1990s.

Among the more influential depictions was offered by *Time* magazine, whose staff had helped popularize the notion of Gen

Xers as "slackers." One 1990 article described those in their twenties as "aimless and unfocused." The film *Slacker* (directed by Richard Linklater) released that year became a cultural touchstone of the generation. It depicts young white people in Austin, Texas, who have yet to find jobs exploring the social issues of their time, including terrorism, unemployment, political marginalization, and social exclusion.

Strauss and Howe argue that Gen Xers were children at a time when Western society was more focused on adults than children. They experienced a cultural shift in family values, from unhappy parents who stayed together "for the sake of the children" to new social values of parental and individual self-actualization. Some Gen Xers became known as "latchkey kids," returning from school each day to find empty homes until their parents returned from work.[4] They were raised to be more peer-oriented than previous generations, something that they seem to have instilled in their Gen Z kids. They are also more independent than Baby Boomers.

Generation X came of age during the war on drugs and the political climate of conservatism championed by President Reagan. During their childhoods, many resources were diverted away from children's programs and directed toward older populations, including protection and expansion of Medicare and Social Security. They witnessed the crack epidemic, which disproportionately affected urban areas and African Americans, and saw the emergence of AIDS. This is also one of the first times that Americans would see and hear discussions of the shrinking middle class, tying this economic state specifically to Gen X and identifying them as the first generation to be "overeducated and underemployed"—a predicament that would affect Millennials far more dramatically. On a positive note, the United States passed Title IX, which allowed increased athletic opportunities for more young women in public schools.

By the late 1990s and early 2000s, as Gen X aged into adulthood, demographers began rethinking their characterizations. Pew researchers Paul Taylor and George Gao labeled them a "transitional generation" because they came of age in an analog world that would soon turn digital.[5] *Time* magazine revised their assessment from slackers to "Great Xpectations of So-Called Slackers" in 1997.[6] The article largely retracted their previous view and reported positive statistics on Gen Xers' entrepreneurial spirit and willingness to fund and support unlikely start-ups.

A 1998 Stanford study conducted on the accuracy of characterizations of Gen X as slackers concluded that while eighteen-to-twenty-nine-year-old Gen Xers did exhibit higher levels of cynicism and disaffection than previous cohorts in that age range surveyed in the 1990s, these dispositions had increased for all age groups surveyed over time.[7] So this was more likely a period effect rather than a cohort effect. The *New York Times* followed not long thereafter in 1999 with a report on Xers' "envious" status as a largely successful, self-employed cohort. The newspaper dubbed them "Generation 1099," the income-tax form for the self-employed rather than the W-2 for employees.[8] Eventually, Gen Xers were credited with creating the high-tech industry and driving the dot-com bubble that helped fuel economic recovery in the 1990s.

B aby Boomers are the parents of most Millennials. The name "Baby Boomers" refers to the large generational cohort born during the post–World War II baby boom, between 1946 and 1964.[9] Scholars hypothesize that the baby boom stemmed from postwar prosperity, which encouraged young adults who grew up during the Great Depression to marry earlier and raise larger families.[10] As these babies grew into adolescents and young adults, new schools and social service institutions were built to accommodate them. Major initiatives were developed and tested in order to meet the perceived needs of this cohort in the workplace. Boomers have been told since birth that their generation is different, special, distinguished by their size—a feature they share with Millennials—and by their coming of age during the most prosperous time in American history.

Especially significant about Baby Boomers is that they are the first generation to be marketed to as a cohort with a distinctive generational consciousness.[11] They played a role in the sexual revolution, rising women's workforce participation, and changes to intergenerational and interracial relationships. The rise of counterculture and the civil rights movement of the 1960s—as well as the second-wave feminist cause of the 1970s—left an indelible mark on this generation. Those who experienced violent confrontations and participated in sit-ins and student strikes saw their protests play out via new and old media forms on the national stage. Boomers came of age alongside a number of technological and artistic advances, many more so than previous generations. Recorded music, radio, and early computing are a few, with television being the most groundbreaking. By the end of the 1950s, there were 50 million televisions in the United States, allowing ideas, events, and people from all over the world to be viewed live in people's own living rooms.[12] Individual choice through consumerism became increasingly important.

Given the immense amount of focus and attention placed on this generation, and their rise during a period of unheralded prosperity in America and the West, cries of narcissism and self-absorption have come to define Baby Boomers. Writer Tom Wolfe dubbed the '70s the "'Me' Decade" and others expanded it to make Boomers the "Me Generation" during the 1970s. This phrase quickly caught on, as cultural aspirations of self-fulfillment and personal achievement began to overshadow the social responsibility that had defined Boomer culture early in its development. These characteristics would be applied to their children, whom psychologist Jean Twenge has named "Generation Me," suggesting that self-absorbed, narcissistic Baby Boomers cultivated those qualities in their Millennial children.[13]

Boomers are the least diverse postwar generation, far less so than Gen Y or Gen Z. According to a 2015 US Census Bureau report, among the youngest four years of the cohort (those born between 1960 and 1964, before new immigration laws passed), only 21.7 percent are minorities as compared to Millennials' 44.2 percent. Most non-US-born Baby Boomers immigrated after 1965, making Baby Boomers today far more diverse. Immigrants are driving diversity across the entire age spectrum, as the foreign-born population is increasing more rapidly than the native-born population.[14]

"How many words can you spell until the dictionary defeats you?" Chetan Reddy asked rhetorically. As he understood the contest, winning meant being the last person standing once the dictionary had slayed everyone else. Chetan began competing in North South Foundation regional spelling bees in first grade and the South Asian Spelling Bee in third grade. By the end of third grade, when he qualified for the NSF nationals a second year in a row, he realized how much he liked competing in spelling bees and became determined to make it to the National Spelling Bee. Chetan had watched winners of the Dallas regional bee do well at Scripps, and in fourth grade he became eligible to compete. He didn't make it until fifth grade, when he successfully cleared the county competition and won his regional bee to advance to the national level.

Chetan told me that it probably should have been intimidating to be at the National Spelling Bee for the first time. That was not his experience. He was calm and levelheaded. Onstage, he was completely immersed in the action. Rather than become distracted by the lights and cameras, he focused on his words and what he had studied. His test score to advance to semifinals was close but not high enough, and he resigned himself to tying for forty-ninth place. The following year, he advanced to the semifinals and finished twenty-seventh. In seventh grade, he made it to the second round of semifinals but misspelled *soboliferous*, producing shoots or suckers, onstage, finishing twenty-second.

Chetan's parents, Vijay and Geetha, worked closely with him for years on his spelling preparation. They each have an MS in electrical engineering and computer science from the University of Texas at Dallas. Mr. Reddy also has an MBA from the University of Dallas. At first they were unsure of what coaching an aspiring speller involved. Chetan's father would quiz him, and their method was effective, but the challenge was getting the pronunciation right. Like many South Asian American spelling bee families

I met, Chetan had a word that he knew how to spell but did not recognize in competition: *righteous*. He would have made it to the NSF finals in third grade, but he had learned it as "ri-tee-us."

As Chetan showed promise, his parents got more serious. His father prepared word lists for him. His mother designed software applications using Excel and Visual Basic. Using the software, Chetan could test and review about one thousand words per hour. An algorithm built into the program tested him more frequently on words he missed. Studying over one hundred thousand words per month allowed Chetan to cycle through the dictionary about seven or eight times during his final bee season. By then, Chetan and his father had whittled the list down to a number they considered more manageable: one hundred twenty thousand. According to Mr. Reddy, in random tests of one thousand words at a stretch, Chetan could spell the core thirty thousand words that are likely to appear in school, county, and regional bees with an accuracy rate of 99.8 percent. This rate dropped to about 92 percent with what he identified as the ninety thousand "expert words" that could appear at the semifinal and final rounds of the National Spelling Bee.

Chetan gradually increased his preparation time from two hours a day in fourth grade to four hours per day in eighth, studying up to eight hours a day on weekends and holidays. Mr. Reddy admits that only a small percentage of kids prefer to spend vast numbers of hours studying spelling bee words over playing games, watching TV, or indulging in other recreational activities. The aptitude and passion "to spend hours doing something tedious, day after day, month after month, year after year," as Mr. Reddy remarked, is limited to an elite few.

"We wanted our son to win. The National Spelling Bee was our Olympics," Mr. Reddy told me. I spoke to him and Chetan via Skype in 2014. During Chetan's final year, 2013, the vocabulary test was initiated just seven weeks before the Bee. The surprise change ate into the time they had allotted for spelling study. Still, Chetan made it to the national finals and finished in seventh place. He dominated the Dallas region during his years of eligibility. He also competed in the national finals of the South Asian Spelling Bee four times and in the NSF national finals seven times at the junior and senior levels.

"I like the thrill of competition. I like seeing my competitors, trying to get better and work harder. For me, it is a big journey. The knowledge you gain makes it worth it." Chetan's family prioritized his spelling career above their own leisure, making his orthographic progress a focal point in their lives. This is not unusual among the Bee Parents I met, who brought a high level of academic intensity and rigor to bear on their children's scholarly and extracurricular activities.

The Generation Z spellers of South Asian heritage I met are mostly children of immigrants who arrived beginning in 1990. They are the latest in the waves of largely professional migration that began in 1965. Even though immigration from South Asia to the United States has a history spanning over 150 years, the last fifty or so have had the most visible impact. In 1965, Congress passed what is widely considered its most liberal immigration law to that point, the Immigration and Nationality Act. It established quotas for skilled migrants. It came into full effect in 1968 and abolished discrimination against immigration based on national origin.

The Immigration and Nationality Act dramatically increased
the number of Eastern Hemisphere visas available per year from
105 to 20,000. It prioritized those working in fields the United
States wished to boost domestically, especially STEM as well as
medicine and other select professions. A significant portion of
migrants from the Indian subcontinent fit the selection criteria,
and their immigration numbers to the United States grew. From
1960 to 1970, Indian immigrants numbered 36,100; in 2000,
their numbers had grown to over 1.5 million.

Thirteen years later, according to the 2013 American Community Survey Data, the South Asian community in America
had grown 97 percent.[15] The 1980s saw a second wave of South
Asian immigration that contributed to increasing levels of po-
larization within the South Asian immigrant community. Some
who came in this wave were sponsored by family members
through the provisions of the immigration act of 1965.[16]

Some immigrants who came to the United States through diversity and reunification visas held lower educational qualifications.
Some found that their foreign degrees and professional credentials
were not accepted in United States workplaces. Many settled into
urban ethnic enclaves and worked blue-collar jobs as store clerks
or taxi drivers, or owned small businesses. More Bangladeshis and
Pakistanis began migrating during this third wave of immigration,
some without professional training or unable to find skilled jobs.
They may have had lower socioeconomic statuses than other South
Asian immigrants who had arrived earlier on professional visas.[17]

The diversity of the South Asian American community is
one that is less represented in the spelling bee world, but not all
elite spellers have parents who work in STEM. This is the case
with Dev Jaiswal, whose mother could only be so involved in

his spelling career. Dev's mother taught him and his older sister Rani how to read when they were young and used to play spelling games with them. Dev's mother cultivated a love of spelling in both of her children but could not continue with their training like some other parents. "I could only help them until they learned how to read and write. Once they got past the second grade, I couldn't help."

Unlike many of the families I met in which both parents had advanced degrees, Dev and Rani Jaiswal's mother does not have a college degree. She and her husband run their motel, the Homegate Inn, in Louisville, Mississippi. Running the motel meant that one parent stayed behind while the other accompanied Rani or Dev to spelling competitions. When Rani was in second grade, she received a notice that the school was holding a bee. Even though she was largely unfamiliar with how it all worked, she recalled, "I knew there was something about the spelling bee, that it's something good to do."

When Rani studied, she would ask her mother questions, including the meanings of words. Her mother told her to write them down and ask a teacher, as she often had not heard of them. She didn't have time to help Rani study, so Rani simply studied lists provided by her teachers. Rani participated each year and made it to regionals a few times but did not make it to nationals until eighth grade. That year, when Dev was in third grade, their family relocated from Oklahoma to Mississippi to operate the motel they had purchased.

Even though Rani and Dev's parents didn't know much about spelling bees, they knew to advocate for their children's extracurricular opportunities. Rani's new school did not administer the bee, so they had to petition for it to participate. The school signed up, and Rani advanced to the state bee. "We brought the bee with us!" she exclaimed. Rani loved her Bee Week experience and remains in contact with the friends that she made that year. At the time, Dev was in third grade. As an eight-year-old, he had a lot of fun watching his older sister. Rani was motivated to help her brother enjoy what she had. Their mother was very encouraging. She explained, "I think anyone can do it. It depends on how much they want to do. For our family especially, we live in a small town without many opportunities. So this is something for them to do."

The immigration wave in which Dev and Rani's parents arrived would be followed by another one of major consequence. In the late 1980s, unprecedented growth in capital-intensive, high-tech industries and in services forecasted a severe shortage of skilled workers in the united states; policymakers and business leaders believed that importing skilled workers was the quickest and most efficient way to address this shortage.[18] The Immigration and Nationality Act of 1965 paved the way for the Immigration Act of 1990. Enacted by George H. W. Bush, the 1990 act's passage incentivized those with advanced degrees and strong technology skills. Colleges throughout the United States began to sponsor a large number of Indian students. India became one of the top five sending countries and by 2000, they constituted the fourth largest immigrant group in America.[19]

Whereas the 1965 immigration act set the number of visas at 170,000 with a per country quota, the 1990 immigration act increased the annual quota of immigrant visas to 700,000 for fiscal years 1992 through 1994, and 675,000 per year thereafter. The act also furthered the expansion of the H-1B visa program, which provides temporary, employer-sponsored visas for college graduates who work in "specialty" occupations that require theoretical or technical expertise in fields such as IT, finance, accounting, architecture, engineering, mathematics, science, and medicine.[20] Nearly three-quarters of the South Asian population in the United States are immigrants who arrived after 1980.[21]

No other immigrant population in the history of the United States has been so carefully curated according to educational qualifications as Asian Americans. According to the US Census Bureau's 2015 report on educational attainment, 53.9 percent of Asians in America age twenty-five or older had at least attained a bachelor's degree or more, as compared to 32.5 percent of the general population age twenty-five or older. A 2016 US Bureau of Labor Statistics report revealed that a staggering 51 percent of employed Asian Americans worked in management, professional, and related occupations (typically the highest-paying careers) compared with 40 percent of employed whites, 30 percent of employed African Americans, and 22 percent of employed Hispanics—even though they account for only 6 percent of all employed workers.

What's more, the majority of all skilled labor to arrive in the United States since 1990 has come from India. Pew Research and US Census data note that the growth rate for South Asian populations between 2010 and 2013 greatly exceeds that of the Asian American population as a whole.[22] Currently, Indians and Pakistanis represent the third and seventh largest Asian American ethnic groups, respectively.[23]

This complex immigration history adds to the range of parenting options for Generation Z. Considering different models of parenting introduced by groups outside of the US mainstream is especially important for this generation. Whereas Baby Boomers and Generation X felt very little impact of immigrants on mainstream culture, Generations Y and Z are coming of age in a far more diverse time. While significant differences separate adjacent generations, the gap between a parent's and child's generation is even starker.

Anthropologist Margaret Mead was highly attuned to these changes in her day, especially as a parent raising her daughter. Insecurities about how to raise children had always existed, but they seemed to be heightened during the tumultuous decade of the 1960s, in which youth mobilized in public ways. One question Mead addressed in 1972 is of particular relevance here: *What has happened to the generation gap?* Mead glosses "generation gap" as "the phrase we have been using to describe the deep break between the generation of those all around the world who grew up before World War II and the generation that has grown up in the changed world of the past twenty-five years." Mead elaborated that the gap consisted of young people being dissatisfied with the world around them and wanting greater freedom and their voices heard.

Most significantly, the priorities separating generations, including the fundamental meanings they associate with being a child, also shift. Mead cautioned, "The generation gap is not something that will go away. It was brought about by changes that altered the life view and the life expectations of a particular generation."[24] Parents project what they believe childhood should look like based on their own upbringing. This can emerge as being at odds with the world as it is now, rather than when they were children.

In the case of immigrants, the disjuncture across time and cultures can be even more stark. Despite differences in languages and social norms, highly skilled immigrants who arrived after 1990 would understandably emphasize for their children the very thing that allowed them to immigrate: academic performance. While Millennials were raised in a much less promising economic landscape than their Baby Boomer parents—facing two major recessions and the decline of American manufacturing—they still carry much of that optimism about the world. For Gen X parents, growing up in an era of less prosperity and hope led to raising kids with realistic expectations about what the world can offer.

Shayley competed in the National Spelling Bee for four years straight. She relied on her audiographic memory, which allowed her to accurately and precisely remember things she has seen and heard. In her final year, Shayley spelled both of her semifinal round words correctly, but missed the cutoff score to make it to the live finals. She accepted the invitation to sit onstage as a spectator during the prime-time event. Shayley has her mother as well as her grandmother to thank for her success. Over her spelling career, Shayley loved learning about words and discovering that there were other kids like her. The highlight was having her grandmother accompany her to National Harbor to watch her compete live. She mourned the end of her spelling career and lamented, "The saddest thing about the Bee ending is that you might never be onstage with people who know the English language so well."

During the summer following the 2014 Bee, I drove past several Civil War monuments and memorials on my way to Harrisonburg, a town in the middle of Virginia, where I was meeting Shayley and Mrs. Martin. They live in Floyd, Virginia, a small town that they told me more about during our lunch at a Thai restaurant. Mrs. Martin explained that tourism and creative work are the main things people do. There is not much industry in her town, and it is far from the interstate. "Nevertheless, it's a vibrant community and people love it." Shayley's county has 15,000 people, and her town had 432 when we spoke in 2014. "One traffic light in the whole county," her mother added for emphasis. Shayley thinks they could use a second one, but her mother doesn't see that happening anytime soon.

Shayley loves writing stories about this area. Over lunch she told me she was in the process of writing one about her grandmother, "to show what the hillbilly culture is really like." She saw the actual experience as quite different from the stereotypes and wanted to capture its authenticity. Shayley's story explores her grandmother's life, her eleven siblings, poverty, and intelligence. She strove to write it "in her voice, with dialogue in hillbilly dialect." Shayley actually wrote the entire story in dialect, which only older people speak these days. She is interested in preserving the culture and foods and writes about sweet potatoes and possum grease. She differentiated the "Deep South dialect" from the "mountain dialect" and wanted to record it, since between television and people moving to the area, people are "just not speaking it anymore." Her mother laughed that she "lapses into it" depending on her interlocutor. "I'm bilingual that way," Lydeana exclaimed, even though she knows that many view this language variety negatively.

Shayley stands out in her region and has advanced further than her local spelling peers, but this is not because her family has shelled out for coaches or other training for her to get ahead. She is not the average, suburban middle-class competitor at the Bee. Mrs. Martin suggested that people think that kids who make it to the National Spelling Bee are "kind of the blue blood," that they are all from educated families with generations of college goers. This is not always the case, she added.

Shayley's community does not recognize the significance of the Bee and did not come out to support her at regionals in the way her mom believes they would for basketball or other sports. By contrast, she identifies Indian Americans as taking it seriously. Earlier that year at the Bee, she and Shayley had run into Sriram and his "entourage" in the elevator, including his grandmother and other relatives. "It's a community, familial thing. They have a network, lots of community and family support." Shayley said it doesn't bother her, but for her mom, it's hard not to notice the difference between sports and academics. "But I guess that's the American way, huh?"

Still, she believed that people recognized Shayley's accomplishments. Her mother reflected, "People in our community are very proud of Shayley for making it to the National Spelling Bee four times. Even though it is not a social event in our region, during Shayley's last year at the Bee, one of her teachers pulled it up online so her classmates could watch her spell. Several people watched her on ESPN and *everyone* congratulated her. It seemed to boost the collective self-esteem of many folks in the community—that someone whose family has been in these mountains for generations could stand on the national stage with the best of them."

In this region once settled by Civil War deserters, residents have consistently voted for lower taxes, meaning little went to educational enrichment. With a growing population and resistance to tax increases in their conservative community, schools often don't have the resources to support talented individuals like her daughter. As a college graduate, Mrs. Martin has been vigilant about creating a path for Shayley to pursue higher education. Because her daughter did a lot of reading early, she knew she was exceptional in language arts.

When she was not challenged in elementary school, teachers had a hard time keeping her interested. Yet when Mrs. Martin advocated for Shayley with school officials, she faced resistance. "People perceive you as this really pushy mom that's trying to torture their kid." Shayley grimaced and interjected, "When my mom talks about this she always sounds like one of those freaky Tiger Moms, because it's like, 'My child needs the best!'" Mrs. Martin laughed this off. Later in our conversation, Shayley walked the comment back and admitted that her mom didn't really fit that description.

If anything, Mrs. Martin fit the description of a Generation X stealth-fighter parent. Over the course of Shayley's public schooling, her mom advocated for educational opportunities that otherwise wouldn't have existed. She had Shayley take the SAT in eighth grade and presented her perfect verbal score to the high school principal as evidence of her needing greater academic challenges, and Shayley was allowed into a German class she wanted to take. She did that while her fellow classmates were learning typing, and it would hold her over for a few years until she could study Mandarin. Mrs. Martin also successfully requested an exception to the policy that students in eleventh grade and above could take classes at their community college. In the end, Mrs. Martin's tireless advocacy for her daughter paid off. She thrived in high school and is exploring her interest in linguistics, among other areas, at Yale.

As Mrs. Martin and Shayley's journey shows, navigating educational and extracurricular experiences can be challenging in a variety of ways. These are stressful times for parents as well as kids, as evidenced by the proliferation of parenting books. By now it should be clear that this book contains no advice but does offer analysis and empathy for any parent, child, or onlooker who finds modern childhood as fascinating and complex as I do. A sampling of the past two decades of parenting studies indicates that competition is a top concern, specifically how to handle it and how it is linked to human capital.

Studies from the 2000s seem to warn against competition and suggest that success comes from children advancing despite it. In their 2005 book, Michael Thompson and Teresa Barker regard alleviating performance pressure from children as important to success. The authors aim to understand the psychological toll that school takes and how parents can be better attuned to its emotional stresses.[25] They identify what they call a "performance-driven obsession" with kid accomplishments as something that families must struggle to cope with and devise survival strategies to navigate. Similarly, Wendy Grolnick and Kathy Seal's 2008 account zeroes in on competition and how much pressure it puts on parents and children.[26] The authors advocate that parents not pressure or push their children and manage their own anxiety about heightened competition. Moreover, they encourage adults to instill confidence in children and let them solve their own problems.

Offering a more damning view, Madeline Levine's 2008
book critiques privilege and misery among wealthy children.[27]
From a clinical psychologist's perspective, she hones in on the
negative aspects of raising "star" children who are expected to
excel. Specifically, she links "intrusive parenting"—in the form
of pressure on kids to achieve—to anxiety, depression, and sub-
stance abuse. Levine's dismantling of numerous competitive approaches as "toxic" stands in opposition to those who value a
human capital model of child-rearing. Levine's 2012 follow-up
offers advice for parents whose kids are struggling with competitive culture. She suggests redirecting focus from grades, winning,
and college-admission success to developing values, interests, and
abilities.[28]

On the flip side, proponents of raising kids to lean into competition argue that parents should find ways to give their children
an edge. Alice Iorio identifies strategies for winning that begin in
preschool and likens parenting to team sports.[29] She emphasizes
that organization, tenacity, and goal setting should be shared
between parents and children. In the case of immigrant and
working-class families, there may not be an economic safety net
and inherited privilege for kids, and they know it. Kids are aware
of how hard their parents work and how much they do for them,
and that seems to motivate them rather than create alienation.

This was certainly the case with Dev, who understood how
busy his parents were running their family's motel. Dev's sister
Rani helped him however she could before she received a scholarship to attend boarding school, but much of Dev's spelling preparation was self-directed. "He really worked hard in those years,"
Rani remarked proudly about her brother. Rani taught him how
to read diacritical markings and initially set him on his path.

Dev used the lists his sister had given him. When I asked Dev if he studied on his own on evenings and weekends, he replied, "Yes, ma'am, I do," with disarming Southern charm. "I try to study every day after school but study consistently on weekends." Dev made it to the state-level bee every year since fourth grade, and in fifth grade he advanced to the National Spelling Bee. He didn't make it in sixth or seventh grade, when he finished in second or third place at regionals. Dev's family strongly believes that anyone can do what Dev and Rani have done.

Dev's mother was supportive and encouraging, but not coddling. She relayed this anecdote to me: "When Dev got out in a regional bee, he ran from the stage and hugged me and started crying. I told him not to do it again. I told him, 'It's okay to get out.' He did not do it again, and he learned how to control those emotions, to be positive." She encouraged him to toughen in the face of defeat, and Dev learned that bracing for disappointment is a central part of being a competitor. "It builds good character," she added. Dev echoed this sentiment, noting, "Spelling has taught me that winning isn't everything. Not everyone can win every bee, and you have to deal with losing. Even if you put a lot of work into something, it's still possible for you to lose. Even if you think you worked harder, even if you think you got a harder word, it happens. It teaches you how to deal with losing and winning." Despite a culture that wants to shelter children from competition, the reality today is that competition is ubiquitous in their lives.

A focus on how to engage with competition is the current parental challenge. Baby Boomer parents approached this through "helicopter parenting," a term referencing the extreme attention and control they are thought to exert over their children's lives.

They hover over their children, involving themselves in every aspect of their child's day-to-day life. Parental coddling, then, is a key feature of this demographic, a condition that is thought to persist beyond Millennial childhood and adolescence. Overall, Baby Boomer parents are thought to have transposed a positive social outlook and emphasis on personal gratification to their Millennial children.[30] Dr. Benjamin Spock, pediatrician and author of the *Baby and Child Care*, influenced Boomers to encourage children to be creative and questioning.[31] First published in 1946, the book's message to mothers, "you know more than you think you do," resonated with this cohort. The core characteristics of Millennials include optimism, confidence, high achievement, sociability, morality, and diversity.

While Baby Boomer parents emphasized positivity and protecting their children through involvement, Gen X parents gravitate toward realism and surveillance to protect their Gen Z kids. Stealth-fighter parents are willing to let minor issues go and not hover over their children in an academic setting but will interfere forcefully should major issues surface. Trends indicate that Gen X parents are focused on raising safe, balanced, well-behaved children who are ready for life's challenges. They value a return to schedules and structure.

Stealth-fighter parents emphasize teaching their children how to be successful rather than simply doing things for them. Education researchers Corey Seemiller and Meghan Grace observe, "The level of independence with which Generation X was raised has set an interesting stage for their own parenting. Taking a lesson from their hard-working parents, they strive to balance work and family. They seek to play active and supportive roles in their children's lives and thus place great value on the time spent with family."[32]

The sense of entitlement many have critiqued about Millennials stems from their being told that they can aspire to do anything and that everyone is a winner. By contrast, Gen Z kids are raised to be more measured in their expectations and find what they are good at. They know that only the best win. Gen X parents want their children to be prepared for the real world. The parental safety net—epitomized by the trend of Millennials returning home after college to live with their parents—is a warning for Gen X parents to do things differently for their children.

Also notable is the push for higher academic achievement, with children starting preschool earlier and many taking advantage of state-funded universal pre-K programs. They are projected to further raise the already record high four-year college degree rate set by Millennials. Gen X parents are believed to have a major influence on Gen Z educational and professional decisions. By contrast, Millennials tend to mistrust their parents and rely more heavily on peers. According to Neil Howe, while Boomers care deeply about the higher civic and moral goals of education for the betterment of all, Gen X parents tend to be more interested in how the right school will create concrete opportunities for their own children. This is likely a reaction to shielding their children from the criticisms of aimlessness and disaffection leveled at them during their own youth.

Stealth-fighter parents are invested in social development, including teaching their children to develop impulse control and polite social behaviors. These practices are also being built into many school curriculums. For instance, my son was taught several "mindfulness" techniques in elementary school that he can draw on to manage stressful situations. My daughter has had yoga in her classroom since kindergarten. In response to the bullying epidemic, schools, summer camps, and other child-focused institutions have created a culture of inclusivity. This adult-guided curation of social life aims to create a way for Gen Z kids to be inclusive and get along with everyone—a core value that underpins Bee Week at the National Spelling Bee. It's clear that kids have already received this message and are well versed in it, such that they fall right into the notion that hanging out in larger groups is preferred to being exclusive and cliquish.[33]

For Chetan, the intense individual competition of national competitions was not antisocial; rather, it offered a major motivation to see friends from all over the country. Staying connected through social media and email builds these relationships and communities in the months between. "You become very good friends, and since you only see them one or two days a year, you become good friends quickly." Chetan is part of a group called the Go Team. In fourth grade, he met two other spellers who would go on to become National Spelling Bee champions while they also competed in the South Asian Spelling Bee. When he was in sixth grade, the three found themselves onstage together at the National Spelling Bee. During a commercial break, one suggested that they make a name for their group, and the other offered "Go Team!" He smiled and said, "It just stuck." The idea of a Go Team is especially endearing considering how solitary spelling study can be.

When Chetan aged out of spelling, friends and families in their community asked them for help with how to prepare for spelling bees. Mr. Reddy created a website called GeoSpell, with word lists, books, and software. Shortly thereafter, he developed a coaching space where students come for spelling bee preparation. This grew into the GeoSpell Academy, which also includes math tutoring for local students. Chetan helps out with the academy while also focusing on his homework, but primarily it is run by Mr. Reddy. Most students are from the Dallas area, but others attend digitally from anywhere in the United States or world.[34]

In 2014, GeoSpell had about twenty-five spelling students, with an additional twenty-five for math. Those numbers have since grown and include 2017 champion Ananya Vinay. Mostly, Mr. Reddy attracts aspiring spellers through word-of-mouth marketing in the Indian American community. In his years of spelling bee coaching, Mr. Reddy has met families who relocate to new towns and change schools for a better chance to make it to Scripps. Parents quit their jobs, move homes, and make huge sacrifices. "So what is it about this particular competition that you don't see with the math Olympiad, or science fair projects? Why do people give up everything for bees?" he pondered. As he sees it, the Indian American community is "focusing on the right things: academics and the success of their children."

Any Gen Z parenting discussion is incomplete without considering the impact of non-US-born parents like Mr. Reddy. The most publicized Asian immigrant parenting style is described in Amy Chua's *Tiger Mother*. Chua is Asian American, the daughter of ethnic Chinese immigrants from the Philippines. In her definition, the term "Tiger Mother" refers to Chinese mothers who believe that their children can be "the best" students and that "academic achievement reflects successful parenting." This logic also implies that if children do not excel at school, blame falls to the parent for not pushing their children hard enough.[35]

The concept of Tiger Mothers is contentious because they use methods some consider extreme, harsh, or otherwise detrimental to the psychological well-being of the child. Chua, however, maintains that these approaches are typical of parenting styles in East Asia, South Asia, and Southeast Asia. The truth lies somewhere in between.

Based on what is known about US-born Baby Boomer parenting approaches, it is no surprise that this parenting style sparked outrage. Three days before her book was released, the *Wall Street Journal* published an excerpt that shocked Americans and led to an outpouring of heated discussion over Chua's seemingly extreme and aggressive child-rearing methods. Chua was lambasted in the media for her rigid control over her children—both psychologically and in terms of their day-to-day schedules—and for imposing her choices on them, which many decried as failing to take the child's own creativity, aptitude, and interests in mind, as was expected in some American parenting models. In America, she was called "the worst mom in the world," "a monster," and her family "the most notorious household in the Western world."[36]

Chua defended herself against these critiques by pointing out the humorous tone and jokes sprinkled throughout her book, as well as her intentions to write a memoir, not a parenting guide. "That list that *The Wall Street Journal* put out—straight A's, only play the violin, no school plays, no playdates—I sort of meant that list to be tongue and cheek, like, a little funny," said Chua in an interview.[37] She added that readers from Singapore, Japan, Korea, and Taiwan related to her parenting style. Supporting this claim, Chua's book was successfully marketed in China as a lenient approach to parenting, foregrounding the benefits of giving kids more freedom and fun. Chua reported that some Chinese publications even contacted her to provide advice on "how to be friends with your kids" and "talking with your daughters about love."[38]

Chua's memoir stood out to me as the most extreme among the works that explore parenting today. However, it's important to remember that her book exists among a sea of books on parenting written by white people, for white people, using white middle-class norms. Economic and social privilege underpin the advice in many of these texts. This safety net is not one that most immigrants have; neither is it available to working-class white or other minority parents. These latter groups are not the intended audiences for those books. The response to Chua's book is expected, as it stands in opposition to a body of work that normalizes white middle-class parenting preferences.

Undoubtedly, Chua is a provocateur. She maintains that Tiger Mothering is superior to American approaches. She argues that the latter tend to favor a child's individuality and personal decisions over the hard work necessary to achieve true academic success. By contrast, the harsh academic regimen imposed at home, the high expectations Tiger Mothers hold for their children, and the psychological control they exert (emotional threats, withholding of support and rewards, and so on) simply work better to achieve academic success. Even so, negative reactions to the book are about defending the validity of white middle-class parenting values as much as they are a critique of how Chua parented. They disclose a set of anxieties in a time when parenting norms are shifting.

Gen Xers with non-US-born parents report that their own childhood may have had elements that Chua describes. Chua acknowledges this, saying, "People who were raised in my immigrant community got it. They were like, 'Oh my gosh, this is so funny.'"[39] While this harsh parenting approach is antithetical to the nurture-based parenting that Boomers practiced, Gen X parents, who nurture differently and grew up in a more diverse generation, may be more sympathetic to the broader takeaways of Chua's book.

Chua's extreme version of parenting has also drawn ire from Asian American Studies scholars, who reject the severity of her approach while still identifying distinctive features of immigrant parenting.[40] Researchers found that highly enculturated Asian Americans, like the children of immigrants, tend to seek a less authoritative relationship with their children than newer immigrants.[41] Even recently arrived parents are found to be far more even-tempered than the Tiger Mother, even if they are demanding of their children and tend to not take their interests into account.[42] Pressure to perform academically is certainly real and highly emphasized in this style of parenting, though threats are not likely to be the way this is accomplished.[43] Parents may be more authoritative than collaborative in decision making concerning their children, but not to the extent of forcing their children to perform to perfection. Bee Parenting shares these traits.

There are overlaps between the US-born stealth-fighter and immigrant Bee Parent styles, even if they differ with regard to intensity. Like scholars who have offered a more balanced view of Asian American parenting, I believe that white middle-class models of parenting can absolutely produce high-achieving children. What Bee Parenting is shifting are the standards and means of achievement and how much more kids nowadays need to do to succeed. Bee Parents unequivocally approach childhood as a structured, education-intensive time to build human capital, making the idea of childhood careers more appealing. Stealth-fighter parents might find this parenting style to be less balanced than what they consider ideal.

Bee Parents draw strength from their children's accomplishments, often more so than their own. This was certainly the case with Gokul Venkatachalam's parents, who immigrated to St. Louis, Missouri, from India. Gokul and his younger brother are their mother's primary focus. Mrs. Venkatachalam does not work outside the home, but she took on the arduous labor of preparing vocabulary and spelling lists for Gokul. This became a time-consuming endeavor.

Mrs. Venkatachalam told me that it was a very slow journey to become familiar and fluent with the dictionary. She struggled in the beginning, but her motivation to learn diacritical markings came from Gokul's keen interest in the topic. In the beginning, neither she nor her husband, who is an engineer, knew how to pronounce words according to the dictionary's "Guide to Pronunciation." We spoke in 2015, the year Gokul won the National Spelling Bee. She admitted, "It was tough in the beginning. We learned slowly, from errors, and from his mistakes. Whenever he made mistakes, I learned from it."

As Bee Parents, Gokul's wins were his parents' wins, and they were willing to do whatever was needed to succeed in the competition. Their dedication to emphasizing high accomplishment for their children is a Gen Z trait that stands in contrast to the

Millennial tendency to defer major milestones further into the future. Stealth-fighter parents may also encourage their children to be more strategic and goal oriented from childhood onward. They are also far more open to the realities of what success in childhood today can entail. They understand that talent alone is not enough. They participate in the cultivation of their children's intelligence and aptitude and help them build expertise. Together, these two parenting styles contribute to Gen Z competitors who are changing the game and raising the stakes of many competitions, including the National Spelling Bee.

Chapter Six

Bee Week

When Ansun Sujoe strolled onto the 2014 National Spelling Bee finals stage in a red dress shirt and black tuxedo vest with matching bow tie, no one seemed to be paying much attention to him. His hair was neatly combed, and he looked serious. It was his very first appearance at the finals, and only his second at the National Spelling Bee. The previous year, he did not advance past the preliminary rounds. All eyes were on repeat finalist Sriram Hathwar, who was heavily favored to win. Ansun had the air of someone who had a lot to prove, but perhaps only to himself. He had known most of the vocabulary words on the written qualifier for the finals, but modestly told me, "I'm not usually good at it." To his surprise, he kept advancing in the competition. He told himself, "I'll just try the best I can, and it doesn't matter if I get out. I still have one more year." What Ansun did not know at the time is that he was about to be a part of one of the most exciting live finals in spelling bee history.

I met Ansun in 2014 and spoke to him on Skype with his mother and younger sister. Ansun's mother introduced herself to me by popping into the screen and saying, "I just wanted to add, I'm the stay-at-home mom. I spend a lot of time with my children, especially Ansun." Ansun is from the Dallas–Fort Worth area of Texas. He initially became interested in spelling in the first grade. Ansun's parents coached and helped him study from the third grade onward, when he became more serious about spelling. Ansun's mother told me that at first, she did not know how to go about nurturing his professed interest in this activity. By the time he was at the National Bee, "he was doing it on his own," she explained. In fourth grade, he won his school bee, which he would win for the next three years as well. In sixth grade, Ansun made it to the National Spelling Bee for the first time. He enjoyed Bee Week 2013 and taking in the DC sights. Compared to spellers who had been competing for several years, he didn't think he did well, but it made him try to make it back.

Wanting badly to represent Dallas again in the National Spelling Bee, Ansun studied with more determination and effort in seventh grade. He increased the amount of time studying. On days when he had a heavy homework load, he would try to fit in an hour. On other days, especially closer to the Bee, he spent the entire day studying, finding a way to balance his schoolwork alongside Bee prep. He easily made it back to the National Spelling Bee the following year.

Ansun gave himself over to the whirlwind of exciting activities before the finals. Back home, he knew his church would be watching him, as would his school. In an interview with ESPN hosts before the finals, Ansun told them he has perfect pitch, plays multiple instruments, and loves classical music. He likes programming robots and builds his own for competitions. He did not expect to make it to the finals, but that was his goal. "I thank my parents and I thank God," he stated as his mother nodded proudly. When asked how he started competing, he explained, "I saw the spelling bee on TV and liked it, and I have a competitive spirit. Putting those things together, with my parents' help and God's grace, they would help me reach that." "Amen!" responded ESPN announcer Paul Loeffler enthusiastically.

Ansun sailed through the early rounds of the finals. Before long, he found himself with only one other competitor remaining. It was Sriram, the odds-on favorite to win. The officials moved on to the championship word list, which contained twenty-five words. When only two or three contestants remain, the list signals the start of the championship round. Because it is finite, cochampions are a possibility. Ansun remained focused on the words he was given rather than on the uproarious crowd reaction after each turn. Improbably, and perhaps because of nerves, he and Sriram both missed a word in the same round. Ansun knew that if either of them had missed their word in a different round, the outcome of the contest would have been completely different.

Eventually they arrived at the end of the list. Sriram correctly spelled his championship word, *stichomythia*, alternating lines of dialogue, and was pronounced champion. Ansun was poised to be named a cochampion for only the fourth time in National Spelling Bee history. The last set of cochampions had been in 1962. He received the French word *feuilleton*, a section of a European newspaper. It was his least favorite language of origin. He asked Bailly to repeat it multiple times but never actually said the word himself. This could have backfired, as the judges couldn't confirm whether he heard the correct word. The audience became increasingly concerned that he didn't know it. Ansun later told me, "I knew it . . . a bit. I was just confused on some of the vowels. I had to keep confirming." When the stage backdrop went red, he knew he could no longer ask questions. He attempted to say the word but couldn't quite spit it out. "Oh, whatever!" Ansun exclaimed, before blurting out a parade of letters. Ansun knew he was right before the judges confirmed it. He and Sriram were engulfed in a sea of confetti.

Ansun caught the spelling bee world by surprise. Viewers remarked, "He came out of nowhere!" Even Ansun's mother didn't expect him to finish so well and was elated for her son. Ansun had not anticipated the commotion that followed. "I didn't know how big a deal it was. Afterwards I saw the big deal," he told me. With his cochampion Sriram, Ansun did the early-morning talk shows followed by network appearances, including trips to New York City and Los Angeles. His parents worked with him further on his public speaking, which he had already improved since his first Bee appearance. Mrs. Sujoe explained to me, "Those skills are needed in a career, so the interviews really helped him." Ansun had embraced his spellebrity status with aplomb.

Bee Week provides a professionalizing and social space for young competitors. A cross between an orthography conference and sleepaway camp, Bee Week acts as a national meeting for young word-lovers, with ample opportunity for socializing and networking. Kids are encouraged to make connections and maintain them throughout the year. Many cultivate them well beyond their spelling careers. Like Ansun, spellers use the opportunity to present themselves and their hometowns in the best light possible. They are ambassadors from their community sent to the national stage. Many understand that they are representing something bigger than themselves and rise to the challenge. Kids learn how to interact with media and present themselves to the press. Onstage, they further the skills they have been working on at home—managing their nerves, operationalizing their knowledge. The events of Bee Week along with the media coverage of this event cater to elite spellers and further their spelling careers.

Since 2011, the Scripps National Spelling Bee has been held at the Gaylord National Resort and Convention Center in National Harbor, Maryland. Before that, it was at the Grand Hyatt Washington, DC, from 1996 through 2010, and at the Capital Hilton from 1980 through 1995. Prior to that, it was staged at various other hotels and auditoriums, including the National Press Building auditorium. During its early years, it was held at the National Museum of Natural History from 1925 through 1939. Planted on one end of the small, fabricated town of National Harbor, Maryland, the current home of the Bee contains several restaurants and shops within a large atrium. The convention center is on the mezzanine level of the structure, often housing several events simultaneously. An instructive sign directs those attending the spelling bee toward the correct hallway, but simply looking up could accomplish the same. Hanging from the rafters are banners of past winners, with their name, championship year, and winning word. These grayscale banners with blue and yellow accents—the National Spelling Bee colors—create a hall-of-champions effect from an otherwise generic convention center hallway.

In keeping with this scale is the cavernous Maryland Ballroom in which the competition is held. From the back, by the sound table and the ESPN sports desk, the stage is distant and small. Spellers onstage are tiny animated figures flanked by massive screens bearing their image. The audience chairs, dozens to each row, are arranged into sections and angled toward the stage. A middle aisle is blocked off so that the cameraperson can film without obstruction. Shortly after a champion is named, the room is reconfigured for a banquet honoring the finalists the following night. On Tuesday, the competition gets under way. Metal detectors and security personnel greet entrants to the ballroom. The bomb-sniffing dogs don't arrive until the following evening, when the largest crowd is expected for the finals.

Despite its multiple uses, the space has its own distinct character for spellers, families, and those who attend annually. It is an echo chamber of memories, elation, and despair. It is a repository of anticipation and hope. Some spellers return annually to this space, optimistic that this could finally be their year. Even when the anxiety of spellers is palpable, their jitters are absorbed by the massive room, in which unamplified sounds are barely heard. Announcements from the judges signal that a competition round is about to begin, and the room becomes completely silent. Ten cameras are trained in several directions to capture the stage, speller, judges, and audience, including a jib camera that usually hovers but occasionally swoops through the room in a hawkish motion. Win or lose, just being on prime-time television for the live finals can be excitement enough for these young spellers.

My first year attending the Bee was 2013, its third year at the Gaylord. That year, like each subsequent one, I applied for and received a media badge, which allowed me to sit at tables reserved for journalists and others writing about the Bee. I arrived on Tuesday evening, to be in my seat by 8 a.m. on Wednesday, when the onstage spelling started that year. I sat with rapt attention until the contest concluded on Thursday night. When I chatted with a Scripps staffer before the finals, she suggested I arrive earlier the following year. Open in front of her was a thick three-ring binder with numerous labeled tabs, starting with Sunday and continuing through Saturday. The binder was open to Thursday afternoon, during which finalists are interviewed to generate "quirky bits of fun" for the awards dinner the following night. There were several other events sandwiched between that and the start of the finals a few hours later. She explained, "This binder contains a detailed schedule for what is supposed to happen every fifteen minutes, for the entirety of Bee Week." She ran her thumb over the tabs to illustrate just how much had already happened.

I was not aware of this thing called Bee Week, which I quickly understood was as important as the competition itself. Returning competitors were thrilled to be reunited with one another. First-timers were heady with anticipation and meeting with fellow spellers. I watched participants flit around with chunky Bee Keepers, the Bee's official autograph book. They line-danced at a barbecue and would attend a dance party the night after the Bee. It was like a high-end camp, with a spelling bee in the middle.

In 2014, I arrived for Bee Week on Sunday, three days before the onstage competition. I attended an orientation meeting on Sunday evening, following spellers and their families as they filed into an auditorium. Kids who knew each other greeted one another excitedly while first-timers sat quietly with their parents. The room exuded a mix of anticipation and mild anxiety. It quieted down as executive director Paige Kimble took the stage. Kimble began by praising the spellers for having made it to the national stage and encouraged them to explore DC and get to know one another. The Scripps staff had planned all year for this week in the "Bee Hive," their nickname for the Scripps offices in Cincinnati, Ohio. Spellers were then given swag bags filled with various branded items and information. Spellers who had competed over multiple years wore retro swag from years past, including watches, scarves, sunglasses, and shirts.

Spellers were then asked to stand and circulate around the room. The Bee Keeper autograph books created an easy icebreaker. Kimble urged contestants to approach one another to get their books completely signed. Each page featured a photograph and biographical information. Some kids were immediately social while others smiled tentatively when someone approached them. Others had not worked up the courage to talk to anyone yet but looked around hopefully. As the flurry of activity built, parents pulled out their phones to pass the time. Someone in the row behind me leaned over to ask me which speller was mine. I explained my research interests and she remarked that she had been coming to the Bee for over five years. Her older two children had each made it twice and her youngest was competing that year.

Before we could speak further, spellers were asked to take their seats for the conclusion of the orientation. Spellers who would celebrate their birthday during Bee Week were called to the stage. Kimble handed each of them a good-sized birthday cake earmarked for their special day. Other announcements included a reminder about the dictionary presentation by Merriam-Webster editor-at-large Peter Sokolowski at 8 a.m. the next morning. She also reminded spellers about the rounds of written tests, their timing, and guidelines on what was allowed into the testing room. Jacket, yes. Dictionary, no. Parents chuckled while their kids smiled, some grimacing.

One of the marquee events of Bee Week is the barbecue. When I attended in 2014, buses lined up in the back of the Gaylord resort to take people to a location about forty minutes away. I sat next to a family from Mississippi. It was their first trip to Washington, DC, and they were very eager to take in the sights. When our bus pulled into the parking lot, dozens of people were alighting from other buses and making their way into a large covered picnic area. Many wore the swag they had received the day before, including their Bee Week T-shirt. That year, spellers' shirts read SPELLED IT! and their families' read WANNA BEE. The buffet lines were staffed by smiling people serving grilled food and fruit. The vegetarian line, offering grilled meatless items, was heavily populated with South Asian American families. Soft-serve ice cream, popcorn, and cotton candy gave the event a carnival-like atmosphere.

Spellers reconnected with their friends and adults greeted others they had met in years past, many sitting down together to share a meal. I sat with elite speller Syamantak Payra's family, whom I had met the previous year at a South Asian Spelling Bee. They were very quiet while they ate. Only later did it occur to me what a tense and anticipatory time it was, the family having spent the entire year preparing. When Syamantak's friend Sriram Hathwar and his family joined us, the conversation became more animated. Sriram's younger brother Jairam was not competing that year, after losing his regional contest to his older brother. He eyed the many entertainment options—including hula-hoop contests, a photo area with props and a photographer, and a DJ for freestyle dancing—and took off. By then, excited children with low degrees of fluency in ice-cream dispensing were lined up at the soft-serve machine. Very little was landing in their cones, but none of them seemed to mind. While the scene was festive, spellers who had spent months preparing for the Bee remained steadfast. Only at the very end of the week would everyone completely relax. The concluding event of Bee Week, the banquet followed by a dance party with a DJ and a lavish buffet of sweet treats, was by far the most joyous and social.

Over my years of research, I came to understand that while the ultimate goal of Bee Week is to stage the spelling bee, the most meaningful aspect for most spellers are the networking opportunities. Social events before and after the competition allow kids and parents to meet others and reconnect. The spelling bee world is reconstituted in these moments, as is the bee community that remains active throughout the year. Seasoned families recalled when the Bee was at the Grand Hyatt, with its large lounge in which spellers gathered for socializing and studying. Now they congregate in the Gaylord's hallways and atrium. This time together allows them to meet like-minded friends and stay connected. Not only does this ensure that the National Spelling Bee is a collegial competition, but it also adds social value to what could otherwise be seen as simply a human capital building exercise.

When Alia Abiad returned home to Western Springs, Illinois, after placing fifth in the 2014 National Spelling Bee, the reception was grand. Felicitations flowed from neighbors, school, church, local television and radio stations, and, of course, her sponsoring newspaper. "I got to meet with the governor. He made June 6, 2014, Alia Abiad Day!" Alia first made it to the National Spelling Bee in seventh grade, after years of being an avid reader. She knew that it was later than many spellers. Alia's success comes from liking words enough to devote time to studying them for long periods. "One can't do the Bee if you don't want to do it," she said. Alia's family is from the Philippines and her parents are Tagalog speakers. They mostly speak English at home, and she considers their pronunciation of spelling bee words to be excellent. They work in the tech industry.

I met Alia and her parents at the Bee in 2014 and we spoke via Skype that August. They both popped into the screen to greet me at the start of the interview, but for the most part, Alia spoke for herself. She first made it to the Bee in 2013, where she advanced to the semifinals and tied for nineteenth place. To prepare for the 2014 competition, Alia relied on her parents as well as her own solitary work. She studied around three hours a day during the summer and on weekends, dropping down to one or two hours a day during the week. "I know a lot of spellers practice several more hours a day," she added.

Alia credits her excellent performance to her method, using a program called Quizlet and occasionally relying on her parents' help. Alia opted to use several books and lists rather than studying directly from the dictionary, which she found deeply frustrating. Alia's mother confirmed that "she tried going through the dictionary for one day but couldn't do it. It was a very inefficient use of time." Alia reminded me that there are so many easy words in the dictionary, or ones she believes the Bee would not ask. She entered over eight thousand words and their definitions into the program herself, which her mother believes led to higher retention. "They were very well chosen, the hardest words," Mrs. Abiad remarked.

Alia admitted that it was tough to sit down and type words for extended periods of time, but she chose this approach because she knew she could read and type faster than she could listen and speak. She typed in the pronunciation and spelled the word into the program. Once the words were inputted, Alia went through a couple thousand per hour. Even though it had been three months since she'd studied for the Bee, her speed was still breakneck when I watched her demonstrate for me via Skype. When she could not stand to look at another word list, Alia drew motivation from family and friends. She did not quit. Even though she worked very hard, she did not feel it was a sacrifice. She studied spelling alongside violin, schoolwork, tennis, and time with friends. She was fine missing her eighth-grade dance for the one held at Bee Week. For Alia, hours of solitary hard work are balanced by the notoriety of being a well-known elite speller in her hometown and in her Filipino community.

Alia's recognition is well earned, as the Bee has become more intense and difficult each year. "You won't find a purer competition than this," Associated Press reporter Ben Nuckols told me. A veteran journalist who has covered the Bee since 2012, he maintained that this is the only true kids contest out there. One way the Bee upholds this status is to consistently update its format and rules, especially to match the competitive mettle of its young stars. Nuckols noted that many small things have changed during his tenure, but the main shift is that the contest has become much harder. "We had ties three years in a row. They continued trying to make it tougher to avoid a tie, and it didn't work. It seems that the spellers continue to surprise Scripps with how many words they know," he explained when we spoke at the 2018 Bee.

Many rules of today's Bee were put into place during Paige Kimble's tenure as its executive director. She joined Scripps in 1991 and has witnessed several changes in the contest format. The most significant rule change in her view is the one that eliminated her in 1980; now once a word is spelled incorrectly, no one spells it again. The second is recalibrating the word list to become progressively more difficult over the course of the competition. This was especially a problem in the early 1990s. Kimble recalled, "Round four in 1991, when kids were getting surprise words, there were two hundred kids in the room and one hundred fifty misspelled." Jacques Bailly and others in the spelling bee world call these "lawnmower rounds." The *Washington Post* ran a story titled "Killer Bees" in 1993, which many lamented as unfair to spellers.[1] In collaboration with Bailly, who worked for Scripps as an associate pronouncer, Kimble was able to advocate for changes to avoid lawnmower rounds. This coincided with the start of ESPN's coverage of the event. These changes, however positive from Bailly's viewpoint, paled in comparison to the introduction of the vocabulary test in 2013. "I was jumping up and down for joy! For years, I'd been trying to think of a way to explicitly reward students for learning what words mean," said Bailly.

One of the most recent rule changes has been to reduce the possibility of cochampions. Ansun and Sriram were followed by two more sets of cochampions, which drew critiques that the contest had lost its edge.[2] By 2017, the Bee instituted a written tiebreaker test, the results of which would be revealed if another championship-round tie ensued. So far, they haven't had to use it, although if two or more remaining spellers had the same score on this test, they would still all be declared champion. Nuckols and I chatted about the difficulty of the words, and he remarked, "If you haven't studied like these kids, then a lot of them are going to be really hard. These are the best spellers in the world. They're not just the best spellers of the United States or of their age group. They're at their peak right now. You can be smart, learned, well-read. You're not going to learn these words." He was right about that.

The kids who do learn these words arrive at Bee Week ready for the action. Each year, the structure is explained to spellers before the rounds of competition begin. On Tuesday evening, spellers were invited into the large ballroom where onstage competition will be held the next day. When I attended this assembly in 2014, the energy of the group was high. Kimble encouraged them to breathe deeply. She offered a history of the Bee and its sponsors. One speller, Shreyas Parab, was asked to help explain the rules. While there were spellers who had made it to the Bee more times than Shreyas, his outgoing personality and stage presence had landed him a speaking role at this assembly. Following Shreyas, Kimble instructed spellers to keep the competition moving, to not give up, to spell before the two-minute clock expired, and to cope with loss graciously. No one was ready to hear about losing, but they took in the message. Kimble reminded them that 281 spellers would start the competition that year, with about 50 advancing to the semifinals and about 12 to the finals.

In 2018, the competition format was updated to accommodate the newly expanded Bee of over 500 spellers due to the RSVBee program. Round one began on Tuesday of Bee Week. Spellers took a multiple-choice test that made up a portion of their preliminary score. This exam, combined with their onstage spelling, determined who advanced beyond the preliminary rounds. Onstage spelling also began on Tuesday in round two, with all the participants; those that spell correctly advance to round three on Wednesday. In these preliminary rounds, parents eagerly watch for their speller among the hundreds onstage while younger siblings try to stay patient. Kids high-five each other when they correctly spell a word, displaying smiles of palpable relief.

Each day the auditorium was packed, with family members and spellers who were not onstage filling up available seats. Hallways were far more populated, and the energy was higher overall. When round three concluded in 2018, 385 spellers remained, only 41 of whom would move to the next round. ESPN3 played an explanatory video of how finalists advance and a "Best of the Bee" compilation video while Scripps finalized its list of advancing spellers. More than 200 were invited back to the stage, of which 41 were announced as finalists for Thursday morning's competition. Before the announcement, Kimble encouraged all participants to return the next day to watch the competition if they did not advance. Each year, spellers seem to need a higher preliminary score to advance, and at least a couple of spellers, sometimes as many as five, are congratulated on having a perfect score. Some are name-checked for how many times they've made it past the preliminaries—each year a few third- or fourth-time competitors are in the mix.

Thursday marks day three of the onstage competition: the daytime finals and the prime-time finals. Whereas Scripps recently required a second written test to advance to finals, a change in the format now names anyone who advances past the preliminaries a "finalist." Starting on Thursday morning, these finalists spell for as many rounds as it takes to winnow down the group. In 2018, sixteen finalists advanced to the night competition. These spellers take a tiebreaker test and ready themselves for the main event. That evening, the auditorium packs to near capacity, with Scripps employees and their families seated in the front rows behind the judges. There is an onstage ceremony prior to the televised portion of the final, in which past champions in attendance are welcomed onstage. Then the current spellers are called onstage, a singer performs the national anthem, and competition begins.

Spellers who don't advance due to their test scores are eliminated quietly from competition, along with hundreds of other kids. Those who misspell onstage have to manage their loss publicly, on camera. When the Bee was smaller and held at the Grand Hyatt in DC, spellers were escorted to a comfort area when they were eliminated. The "cry room," as spellers called it, was described as a dimly lit, secluded area behind the stage that provided privacy, tissues, and candy. Spellers were welcome to stay for however long they wished. Commiserating with other eliminated spellers could be as therapeutic as the refined sugar on offer. At the Gaylord, the cry room has been replaced by a comfort couch, a highly visible lounge area to the side of the stage where a speller and a handler sit until a parent comes to collect them. Well-dressed women wait in the wings to escort those who misspell off the stage. They lead each speller down the stairs on the left side of the stage, where they sit on the sectional sofa until their parents make their way over, often with a camera pointed at them while they wait. Depending on where in the massive ballroom their parent is seated, they can be there awhile. Once the parent arrives, the pair have to walk the length of the auditorium to exit via a rear door. In short, it is a long time in the public eye for kids to have to control their raw emotions. Most do it surprisingly well, but everyone would prefer to avoid the comfort couch.

S hreyas considers himself one of the first elite spellers in his small town of Aston, Pennsylvania, which is forty minutes from Philadelphia. He believes it to be less competitive than densely populated regions like New York City or Houston. In his community, no one was terribly interested in the spelling bee. "Spelling wasn't their number-one concern; most people didn't care about it." His non-spelling friends did take note when he went to nationals in DC and missed a week of school. But missing school wasn't the important part for Shreyas, who was far more interested in seeing spelling pals.

Shreyas also relished talking about the significance of spelling on different media platforms. His CNN interview focused on the impact of the Bee on his community. At the local Hindu temple that he attends with his family, young children look up to him and congratulate him on his path-breaking spelling career. He encourages them because it has changed his life so substantially. He believes his media appearances have raised the profile of spelling in his region. "Nowadays more people in my school like spelling because they saw me on TV and on CNN." His television interviews have made a positive impact on his community.

Media has always been the cornerstone of the National Spelling Bee. Newspapers were the original speller sponsors of the

Scripps bee and, along with public television stations, continue to be the primary sponsors of spellers from different regions and states today. As sponsors, they stage regional competitions and fund their speller's travel to DC. Many sponsors also send a reporter and possibly a photographer to closely follow their speller. These credentialed media sit close to the stage, behind the judges. They write and send back multiple pieces over the course of the competition from the auditorium or media break room. An entire town or city may eagerly await news about their hometown speller. Professional photographers sent by sponsoring newspapers crowd into the pit in front of the stage when their speller is up.

Capturing the drama or creating it when none is forthcoming are ways that journalists keep the Bee engaging. None knew this contest like the seasoned reporters I met. In 2013, I sat next to then Scripps Howard journalist Bartholomew Sullivan. He introduced himself over the music blaring during the setup and sound checks and said he was following a particular speller who unfortunately had not advanced to semifinals. Later that day, before the finals, I asked how his story was developing. He was way ahead of me. The finals were still hours away, but he had already released a version of his article. In it, he had interviewed his speller and me, about my research project. He would simply update the piece when a champion was named. "I've already written nine different ledes," he told me. I was impressed, but not as much as I would be from what he told me next.

"I have a good sense of who will win," he declared confidently. As a newbie, I was skeptical and questioned his certainty. He explained that, like others who cover the Bee every year, he observed which spellers returned repeatedly. He was practiced at gauging their performance and skill level. His pick for that year was Arvind Mahankali, "the *New York Post* kid," he said, referring to the speller by his sponsoring newspaper. As the finals continued, it seemed like any of the remaining five could win. In the end, Sullivan was right—Arvind won. He had barely hoisted his trophy when Sullivan sent out the story with the first lede and began to pack up.

Journalists like Sullivan not only have an excellent sense of the current action, but also know how the Bee has changed over the years. Journalist Anne Rosen, whom I also met in 2013, told me that the Bee had become far more official in its format. Its growth in size made it completely different than the one she'd covered in the early 1980s. Even back then, she mused, there was a good deal of pressure associated with the activity. The auditorium was arranged such that spellers sat on a lower stage and audience seating began just as the stage ended. One speller in particular stood out in Rosen's mind. When this speller's turn came up, she approached the microphone as expected. She wore a paper name tag with her speller number and sponsoring newspaper. This was not a laminated, graphically ornate placard created for today's contestants that are sometimes wider than the smaller children who don them.

As Rosen told it, when the speller received her word, she went completely pale. "White, even," she embellished. Time seemed to stand still, with the audience and fellow spellers wondering what was happening. They soon found out. The speller vomited, all over herself and then on the mic in a projectile fashion. Some of it even splattered onto the front row of the audience. The story reminded me of those water-park shows with marine animals in which those in the front rows are warned that they might get splashed. Shaken and crying, the wilted speller collapsed into her mother's arms as she rushed onstage to aid her.

"Back then, there were no handlers," Rosen reminded me, gesturing to the comfort couch and the well-dressed women who smiled kindly as they escorted spellers off the stage. The speller in her story had yet to complete her turn and so was still in the competition. Getting timed out for vomiting would be unduly harsh, so the spelling bee organizers called a break. They got her and the mess cleaned up. Shortly thereafter, Rosen explained, they resumed the competition and brought her back onstage to finish her turn. Her paper badge was moist and streaky. She proceeded to misspell and was eliminated.

Kids today seem to expect the pressure and handle it better. In those days, kids were onstage for two days straight. Bailly and Kimble have both commented that this format was exhausting for the spellers and taxing for the officials, and none of it made for good television. Those familiar with ESPN's "Best of the Bee" reels may remember seeing a speller faint onstage in one of them. That video features Akshay, younger brother of 2002 champion Pratyush Buddiga. When given the word *alopecoid*, foxlike, he repeated the word with a look of grave concern. His eyes rolled back in his head and he collapsed. There were audible gasps of concern, but in the next frame, he was standing again, ready to spell.

Journalists that year attributed the collapse to stress and used it as evidence that the spelling bee causes far too much anxiety in and pressure on young people.[3] Kimble offered an alternative explanation, as someone who saw it live and up close. She reported that the entire incident lasted only about ten seconds. Akshay had told her he had not slept well the night before or eaten much before the contest. He stared into the bright lights with locked knees and went down. He quickly recovered and successfully completed his turn.

When one reporter asked about whether kids still find this stressful, Kimble responded, "The kids are excited for their moment." Another year she explained, "Being on TV energizes kids. They enjoy the challenge of figuring out patterns and coming up with answers coolly." She added, "They have a lot of poise too." Bailly told me the same when we spoke, remarking that being onstage was enlivening for these kids, more than anything. "I've seen very few of them get nervous about it," he said. He tells them, if they have not already learned this from each other, to block out the cameras and just focus on him. Most seem to do that as a matter of practice.

Each year, select spellers are tagged as the ones to follow, while others are showcased for their age. The youngest spellers are introduced and perennial questions about the contest format addressed at the Bee Week press conference, held each year for the media. Box lunches that contain crinkly bags of chips, sandwiches wrapped in the loudest of plastic wraps, and crunchy apples are served. Attendees seem nonplussed by this ambient food noise and proceed to film and record the event. Each year they invite "buzzworthy" spellers—a term Scripps has worked into their branding of the Bee—whom they anticipate many reporters will want to interview. Usually these are the youngest spellers, the precocious five- and six-year-olds whose parents are on-hand to help them navigate the questions asked.

In 2013, the youngest speller was eight-year-old Tara Singh. Bespectacled with a bob of black hair, she was absolutely tiny amid the throng of adults looking to interview her and holding microphones in her face. Incidentally, Tara was once again in the spotlight in 2017. By then, she had developed her own style and was an avid fan of the musical *Hamilton*. The National Spelling Bee tweeted this out in her speller bio prior to the Bee, and the show's creator and former star Lin-Manuel Miranda tweeted supportive messages to her during the Bee.

In 2016, the speller receiving all the attention was Akash Vukoti, a six-year-old who could spell the longest entry in the dictionary the way the rest of us might spell *dictionary*. *Pneumonoultramicroscopicsilicovolcanoconiosis*, a forty-five-letter word for a lung disease, rolled off the tiny first grader's tongue before he began reciting a procession of letters. In 2017, the youngest speller ever to win a regional contest was Edith Fuller, at five years old. She had just turned six before coming to the Bee. Reporters and the media in general were enamored with the petite speller dressed like an American Girl doll with ringlets of blond curls to match.

Every year, Kimble and Bailly field questions about the format of the contest, the spellers, and the difficulty of the words. Seven nations participate in the Scripps National Spelling Bee by holding the contest in their own countries: the Bahamas, Canada, Ghana, Jamaica, Japan, South Korea, and United States. Kimble has commented that several others are interested. Doing an international version of the bee is "still on the shelf," she remarked at the 2015 Bee Week press conference.

One of the most mysterious aspects of the National Spelling Bee is how words are chosen for different rounds of the program. There is no question that the words have become more difficult overall, but beyond that there is little information forthcoming. Reporters routinely ask how Scripps determines a word's difficulty, and Kimble gives a version of the same answer each time, which is, "I'm going to say that's part of our secret sauce." Journalists laugh but know they won't get any further elaboration on this subject. Personal background, the region of the country, and other factors can all influence whether a speller might know a particular word. There are "happy coincidences," as when a speller named Marieke got *maraca*. Generally, however, it is luck and preparation that determine the difficulty of a word for any one speller.

When pressed about what it takes to win, Kimble added, "Intellectually, there are just a few kids in each class that are at the top of their game. This is a good opportunity for all kids." Being at the top, or near those who are, has its own benefits. She noted "special stories" of students who were first-generation academic achievers, some of whom the Bee had kept in touch with through their education into elite colleges. She emphasized, "The Bee can be a stepping-stone for children to get confidence for greater success in life."

According to Kimble, kids who make it to the Bee are avid readers, a claim amply supported by my research. She remarked, "They love reading. These kids have books in their homes. Their parents read to them, they are early readers." While this trend is undeniably positive, scholars have also noted that not all children have books in their homes and that having a parent on hand to read to kids is a great privilege that not all communities can enjoy. At the 2014 press conference, Kimble acknowledged this: "In the Bee, some have very privileged walks of life and others not at all. We hear stories of children who can't make it. We like to bring these kids in so they can get the recognition they deserve, to do more in life."

At the 2014 Bee, Alia knew far more of the words than she thought she would. She was delighted to make it to prime-time finals. She told ESPN hosts Paul Loeffler and Chris Mc-Kendry that she'd studied hard and without expectation: "I wanted to see how far I could take it. My goal was to make it to finals, so everything after this is icing on the cake." She cheerfully told them that she enjoys travel and plays violin with the Chicago Youth Symphony Orchestras. If she could meet anyone in the world, she said, she would meet Pope Francis. Alia's role model is her great-grandmother in the Philippines. She is a tennis fan, and Roger Federer is her favorite player. She admits having a difficult time with Welsh and Irish words. "I'm ready for the big jump to ninth grade next year," she stated confidently.

When the hosts asked her parents what made them most proud about their daughter, they named her work ethic, discipline, and ability to hold up under pressure. "She *is* grace under pressure," concurred Loeffler. Turning to Alia, he asked, "How can you stay that way?" Alia explained that she focuses on the moment and takes deep breaths but does in fact worry about getting words she doesn't know. At the microphone, however, she knows how to remain calm and steady.

Alia's school televised her National Spelling Bee appearances in the cafeteria. The finals coincided with her eighth-grade dance, so the school brought a television to the dance and friends stopped to watch her spell. She didn't want to let down her friends at home, especially given how supportive they were.

"They sent us videos of them cheering me on," she told me. Her excellent run at the National Spelling Bee left her well recognized and regionally celebrated. Still, she was sad, because the Bee was a wonderful experience that she did not want to see come to a close. "I think it gives all the spellers their own chance to shine, step out of their comfort zone."

Alia's spelling career inspired her to undertake public writing and participate in other events as well. In 2015, as a sophomore, she was one of 16 winners selected from over 1,300 entries for a *New York Times* Voices of Students: Letters to the Editor contest. In her junior and senior year, she ran the Chicago Marathon. Like many Gen Z kids, she is also interested in doing social good with her hobbies. Alia volunteers with Back on My Feet, a nonprofit organization that uses the power of running to address homelessness in Chicago.

Alia has blogged about her experience at the Bee and appeared on Filipino television stations. She hopes to motivate other Filipino Americans to participate. "I think that with Filipino Americans there's a culture that they would be great at it. They would be able to work hard and spell and love language." She told me that she would love to have the impact that Nupur Lala has had on South Asian Americans and says that anyone can do this if they work hard enough. "It would be amazing if I could have that effect, but really I think that anyone can do it as long as they're willing to work hard enough." Alia remarked confidently, "If you learn to make good use of your time, you can do everything you want."

Spellers like Alia are ideal ambassadors for the Bee, on television as well as social media. The individualized promotion of each speller has increased on Twitter since Alia's time, with the

Bee growing its social media presence while spellers do more to share their experiences. In the weeks leading up to the competition, @ScrippsBee tweets out bios of that year's spellers, tagging people who might be interested. This is how Lin-Manuel Miranda learned in 2017 that speller Tara Singh was a big fan. Fans cheer for spellers, read their blogs, and check out Bee Week podcasts. Merriam-Webster, which maintains an active Twitter account in general, is especially busy during the Bee.

During competition, Bee Week staffers tweet out each word along with its speller's name, number, and whether it was spelled correctly. In 2016, Snapchat also covered the contest. Before the live final, the company representative asked well-known spellers and past champions to record snaps that he would release during the live broadcast. I sat next to him for a while and watched him record snaps of 2008 champion Sameer Mishra and 2010 champion Anamika Veeramani, both of whom were fluent in this platform. Snapchat planned to release the snaps during the competition. The rep politely asked if I wanted to "do a snap" as well. I thanked him and declined, responding that I was outside the Snapchat demographic. We both smiled in relief.

Social media at the Bee fuels friendships as well as spellebrity sightings. Kids post and tweet about their National Spelling Bee apiary-themed swag as well as their "spellfies," or speller selfies. Most Bee Week tweets are positive and encouraging, with some expressing outright awe about particular spellers. Former spellers make excellent tweeters, deftly offering complex etymology within character limits. At the 2018 Bee, I sat near Ben Nuckols and former speller Amber Born, who were both live tweeting the action. Nuckols won his county spelling bee in eighth grade and went to state but didn't advance to nationals. "I didn't make the leap that these kids make, studying roots and language patterns. I did it all because I was a big reader and had a good memory. That was good enough to get me as far as I got."

Perhaps because of this, Nuckols is deeply appreciative of the skill that elite spellers exhibit, admiring their prowess onstage and, when they age out, on Twitter. He tweeted to his followers to check out former finalist Siyona Mishra, @SiyonaMishra, which I did. I had watched her onstage for years at different contests and was duly impressed. Her Twitter game was tremendous and lightning fast. She offered etymological information in real time, including root-word analysis and possible reasons for misspellings. It was evident that she had this vast knowledge at her fingertips, without needing to research a thing. "That's the brain of a speller at this level. She's showing you the thought process," Nuckols commented.

While most #spellingbee social media is positive, a few take advantage of the anonymity of social media to tweet @ScrippsBee in hostile ways. For instance, one viewer of the 2016 Bee took issue with the idea of a comfort couch. Some viewers do not seem to understand the difficulty level of the Bee, and one in particular berated Scripps for coddling kids. During the finals of the 2016 National Spelling Bee, @kchapman_88, aka Kyle Chapman, tweeted: "Unsure of why the national spelling bee has a 'comfort couch' you fucking lost suck it up quit teaching kids it's okay to loose @ScrippsBee," notably making grammatical errors and inadvertently tweeting the opposite of what he meant (that the Bee should *start* teaching kids that it's okay to lose). @ScrippsBee responded tersely: "@kchapman_88 *lose." The reply brilliantly showcased the importance of orthographic accuracy. The tweet went viral, and @kchapman_88 temporarily shut down his account, only to reinstate it and alter his bio to "catch me on CNN." The exchange was widely covered by a number of media outlets, all of which declared it a decisive victory for @ScrippsBee.

Bee Week, including the onstage competition, welcomes kids to get to know one another, grow, and become more ambitious competitors. Every elite speller I met desperately wanted to make it back after their first time. At the Gaylord, they tend to be polite and collegial. Occasionally kids do get ruffled, but Kimble's priming about how to react to loss, exit the stage, and keep the competition moving are lessons that elite spellers internalize. Dev Jaiswal had figured this out early on, when he made it to the Bee in fifth grade. In eighth grade, he told himself, "I hope to make it to nationals again, but if I don't that's okay." Dev not only made it to the 2015 Bee, but also had the top written test score heading into the semifinals, and again heading into the finals.

Dev knew the stakes of what lay ahead that evening. He was representing his state, and this was his last chance to do so. For the live prime-time finals, Dev donned a dress shirt and slacks and styled his hair neatly with a portion combed forward onto his forehead. Earlier he had told the ESPN hosts that his approach was to stay composed and take deep breaths as a calming mechanism. "I took a lot of those today," he told them. When asked what he would do if he won, he seemed overwhelmed by the very possibility. "It would be the greatest thing in the world. I don't know what I'd do—run up the wall or something!" he exclaimed. Registering the amused faces in the room, he quickly added, "I'm working on that." After he left, Loeffler remarked, "He just loves it. This is a sport to him."

Dev relishes Bee Week and the memories he formed there. He sees this time as a basis for lifetime friendships and wants to return to see people. They keep connected through Facebook and Instagram groups. He finds a comfort and understanding among speller friends. They discuss new words that are added to the dictionary—something that excites them, but "with an average person at school, it would just die off." His sister, Rani, described Bee Week in similar terms, noting, "It's about the passion and going after your goals. The kids are interesting with real personalities. There is an atmosphere of friendship. It's not just nerds going on a stage and spelling a big word."

In the finals, with only five spellers left, Dev received *iridocyclitis*, inflammation of the iris. The audience gasped in sympathetic acknowledgement of the word's difficulty. He misspelled, and the auditorium uttered a collective "aww" and arose in ovation. This response came as no surprise to those who knew him. Dev's mother and sister flocked to the comfort couch to collect him. A cameraman moved in close to capture a big hug from Rani, followed by an even bigger embrace by his mother, who kissed his forehead and beamed with pride.

That year, Dev's school and state legislature celebrated him with "Dev Day." Dev would follow the same ambitious path as Rani; he was accepted into the Mississippi School for Mathematics and Science and started attending this boarding school in eleventh grade. Chess club, astronomy, and intramural basketball are among a few of his interests. What excites him most is his foray into spelling bee coaching. Of his three students in 2017, two made it to the Bee; in 2018 he expanded his roster. He hopes they can experience all that he did during his days as an elite speller.

Chapter Seven

Becoming Elite

"When you come to this level, you're sort of a master of semantics and linguistics," began Syamantak Payra. "A veteran," interjected his mother. He agreed. "Yes, a veteran. There are other spellers of this level you can relate with and discuss words." Syamantak first got excited about spelling when he watched the Bee on television in third grade. That year he won his school bee and became the first third grader to go to district. Even though he was eliminated in the second round, he emerged as a serious contender. His love of reading, developed when he was three, fueled his love of spelling.

Syamantak began to routinely win regionals and make it to the nationals of the South Asian Spelling Bee and NSF. The Houston area is one of the most competitive regions in the country due to the population density, regional institutions such as NASA and Rice University, and oil companies like Exxon, BP, and Shell. "Too many smart people," his dad summed up.

Syamantak's family, along with others, petitioned Scripps to send two people, and Houston PBS agreed. Syamantak attended the National Spelling Bee multiple times. In 2014, his final year, ESPN visited him and his regional cowinner, Shobha Dasari, to shoot features in their homes.

When I saw Syamantak at the 2014 National Spelling Bee, his mother invited me to visit their home later that summer. They live southeast of Houston, close to where I had planned to attend a South Asian regional spelling bee. I drove my rental car to their home in what appeared to be, from the small trees and bushes, a newer development. Their ranch-style house is spacious, sunny, and lovingly decorated. One grandparent from each side of Syamantak's family was visiting. They joined us for the interview but said little. About ten minutes into our conversation, I heard a rice cooker start to beep. Mrs. Payra kindly invited me to stay for dinner and I accepted.

Over the course of our sprawling, three-hour conversation, Syamantak and his mother, Dr. Sanjukta Payra, had a lively back-and-forth about the letters he missed on particular turns in which he was eliminated, including single-letter mistakes from several years prior. "You never forget them," Mrs. Payra said, reminding me of how many years they had spent on spelling bee preparation. Sometimes she and Syamantak would bicker over a particular word and which letter was uttered. Syamantak's father, Dr. Pramatha Payra, sees himself as a peacekeeper. Like his wife, he also has a PhD in chemistry, but unlike her, works outside of the home.

Mrs. Payra views herself as a "production manager" for Syamantak, primarily for spelling but for other areas as well. While developing his spelling career, Syamantak also published poems and essays in various anthologies, magazines, and books. "Might as well do something fun with it," he remarked about his vast body of linguistic knowledge. Alongside this, he became an accomplished violinist who plays in his gifted middle school's chamber orchestra and is active in Mathcounts, a national math enrichment and competition program.

Given his many interests, Syamantak and his parents did not think spelling would become such a major part of his childhood. Yet he became immersed and so did they. They have no regrets about the years they had invested; they only wish it had not taken so long for them to figure out how to prepare and build the right kinds of skills. "It was a Herculean task," explained Mrs. Payra.

Becoming an expert as a child—whether in spelling, chess, violin, dance, soccer, or something else—has become increasingly common among Gen Zers. While there have always been child prodigies who require copious time and parental guidance to transform their gift or talent into a skill, kids are now becoming experts in more than one area. It is not unusual for Gen Z kids to spend hours a day, for months or years, to master a chosen field. Some train in an instrument or sport with the expectation of continuing through high school, college, and even beyond. What is curious about elite spelling is that kids age out when they turn fifteen or finish middle school. Yet this career can consume their entire childhood.

In this chapter, I explore what makes kids want to become elite spellers and the significance it can hold for life after the eighth grade. Elite Gen Z spellers take a professional approach to their spelling training in order to keep up with the high level of competition. At the center of my investigation is their method of building expertise and how they learn to do so. Many work with their parents or coaches to devise their own curriculum. Whether it comes down to grit, deliberate practice, or some other method, spellers who want to advance prioritize this activity. Parents play a key role here, as facilitators, coaches, and providers of economic and emotional support. The Bee Parents I met invest themselves fully in this activity, sometimes at the cost of their own careers and leisure activities. This commitment is mirrored in the spelling bee infrastructure the South Asian American community has established and maintains for their children.

When Sriram Hathwar was in first grade, he watched a family friend compete in regionals. Dr. Roopa Hathwar, his mother, advocated for Sriram to study spelling with an upper-grade teacher at his Montessori school. In second grade, he won his school bee, advanced to regionals, and beat out the previous champ. He is one of the few second graders to make it to the Bee. Sriram's mother has worked as a physician throughout Sriram and Jairam's lives but decided to drop down to four days per week when Sriram was born.

The Hathwars' upstate New York town was not a highly competitive spelling bee region like Houston. "Painted Post is an unheard-of place, we didn't get much exposure to spelling bees," she told me. Even though other spelling bee families they knew were studying word lists, she decided that no list would prepare Sriram like the dictionary. "Scripps says *Webster's Third* is the gold standard, so why not go for that?" she asserted. Sriram made it to the Bee every year except 2010 and 2012, when he came in second in his regional bee. "We didn't give up, but the results aren't always in your favor," she recalled, while also acknowledging the team effort of his preparation.

Sriram's mother helped him section the dictionary into "chunks" according to the number of days until a particular bee. From second grade to sixth grade, she helped Sriram study. After that, he became more independent. Before Sriram spelled a word onstage, he would chant a Vedic phrase such as *Om Namah Shivaya* or *Jai Hanuman*, both referring to Hindu gods. "I repeat it to calm me down sometimes," he explained. Mrs. Hathwar taught him this technique, as well as the lengthy Vedic prayers that Sriram is able to chant for over an hour at a time. Learning aurally "opens up more synapses," she said. "When I've learned a new chant, it opens a new avenue in my brain. I can do more stuff because of that." According to them, chanting has been helpful in learning new words and retaining them.

Sriram spent countless hours of study devoted to becoming an expert, and he triumphed in the face of obstacles. How kids become elite like Sriram is up for great debate. Some researchers downplay the importance of talent, arguing that many activities do not call for any innate abilities that cannot also be learned. Others do emphasize the importance of being gifted, like having a particular physique for basketball or gymnastics. Most researchers agree that talent alone does not transform into expertise without a great deal of effort.

In his book *Outliers: The Story of Success*, journalist Malcolm Gladwell aims to understand what makes some people highly successful. These outliers, as he calls them, are exceptional, but they rely on more than talent. Gladwell draws on a study by Anders Ericsson to offer his "10,000-hour rule." This enormous block of time is what is needed to make someone an expert at something. Gladwell's theory gained much public traction, but detractors continue to identify flaws in his reasoning. One such counter-argument was offered by psychology professor Ericsson himself in his book *Peak: Secrets from the New Science of Expertise*.[1]

Although Ericsson's work provides the basis for Gladwell's, the former believes deeply in deliberate practice.[2] How much a person practices is less important than how they approach their practice. Deliberate practice calls for specific goals, a defined area of expertise, and a skilled teacher or coach. The continuous feedback offered by this expert should be coupled with practice outside of one's comfort zone. Ericsson argues that serious practice as a child may correlate with becoming elite at an adult level. This, he argues, is through neurological changes that occur in particular brain regions. When people embrace challenge, he contends, transformation may occur.

Others take issue with Ericsson's emphasis on instruction and perseverance, pointing to the importance of intelligence, motivation, personality, and aptitude for a particular activity as key factors. Some find the concept of achievement itself quite difficult to pin down. Developmental psychologists have looked both at beliefs about the capabilities needed to complete different tasks and at students' reasons for doing them.[3] Although capability research dominated early work on achievement, more recently researchers have focused on the second category, which encompasses interest and intrinsic motivation, achievement values, and goals.

This was relevant for Sriram, who was not only interested in and motivated to win the National Spelling Bee, but was destined to do so. Or at least that is what everyone from fellow spellers to TV producers thought. As a regular contestant for several years, the sheer odds favored him to eventually win. At his final trip to the Bee, the ESPN production crew welcomed him back warmly. Some who had worked on the Bee for years remembered his first visit to their studio in 2008, when he ate an entire plate of cookies.

Sriram told them about his game-day rituals and superstitions, akin to those of other elite athletes: he prays with his family and eats oatmeal on the day of any spelling bee. They asked him to talk about his fifth time at the Bee and what it felt like to be heavily favored to win. "My intention is to win," he stated, even though his voice betrayed a slight hesitation. He added that he had been studying spelling for at least one to two hours a day since second grade. Rather than asking him to spell out his favorite word in tiles, they decided to set up the word *champion*. Noticing his concerned look, they suggested that he say "Maybe?" in a hopeful way for the camera. When we spoke months later, he admitted that the word had of course been on his mind. "I'd been preparing to win, thinking about it for a long time. I imagined holding that trophy. I dreamed about it."

By his last National Spelling Bee in 2014, Sriram Hathwar had spent half his life on competitive spelling. Heading into the prime-time finals, Sriram was the only one who had been there before. Sai Chandrasekhar and Syamantak Payra, two spellers with high written test scores, were expected to advance along with Sriram but both misspelled during the semifinals. Sriram breezed through several rounds with seemingly no difficulty. He later told me that he knew most, and possibly all, of the words asked. When only three finalists remained, the judges commenced the championship round of twenty-five words. The third-place finisher that year, Gokul Venkatachalam, was eliminated early on.

Sriram and Ansun Sujoe went head to head, battling it out for the title. In round sixteen, Sriram misspelled *corpsbruder,* close friend or comrade. That same round, Ansun received *antigropelos,* waterproof leggings. Sriram winced with a look that suggested that he knew the word—a look very much like Ansun's when he'd heard *corpsbruder.* When Ansun also misspelled his word, Sriram's face melted in relief and disbelief. It seemed unlikely that both spellers would misspell and be reinstated, but that is exactly what happened. Eventually, he and Ansun were named cochampions.

What keeps a speller like Sriram going, even in the face of elimination? Angela Lee Duckworth calls this grit. As I discussed in Chapter 2, grit is what propels people to persevere in an activity, despite setbacks and even failure. Duckworth examined grit across a range of contexts, including data collected from participants in the 2006 National Spelling Bee. She and her colleagues tested what they call an "expert performance framework" to map and analyze how children improve in an academic skill or discipline.[4] This framework distinguishes between deliberate practice performed in solitude and less rigorous forms of preparation, such as word games played at leisure or being quizzed by another person. Duckworth hypothesized that as spellers accumulated experience, they would increasingly privilege deliberate practice when preparing for competition over less intensive methods like group study.

Similar findings are presented in Aige Guo's doctoral dissertation, which examines preparation and competition at the 2005 National Spelling Bee.[5] Guo applies the concept of deliberate practice to refer to well-structured, effortful, and purposeful work undertaken to become an expert in a specific domain. This differs from "informal practice," which is nondeliberate. Put another way, spelling bee deliberate practice could look like a kid studying the dictionary, followed by a parent quizzing them and noting errors that they address as they move forward. This would be more effective than a group of kids who enjoy spelling and each other's company running a mock spelling bee on Facebook. With the latter, there would be less indication of each one's progress and areas in need of improvement.

Through interviewing spellers, parents, and teachers, Guo discovered two levels of spellers—Level I, those who focused on vocabulary building through memorizing words, and Level II, those who focused on learning spelling rules, etymology, and root words. Guo concluded that expert proficiency came with knowledge of a large vocabulary and a large base of words, which typically developed through formal practice. Finalists' level of spelling proficiency was linked to their level of spelling practice. Level II practice is extremely challenging and work-intensive, as spellers who engage in it know.

Ultimately, a combination of deliberate practice and grit together proved the best predictor of success at the Bee. Perseverance and passion for long-term goals enabled spellers to persist with practice activities that were less immediately rewarding. Delayed gratification could be challenging for kids wishing to see immediate results but was effective preparation in the long term. Spellers became more skilled at learning and were able to engage with the material in more advanced ways. Guo's work suggests that deliberate practice requires ongoing evaluation and recommendations for remedying problem areas at each stage. The person providing this, often a parent, learns as they go along, diligently correcting their own mistakes alongside those of their speller.

Whatever happens in the brains of highly skilled spellers, there is no question that they do become elite. They display as kids a level of mastery over an area that few adults can match. Their version of deliberate practice looks something like this: they begin early, work with an expert, and push themselves to master words of increasing levels of difficulty. They don't see themselves as simply talented. One told me, "Even if you're naturally good at spelling you still have to study, because the language isn't just imprinted into your brain when you're born. I was pretty good at spelling when I was little, but you have to put work into it if you want to get somewhere. You can't just rely on your natural ability, even if you have it."

Elite spellers also require growth mindset, Carol Dweck's concept discussed in Chapter 1. Growth mindset leads spellers to view less-than-perfect results as a challenge rather than failure. In this vein, another speller emphasized perseverance, adding that not knowing how to go down is a major liability, because it often leads to quitting. "If you only love to win, you have no idea how to lose." While I never asked if they had clocked ten thousand hours, the hours they reported spending on spelling during peak preparation—two to three per weekday, all day on weekends— suggests that at least some of these kids are certainly outliers in Gladwell's sense of the term.

Syamantak made quick work of word lists and moved on to the dictionary. "Once you're done with that, you're pretty much free to explore the English language," he quipped. His mother and I smiled, she in amusement and me in awe. Syamantak says that his ability to understand language patterns increased over the years. With "easy" lists that posed no challenge, Syamantak could rapidly spell words backward as well as forward. *Narcissistic*, extremely self-centered, was his favorite for this early activity, and he and his mother both laughed remembering those days. Studying from the paper dictionary proved challenging, flipping through its pages and squinting at its small font. A searchable online dictionary, however, changed how much they could accomplish and the effort involved with doing it. Using it, they could generate lists of words ending in *-ible* versus *-able*, for instance, which were very helpful for visual recollection.

According to linguist Geoff Nunberg, people with "retentive visual memories" excel at spelling bees. He glosses this as "the kinds of people who can tell you how many states border on Missouri without having to look at a map."[6] Since any word could appear at the Bee, Syamantak and his mother employed a methodical approach to cover as many words as possible. In addition to building his knowledge, Syamantak thinks being bilingual in Bengali and English also helped, listening to and speaking two languages and figuring out meanings in each.

The sheer amount of labor involved in cultivating an elite spelling career is mind-boggling: combing through the dictionary, creating lists, developing a classification system that both makes sense to the speller and identifies areas in greatest need of improvement. Even with her clinical, highly ordered approach, the dictionary still overwhelmed Mrs. Payra on some days. She and Syamantak have had their share of impasses. Like many of their peers, Mrs. Payra lamented the early incorrect pronunciations and word misrecognition that kept Syamantak from advancing.

As he became older, she worked hard to keep the material he studied fresh in his mind. She offered the analogy of a blender, and how one has to keep the machine on to keep all of the ingredients in action. Once it is turned off, knowledge settles and is not top of mind. "You constantly have to keep churning stuff up from the bottom to the top, and likewise from the middle, for it to be homogeneous." With over ten gigabytes' worth of spelling study on his computer (the pronunciations take up graphic space as tiny bitmaps), it is enough for a lifetime.

By the end of his career, the collective expertise of Syamantak and his mother could have rivaled that of a lexicographer. Their knowledge of language roots and exceptions was extensive, easily among the greatest of the families I met. The sheer volume of rarely used words they generated effortlessly was staggering, such as *dghaisa*, a small boat common in Malta, and *phthisic*, relating to pulmonary tuberculosis, both words Syamantak had received in competition. Through their deliberate practice, they developed a love of words. A "good year" at the National Spelling Bee is determined in part by the quality of the words—those with an intriguing meaning or illustrative origin story. Scientific terms for obscure processes and lesser-known species are also favorably regarded. Mrs. Payra and Syamantak exemplify the kind of discipline and deliberate practice required to lift someone into the elite rankings.

Are elite spellers like Syamantak naturally off-the-charts talented in this area? Or are they so persistent that they make their talent seem pronounced? These are questions that Adam Gopnik raises in an article for the *New Yorker* magazine.[7] Gopnik asks whether achievement can be engineered, in particular with child prodigies, and examines the role that parents play in elevating such children. Elite spellers, especially those who win or come close to winning, are certainly prodigious. Yet it is less clear whether one has to be a language prodigy to win the spelling bee or if it simply comes down to hours of practice and, as noted earlier, grit and deliberate practice.

Spelling is not the only activity calling for this approach. Looking at competitive dance, for instance, offers useful parallels. This intense activity requires lessons, costumes, rehearsals, travel, and parental attention. Traveling to competitions, doing their child's hair and makeup, and dressing them in custom-made matching costumes are all part of being a dance mom. The competition is fierce, with some event judges assessing over five hundred performances in a weekend.[8] Dancers today not only draw audiences when they perform, but can also have major social media followings, as can dance teachers. The growing interest in dance has led competition to become far more technically challenging than adults in that world remember. Like spellers, dance kids can train up to thirty hours per week on evenings and weekends, while attending school full-time.

In a similar world with analogous levels of intensity, young elementary school students compete to become chess champions.[9] As early as first and second grade, they are trained to be diligent, patient, and delay gratification. Chess is a paid extracurricular option in some schools, in which parents can elect to hire professional chess players to coach their child. Children in these programs compete against one another in lengthy day-long

tournaments. Their parents fly them to contests, usually waiting
outside the room as their children compete.

In spelling, dance, and chess, talent certainly does play a role.
But the parents are also deeply involved and invested in the outcome of their efforts. This reminds me of an analogy that several
people made, by way of helpful recommendation, when I first
began exploratory research for this project in 2012. "Have you
watched *Toddlers and Tiaras?*" they would ask, referring to the
reality television show in which mothers doll up their daughters
to compete in child beauty pageants. If I didn't know some of
these people well, I would have assumed they were joking. When
I invited them to elaborate, they noted that both that show and
the National Spelling Bee involved young children performing
on television and parents "pushing their children against their
wills." It's a valid concern, but I didn't see evidence of this. While
parents may push their young ones in certain ways, it is very difficult to make someone spell correctly on a stage. Kids who are
elite spellers want to do this.

I am still often asked whether elite spellers at the National
Spelling Bee have "show parents." That is, do they belong to that
special class of individuals who stake their livelihood on their
young child's acting, modeling, singing, or celebrity activity in
hopes of striking it rich? The truth is, no one gets rich from the
Bee. In 2018, first place was awarded $40,000 and a variety of
prizes and media appearances; second place received $30,000;
third place $20,000; fourth place $10,000; and smaller cash
prizes through seventh place. Considering all the work hours and
monetary outlay it takes to win, it is not a major windfall. So
elite spellers don't have show parents, but they do have highly

involved, very invested parents who foster their child's interests and passions—stealth-fighter parents and Bee Parents. They also have a broader network of people who look out for their advancement in the spelling bee world—their family, friends, and the broader spelling community.

For South Asian American spellers especially, this community model has been proven successful here, as it has elsewhere. A fascinating study of how people parent Olympic athletes shows that it literally takes a village.[10] *New York Times* sportswriter Karen Crouse researched the small Vermont town of Norwich, which has sent athletes to almost every Winter Olympics for decades. It is white and middle-class, and all kids are encouraged to compete in sports. These Norwich parents frame sports as fun and encourage each other's children as well.

Here, individual parental pressure is replaced by a larger adult population that shares the same values and beliefs concerning the kind of achievement they hope to see in their children collectively. I see parallels between this approach and the South Asian American spelling bee world, except for the regional proximity of families. "Communities have a culture of entering the Bee, with teachers and families involved," Jacques Bailly told me. He drew an analogy to the Olympics and how records began falling to new competitors when it was not simply upper-class Europeans competing. "We have a broader pool coming to the Bee now." He mentioned that he knew of North South Foundation bees. "I think it's wonderful, it's great. Imitation is the greatest form of flattery." Other case studies of parenting from France, Germany, and other closely knit cultures indicate that "unusual excellence emerges within tightly structured local traditions."[11] The emergence and growth of a minor-league spelling bee circuit for South Asian American kids has deepened their commitment to this activity.

Gopnik raises another question that pervades this literature, which considers the benefits of results-driven parenthood. Much of the inquiry on this topic focuses on academic achievement, rather than extracurricular parental involvement. Researchers have probed the relationship between parental involvement and academic achievement from every angle. In one mega-study, authors reviewed thirty-seven studies of parental involvement and academic achievement that span kindergarten and primary and secondary schools.[12] Focusing on research carried out between 2000 and 2013, they examined the relationship between parents and achievement and identified characteristics that moderate it. Variables included the type of parent involvement (reading, supervision, expectations, etc.), the measure of achievement (math, reading, science, etc.), type of achievement measure (standardized, nonstandardized, or not specified), and the educational level (kindergarten, primary education, secondary education, or some combination of these). The researchers concluded that the strongest associations between type of parental involvement and academic achievement were found when parents had high academic expectations for their children, developed and maintained communication with them about schoolwork and activities, and promoted strong reading habits.

Studies also reveal significant racial and ethnic variation in the level of parental expectations, the role of students' academic performance in determining parental expectations, and the effect of parental expectations on student outcomes.[13] Common across these studies is the generalization that parents' expectations about their children's schooling will be partially dependent on their racial or ethnic heritage. Examining linkages between socioeconomic context and parental expectations is important, as is exploring the culturally based beliefs that parents have about their own role and the role of institutions such as schools. For Bee Parents who involve themselves in numerous aspects of their children's educational and extracurricular lives, their expectations are commensurate with the time they invest in their children. They believe that their increased engagement plays a vital role in their child's success.

This South Asian American parent-child relationship is something ESPN sportscaster Kevin Negandhi likes to explain for home viewers. When we spoke in 2017, he explained, "The parents demand excellence while they also comfort and support the kid. My dad's homework was tougher than any other at school. I knew about the pressures and I understood the demand for excellence. Kids just want to do what's right and not disappoint their families." The desire on the part of children to not disappoint their parents is palpable. Parents of South Asian American elite spellers are deeply invested in their children's spelling success and take a central role in furthering it. They know that they are part of a very small portion of the South Asian population in the United States that gravitates toward competitive spelling.

"I've never been at the top of my field again like I was at fourteen," Nupur Lala told me. The then-bespectacled Nupur, wearing a white polo shirt issued by Scripps, performed an ebullient two-legged leap upon being named 1999 National Spelling Bee champion. Her joy in the moment was contagious, but few could have predicted that her ardent interest in spelling would be too. Unlike other champions who are only commemorated on the National Spelling Bee website, Wikipedia, or in occasional "Where are they now?" articles about past winners, Nupur's victory had numerous afterlives. As one of the eight children featured in the documentary *Spellbound*, she enjoyed her initial fame from winning and another round when the film was released and nominated for an Academy Award.

Several years later, Scripps distributed copies of the documentary to schools, to renew interest among a younger generation of spellers. This cemented Nupur's celebrity status for a whole cohort of spellers too young to have watched *Spellbound* when it was first released. The film continues to be heralded as a classic, but its depiction of Nupur took on a larger-than-life quality for South Asian Americans. More than any previous winner, Nupur's success suggested that they too could win this contest. Even though the film did not glamorize the grueling work and familial involvement needed to win, many emulated her approach in building their own spelling careers.

After her win, Nupur did not return to the National Spelling Bee until 2014. That year, two Australian documentarians wanted to include her in a project about the Bee, and she attended under those auspices. "When you go back to Scripps as a national champion, you are treated as a celebrity for those five days," she told me when we spoke a few years later. She certainly looked like a celebrity onstage in a line of other past champions at the start of the prime-time finals. She was in her late twenties and had transformed from the teen in glasses and a white polo shirt into a lovely adult wearing a stylish dress and heels. The crowd cheered loudest for her, confirming that her fifteen minutes of championship fame had been extended manifold by her appearance in *Spellbound*.

Nupur ignited what would become a much remarked-upon, curious phenomenon of South Asian American dominance at the Bee. In the ensuing years, the contest saw both white and Indian American champions, until 2008. Since then, only the latter group has won. I was not planning to reach out to Nupur, primarily out of respect for her privacy. Yet when nearly every South Asian American family I spoke with named her as their inspiration, I decided I had to try. When I finally contacted her via Facebook Messenger, she was exceedingly gracious and very helpful in finding a time to speak in May 2017, after a grueling month of night shifts as a medical student.

Nupur remarked that the "same streak of stubbornness" that motivated her to win the Bee resurfaced with regard to following her intellectual passion: cognitive neuroscience. At fourteen, she had told interviewers at the Bee that she wanted to be a neurologist. "I marveled about how words pop into my head fully formed, especially when I could not recall having seen them." Having graduated from the University of Michigan in 2007, she took what she describes as a "nonlinear" path to medical school, which she was completing when we spoke a decade later. She has since begun her residency. Along the way, she completed a master's degree in cancer treatment. She had been diagnosed with thyroid cancer and wanted to become a practitioner to treat others. "You're the first person I've mentioned this to publicly. But I want to be open about it, because now I'm becoming a physician," she reflected.

Winning the National Spelling Bee was transformative for Nupur. She demarcates her pre- and post-spelling-bee life, calling the 1999 Bee "an absolute defining point in my life—no pun intended!" I enjoyed the pun. "Now that I'm thirty-two, I've lived a bit and accomplished other things. Still, it comes up all the time," she told me. World-class surgeons recognize her and congratulate her, which she finds very amusing as a medical student. "I'm thinking, 'You save people's lives and you are recognizing me for spelling twelve words correctly in middle school,'" she laughed.

The Bee was smaller and less dramatic when Nupur competed in 1998 and 1999. "The spelling bee today is an almost inscrutable phenomenon to those of us who competed in the '90s," she told me. "Now there's no camera shyness. Kids really enjoy the spotlight. Their sense of self-presentation is very strong." Unlike Nupur, who was asked to wear a National Spelling Bee polo shirt for the onstage competition, current competitors can "dress to put forth their personalities," she suggested. In her memory, her own sense of self was not nearly as well-formed when she was a speller. Whereas her aim was to compete in spelling bees and simply do the best she could, kids at the 2014 Bee told her that their childhood goal was explicitly to make it to Scripps. They had seen it on television as kindergartners and started working accordingly. In her view, Scripps had done a great job of appealing to kids and inspiring them to make it to the Bee.

By contrast, when Nupur told friends she was going to DC to compete in the 1998 National Spelling Bee, no one seemed particularly excited. She learned that there was limited public recognition of the event in her region. "There was much less visibility, perhaps because it was a pre-Internet era," she remarked, describing it as a smaller, more contained phenomenon. She and her mother studied an hour or two per day and she was excited to have a chance to compete on a national stage. At that time, the competition had been televised for just three years on ESPN. Only when she arrived in DC did she understand the scale of the contest and what a monumental feat it would be to win it. "We were flying blind the first time," she admitted.

Like Nupur's parents, South Asian Americans who moved to the United States to perform skilled labor have high academic expectations for their children. As I described in Chapter 5, the majority of Bee Parents are Indian Americans who immigrated based on their exceptional education and professional training. Since they came for the opportunities made possible by their academic qualifications, it should come as no surprise that they highly value education. What's more, they consistently prioritize academic opportunities for their children, often above their own social lives and leisure. Sometimes there is a happy confluence of families finding social opportunities and other personal connections through their children's spelling careers. Still, the majority of their collective time is structured around education and academic enrichment. Many also enroll their kids in supplemental math and reading through Kumon or Sylvan enrichment programs.

The spelling bee is somewhat different from these academic activities, but the winning streak does underscore this community's heavy emphasis on education-related achievement. The spelling bee used to be called the "orthographic Super Bowl," but has since been renamed. "I've watched the National Spelling Bee for years and commented that it is the Indian American Super Bowl," ESPN host Kevin Negandhi told me. "I've spoken to so many Indian Americans about it. We know it is our night, and it is a night of pride." He drew an analogy between spelling study and the kind of involvement, practice, and cultivation that white middle-class American parents do with team sports. "Parents here play baseball catch with their kids. They take them to practice for hours and hope that they make it into travel leagues and win athletic scholarships. This is what Indian American parents are doing, the same thing as a parent on a baseball team would do. They work with their kids and help them practice every day, only inside, with flash cards and a dictionary. Instead of training their bodies, they are training their brains," he analogized.

Indian filmmaker Tanuj Chopra has even dubbed spelling bees the "*desi* Hunger Games" (a word used to refer to the South Asians in the diaspora). This intense desire to win is also captured in *Spellbound*, raising questions for some about whether the Indian American parents put too much pressure on their kids. "What you have to do after you immigrate is so competitive," Nupur mused. For example, her calmer, self-driven preparation stands in contrast with the other Indian American contestant featured in the film. Neil Kadakia, also a repeat competitor, is coached by his father. Viewers are not offered a deep sense of what makes Neil interested in this activity. Neil's father appears to be fueling the process, urging Neil to continually improve. He takes a very involved approach, priming his son for what at times feels like a prize fight and cycling through word lists at warp speed, all the while referring to him as "champ." It certainly seems like Neil really wants to win, but also that he is nervous about letting down his father. We can only interpret the small slice of his life featured on-screen, which includes Neil's rigorous training at home and his father's copious hand-wringing and prayer at the Bee.

Several Bee Parents I spoke with criticized Neil's father's feverish desire to see his son win the National Spelling Bee. Clearly a major point of pride for him, he linked the win to a feast he would sponsor for his entire village in Gujarat, India. Though heavy-handed compared to Nupur's parental involvement, Neil's family appears to be motivated by a similar desire to help him achieve greatness but goes about it differently. "This is where I feel conflicted about the spelling bee," Nupur admitted to me. She wondered how much agency these children had in deciding how much to prepare or how seriously to compete. She suggested that parents can be quite invested in the spelling identity of their child. With elite spellers, the drive comes from within, but with others, even those who perform well, the question of how much a kid wants it versus a parent's desire is very difficult to discern.

"When I was younger, I wanted to be an artist or a novelist. My mom used to say that Indian kids don't succeed in those fields and that we are subjected to a different set of metrics," Nupur told me. This idea played some role in why she chose spelling, which was far less subjective than the arts. She did well in her school bee and won her regional competition. As she prepared for the Bee that year in 1998, Nupur learned that at least six of the top finalists the previous year were Indian American. It led her to a realization: "There were no barriers to my success. It was profound. This was the first activity that I had participated in where my ethnicity, my gender—none of this was holding me back. I saw it as a wide-open arena."

The first year she competed, Nupur was eliminated in round three for *commination*, denunciation, which she spelled C-O-M-A-N-A-T-I-O-N. In retrospect, she believes she could have figured it out, but being onstage for the first time was nerve-wracking. She panicked and rushed through her turn. The following year she became more strategic and deliberate in her study and set her sights higher. Nupur was quiet about her spelling career in middle school, concerned that other kids would not relate to her passion for words. "I'm still not sure what motivated me to work as hard as I did," she reflected. When her mother saw how dedicated she was, she helped her daughter as much as possible. Nupur describes her parents, and especially her mother, as being crucial to her success, in addition to Nupur's own motivation. Her mother looked up words for her to learn while she was at school and had them ready each evening. With her mother's assistance, Nupur patiently built up her knowledge reserve and slowly became more accurate as well as efficient. Nupur's working dynamic with her mother is nicely captured in *Spellbound*. Their interaction is calm and focused, with her mother helping her develop ways of studying and learning. They make no mention of the number of words they can cover in an hour, or what the win would mean for Nupur's parents or extended family.

Nupur is one of the few spellers of her era I interviewed who was open about her intense love of competition. For her, it was not just a passion for words that took her to the top. This was certainly a part of it, and one that kids commonly name as their reason for developing their spelling career. The other part was her drive to play hard and see how far she could go. Her second year at the Bee, she thought she stood a chance to advance beyond the preliminaries. Given her eighty-third-place finish in 1998, no one had her pegged to win in 1999. This lifted a great deal of pressure, although she still struggled with her nerves in the third round. She initially froze on *corollary*, something that naturally follows, but eventually came up with the right spelling. When Nupur saw one of the favored competitors spell out, she became somewhat alarmed, remembering the luck involved in the words one was given. In the late rounds of the Bee, she was given *poimenics*, the study of pastoral theology, and simply did not know it. Yet her myriad hours of preparation allowed her to use her etymological knowledge to venture a guess, and she did so correctly.

Even as she advanced through the rounds, she did not want to think about winning. "There is a lot of psychodrama," she explained, referring to spellers thinking about how others may have prepared better than them and getting "nerved out" during the competition. Nupur spelled all of her remaining words until she was the last one standing, with one word left to go: *logorrhea*, excessive talkativeness. She knew the word and contained her excitement until she had been named champion, breaking into a triumphant leap. Media requests began that night, resumed at 5 a.m. the next morning, and continued in the ensuing weeks. When we spoke, Nupur reiterated that there is a huge element of luck in winning. "And," she added, "I was very lucky that Sean Welch and Jeff Blitz were making a documentary and included me."

Over a million Indians, many well-educated engineers and their professional spouses, came in the 1990s as a result of the Internet revolution. Their kids were at the right age for spelling. They thought, 'If she can do it, we can do it!'" speller Aditya

Rao's father exclaimed about Nupur Lala's win. Arguing that these kids possessed all the things they needed—intelligence, memory, English-speaking parents, and financial resources, he posited that "all they needed to see was someone winning." Aditya's father, Mohan Sowlay, views a critical mass of Indian Americans as helping to maintain their success at the Bee, including circulating strategies for preparation within their communities. Starting early and participating in all the available bees—especially NSF's and the South Asian Spelling Bee—are vital to their success.

I met Aditya and his family during the summer of 2014, at the New Jersey regionals of the South Asian Spelling Bee. Aditya is soft-spoken and composed. His mother, Shaila Nanjundiah, was proud to speak to me about Aditya's spelling career, especially as it was ending. "This is his cricket. This is his sport. We are sad that his competitions are coming to an end." Aditya was motivated to make it to one last South Asian Spelling Bee finals. His friends, other elite spellers, encouraged him to do so in hopes of seeing him there. This group stayed close through email and social media, even though they rarely saw one another. "They still remember the words other ones missed in each competition," she said, impressed by their commitment.

Aditya's mother described the several years of disciplined study her son devoted to spelling. Aditya first entered a South Asian Spelling Bee competition in second grade, in 2007. Even though the contest was smaller then, the New Jersey regional always drew a big crowd of competitors, given the state's large population of South Asian Americans. Aditya was only seven but competed for about ten rounds with a speller several years his senior, Sukanya Roy. He eventually placed fourth in that bee, and

Sukanya would go on to become the 2011 National Spelling Bee champion. The judge told Aditya's mother that he thought her son had a gift.

Seeing her son's potential, and Aditya's drive to excel, she was determined to find a way to enable him. "Indian moms are like those Tiger Moms!" Aditya's father exclaimed as Aditya and his mother both shook their heads in disagreement and laughed. Joking aside, the cutthroat competition Aditya's father experienced in India has made him adamant that his own kids not be left behind, whether or not they have an innate ability for a particular activity. As he saw it, immigrant populations have a lot of energy because they have to break bonds to move and they make sacrifices; they have the drive to succeed, the desire to pass on what they've achieved. "We have that energy, and as parents, we transfer that energy," he remarked about propelling his children into activities.

Along the way, another brain sport caught Aditya's eye. Aditya aced the *Jeopardy! Kids Week* online quiz and qualified for the written test, ultimately traveling to New York to audition. According to Aditya, thousands of young people take the online test but only two hundred go to the audition at each of the five locations. He scored high on the test, but the interview part did not go as well. He quietly explained, "I didn't have the vivacious personality they wanted for TV." "Energetic at home" is how he described himself during that phase of his childhood.

After that, Aditya aimed to return to competitive spelling. His father was less enthusiastic about him doing the intense preparation required for this brain sport. Yet he saw how his son was able to match patterns and discern clues on *Jeopardy!* and began considering his potential differently. "He's got a flair for this," he admitted. "There are benefits to this, even if I disagree with the idea," he added, recalling how spelling preparation was instrumental in helping Aditya work his way through *Jeopardy!* trivia.

Aditya first made it to the National Spelling Bee in eighth grade. While first-time entrants had won in the past—it was Bee pronouncer Jacques Bailly's road to becoming the 1980 champion—it was unheard of by the 2010s. Aditya knew that compared to many other national competitors and their lengthy careers, his one year of focused preparation was relatively light. At the 2014 Bee, Aditya was only sure of about three of the twenty-five words on the written test but was able to piece together the rest through his knowledge of etymology. He would have advanced to the finals based on his written score if he had correctly spelled onstage during the second semifinal round. He subsequently won his regional South Asian Spelling Bee and advanced to the national levels of that contest.

Families like Aditya's who participate in South Asian Spelling Bees or NSF bees do so enthusiastically. This is their summer brain sport, which many prioritize over other leisure activities and vacations. From 2012 to 2015, I attended eight regional South Asian Spelling Bees, as well as three national finals. The regional contests are day-long affairs for the entire family, usually held at community centers or on college campuses. Each follows a set schedule of speller registration, T-shirt distribution, a written test, and an onstage competition. Regional pronouncers use lists prepared by Touchdown Media, and the first-, second-, and third-place finishers receive trophies plus $500, $300, and $200, respectively. The winner of the national finals wins $10,000.

The South Asian Spelling Bee's finals are held in New Jersey. The years I attended, the contest was staged on a Friday afternoon in August, with spellers arriving Thursday evening. In a welcome banquet, founder Rahul Walia made opening remarks about the development and growth of the contest and spellers taped a short video greeting featuring their interests, hobbies, life mottos, and what they would do with the prize money if they won. On Friday, spellers were convened for lunch and conversations with the Sony TV host. That evening at the finals, the spellers lined up according to their name-tag number and clustered around a large Snoopy mascot, the MetLife brand ambassador, for photos against a screen bearing the logos of Touchdown and all the event's sponsors. The champion from the previous year was invited to review the rules of the contest and kicked off the proceedings. Eventually a champion was named and photographed with Snoopy, Walia, and an oversized check.

While the North South Foundation is a volunteer-run nonprofit and has no broadcast component, the South Asian Spelling Bee interviews spellers and families on camera before each bee. Siblings, parents, and grandparents are presented as a unit, even if not all of them are urged to speak, underscoring the community-based feel of the event. Audiences are asked to applaud, cheer, express disappointment, and sit silently as the camera films their range of responses. Eventually Sony airs a "live-to-tape" version of the competition that includes highlights from the season's regional contests as well.

"Now if you're an Indian child, you try spelling bees. This is a common thing now," Nupur told me. She still does not know why it has become a popular activity among many South Asian American families, and why it still seems to hold more prestige than the math or geography bees. "It is a safe route to success," she mused. Nupur asked me whether my children like spelling and whether I've steered them toward this activity. I told her I had never enrolled them in a competition outside of their school. "If I had kids, I wouldn't push them toward it either," she said, adding, "If my kid wants to spell, my mom can be the coach. She misses it."

This comment is similar to one Aditya's father made, in which he contended that immigrant energy is finite, and that it may not last across several generations. Once his kids have it easier, they won't need to extend themselves the way he and his wife do. Aditya mused, "I mean, *I* liked it, but my children aren't going to do the spelling bee." Aditya's comment is curious and yet very consistent with what I observed about Indian American elite spellers. By and large, they all had at least one, if not two, non-US-born Bee Parents. They greatly value spelling in their own lives but are not certain about introducing this activity to the next generation. These are hypothetical musings, given their young age. Perhaps a better indicator of the lasting legacy of South Asians in spelling are past champions who have had children or have otherwise remained connected to the Bee.

Balu Natarajan, the 1985 winner, is the only former champion whose child has made it to the National Spelling Bee. He is a sports medicine doctor in Chicago. Balu responded to my email queries, and we met at the 2018 Bee. He reflected, "The whole 'immigrant' notion was a big deal back then. My victory made the front page of the *USA Today* because I was 'the son of immigrants.'" He commented that today people would just report that another Indian American won. Balu's older son Atman became interested in it because of his father's legacy. Balu and his wife were ready to support their son, but only if Atman wanted to do it. Balu recalled, "We told him we would support him. But if he got tired of it, because it takes a lot of work, we'll back you up on that too. He's been unwavering."

When the coach they hired told Atman that he had to study two hours a day, the speller realized he'd need to wake at 5 a.m. to make that happen. "Every now and then there were some blood-curdling screams because he didn't want to get up," Balu said of Atman. "But now, when it's a bad day, the younger brother says, 'You have to get up!' And he's nine. Those to me are the most powerful things from all of this."

Atman had been working to get to the Bee for four years, since third grade. Each year he won his school bee. In 2017, he placed second in the DuPage County bee; in 2018 he won it. Balu said, "I didn't have to study nearly as much. A simple look at the words posed in 1985, compared to those of today, tells the majority of the story. The current competitors are simply of a higher standard." Balu reflected on how hard it is to groom a speller for nationals, and why it is mostly first-generation immigrants who take it on. He mentioned another elite speller from his day, Lekshmi Nair, whose daughter Mira finished third in the 2017 Bee. As former spellers, he and Lekshmi could share with their children why this kind of intensive investment is worthwhile. He explained, "Those of us who were in it, who have tasted that, were able to pass that on. But if you're second generation and didn't taste that, you don't know what it takes and you can't convey that appreciation to your child."

Balu differentiates this view from that of a non-US-born immigrant parent, like his wife. "My wife grew up in India, so she's very clear on 'this is how you study.' She had to beat out people to get to each next level of schooling. Just getting a seat in school is this elbowing-out contest in some cases. There's a mindset that goes with that." Balu admires that Lekshmi is Mira's coach, adding, "That's hard! To be a radiologist, two doctors in the house, and then coaching your kid to get here, and your kid comes in third. I was thoroughly impressed! She had an understanding and appreciation for what it takes, and she was able to convey that to her child."

Balu and Lekshmi's paths are unique in that none of the other former champions I interviewed spoke about spelling bees in their future plans. Rageshree (Raga) Ramachandran, the 1988 champion, corresponded with me via email and phone in 2017. When Raga participated in the 1986 and 1988 Bees, there were several Indian American participants but no winning streak. Raga was delighted to be the first winner from California. "I'm pleased to see we've had several champions from California since then," she wrote. She enjoyed the post-Bee celebrations and copious national and regional press coverage. Her relatives in India sent her an article about her win in a Tamil-language newspaper. In the short term, the media coverage was quite intense. The family decided to invest in their first answering machine to field all the phone calls.

Raga credits her parents, noting that her win was a family affair. Both of her parents were busy university professors with numerous community and personal commitments as well, including raising her younger sister and herself and supporting their extracurricular activities. "We all learned a lot together about spelling bees, and I'm proud of our participation in this unique American pastime." Yet the first time Raga's daughter learned about her win was when they visited the *Beyond Bollywood* exhibit at the Smithsonian and she saw her photo on display. "She knows a bit about my experience, and I'm curious to see if she is interested in competitive spelling." As of our 2017 conversation, Raga had not brought her daughter to participate in the South Asian American spelling circuit.

Younger former champions I spoke with had remained connected to the competition themselves by serving on the Bee Week staff. They shared their thoughts on their win and the South Asian American spelling community more broadly. The 2000 National Spelling Bee champion, George Thampy, drew inspiration from Natarajan and Ramachandran, the two Indian American winners he observed as a child. He never expected to be part of a multidecade phenomenon. George believes that the South Asian American community thrives in spelling because it strongly encourages only some kinds of academic success. These include competing in the spelling bee and going to medical school. He contends that this is one of the reasons that South Asian Americans are not well represented in the arts, politics, or sports. Offering an illustration, he remarked that in his generation of Indian Americans, there was a common pressure among those academically inclined to pursue medicine. "Of my six siblings, four of them are in the medical profession, while two are training to be physicians." In short, he wondered if many Indian Americans simply stay with what "legitimizes them in the Indian American community."

Compared to his competition years of 1998 through 2000, George notes a far greater number of Indian American spellers at the finals today. He pondered why the number of South Asian

American families at the Bee seemed to swell each year and how they all seemed to know each other. "Why is it that there are so many Indians coming to the Bee?" he mused. He speculated that they could be encouraged by their successes at the North South Foundation's bee or other arenas where young people gather to test their academic mettle. George remains active with the Bee and serves as a judge for the national finals. He records Bee Week podcasts and video footage as a role model to aspiring spellers. He sees it as an opportunity to perform service like his parents did, when they sacrificed so much time to coach him at the expense of their own interests.

Another member of the Bee Week staff is 2008 winner Sameer Mishra. Sameer knows that all champions are notable in their own way, but his fame also stems from his appearance on a frequently played ESPN "Best of the Bee" reel. He is shown being asked to spell *numnah*, a cloth placed under a horse's saddle, but repeated the word back as *numbnut*, slang for a dimwitted person. For that, he is known as "the numnah guy," with people forgetting that he actually also won. Sameer and I spoke in 2017, having met at the Bee several times prior. He admitted, "At first I didn't understand why it was funny. I was focusing on understanding the word. When I said *numbnut*, I wasn't making a joke, that's just what I heard. People tell me I'm a funny guy, but that joke was made out of complete coincidence!" Reflecting on his time at the Bee, he remarked, "I'm privileged to have been around the Bee for twelve years: four as a competitor, three as a younger sibling watching my older sister, and five as a staff member." Sameer's sister made it to the Bee three times but never moved past preliminaries.

As a younger sibling, Sameer got drawn in by the Bee Week social events and decided he wanted to experience them for himself. When their mother quizzed his sister, he started to participate too. In addition to eventually studying the dictionary, Sameer was part of a community of spellers called Speller Nation. They had practice bees using AOL's chat interface AIM. Sameer's family has been dedicated to education since they arrived and settled in West Lafayette, Indiana, where his father initially had a research fellowship. "Education is a path to financial success. As immigrants, they want us to have the secure life and understanding of the American system and way of doing things, that whole experience, and one of those things is the spelling bee."

Sameer is reflective about what winning did for him. In addition to the skills he honed that helped him get organized and stay focused, including developing a work ethic, working toward a goal, and creating time lines and to-do lists, he also learned how to build a public personality. He recalled an event his school arranged to celebrate his becoming champion. He couldn't muster anything to say when asked to address the room. The newspaper headline the next day read, "Spelling Bee Champion Finally at a Loss for Words." Realizing that was not a way forward, he figured out how to be friendlier and more outgoing and cultivated a social persona. He remarked that now spellers seem to already understand this.

During his years as a Bee Week staffer, Sameer has spoken extensively to finalists. He believes that, regardless of ethnicity, certain things are shared among the spellers. "What I've noticed is that there's a lot of interest in the competition from the entire family. The mom and dad are very involved. They know what the dictionary is, how big it is; they understand the complexity of the task. And there is someone who has spent a disproportionate amount of time helping that person prepare for the Bee, whether it's a teacher, family member, or parent, sibling, or friend. Or, with the more recent trend, a hired coach. It's now a team effort."

Anamika Veeramani, the 2010 champion, also finds it curious to be part of this Indian American winning streak. Having grown up in Cleveland, Ohio, she remarked upon how different she thought her upbringing was compared to many of the South Asian American kids currently competing in the Bee. She finds the large numbers of South Asian American parents and kids at the Bee perplexing, not understanding why so many of them now flock to this activity. Even though she is also part of this phenomenon, she does not think she participated in it as intensively as she sees families doing so now.

Anamika suggested that the phenomenon likely increased in the years after she finished her spelling career. She was also involved with many other activities alongside spelling—science fairs, math competitions, and the like—making spelling bees one activity among many, rather than her sole focus. Anamika was happy to help her younger brother Ashwin, who advanced to the 2014 finals, but is unsure of whether she would work as intensively on spelling as her mother did if she had children.

The 2011 champion, Sukanya Roy, described her win as "coming from a place of community, being part of this really tight-knit community of spellers who had all been coming back to Scripps year after year." Sukanya remarked that while people had identified the South Asian trend before her win, it now has far greater visibility. She links this to the rise of social media, especially in the Bee's expanded coverage that includes tweeting every word and bios of spellers. As a Bee Week staffer, she does go out of her way to be helpful to families who approach her and ask for advice.

What is clear with these winners and today's elite spellers is that the competition continues to become more intense and grow more important in the South Asian American community. As long as there are new non-US-born, highly skilled immigrants entering their children into the South Asian American spelling circuit, it will continue to thrive. As a result, the difficulty level of the National Spelling Bee will continue to rise. Kids who aim to be contenders will need to invest the intensive time and resources required to make it to the Bee and develop the grit to persevere, even in the face of repeated failures.

During the 2014 National Spelling Bee semifinals, Syamantak Payra misspelled *circumforaneous*, wandering from place to place. The auditorium uttered a collective gasp and silence hung in the air after the bell dinged. Spellers rose to give him an ovation, and the audience and press stood to do the same. It was lengthy and enthusiastic, recognizing his immense talent as well as deadening the sting of his being eliminated before the finals, especially because his test score was high enough for him to advance. Syamantak views his spelling career as a "journey of seven years." He is interested in passing that knowledge along to new budding spellers. His mother referred to the growth of his spelling career as "standing on the shoulders of giants to look further ahead."

Former competitors like Syamantak who advise up-and-coming spellers not only impart practical information, but also empathize with them about the emotional toll this kind of participation can take after years of competition. Syamantak's disappointment with the end of his spelling career was palpable. "The thing is, we all know about the vicissitudes," Mrs. Payra said softly. "But when you see there is so much promise in the kids, it is hard to say that there might be heartbreak involved, so we don't go there. You still want to take your chances and see how you fare." Those who do will find that there are many benefits to becoming elite, despite the anguish of dictionary defeat.

Chapter Eight

Making Spellebrities

ESPN on-air host Paul Loeffler has announced the National Spelling Bee for over a decade. When the camera is focused on the stage, Loeffler speaks to ESPN viewers in hushed tones, narrating the intricacies of the word or offering relevant contextual information about a participant. This kind of commentary is intended to help viewers better understand the activity and also give them reasons to root for the speller onstage. "So much of what everyone would consider a sport is mental. It's processing," remarked Loeffler when we spoke in 2015. Like NFL quarterbacks or star baseball players, being an elite speller is about intelligence and thinking quickly. Spellers prepare as athletes would and have to perform under pressure, within time constraints, in front of an expectant audience. "It's every bit as intense and competitive as any athletic event you could think of," Loeffler remarked.

Play-by-play commentary elevates the spelling bee to a major sporting event for live broadcast, and Loeffler is a natural. He has been announcing sports to anyone who will listen since he was twelve. He is also a former National Spelling Bee finalist who competed before the network began to broadcast the event. ESPN likes to include a throwback photo of young Paul onstage at the mic at some point during the broadcast. In sixth grade, when Loeffler came close to winning his state bee, his mother encouraged him to study harder. "She coached me and bribed me with baseball cards," he laughed. It worked. Two years later, he won his regional bee and made it to Washington, DC. "It was an eye-opener. I really wanted to win, but I didn't," he told me.

Loeffler grew up in a white middle-class family in Fresno, California. With his thirteenth-place finish in 1990, his mother became more invested in the activity and began to work with his younger sister Corrie. "She competed here three times. She was good enough to win," he said. Corrie continues to be very involved in the Bee, working for Scripps and serving as one of the Bee Week judges. Loeffler remarked on how much had changed since their time onstage. In addition to the venue moving to the Gaylord in National Harbor, Maryland, there used to be no time limit to spell, no Internet or online dictionary, and the Bee was not on national television so there was no pressure of audiences and viewers outside the auditorium.

Around 2005, ABC contacted Loeffler to gauge his interest in hosting the Bee. "I thought it was a joke! I must have been the only former Bee kid on TV somewhere, and they found me," he recalled. Modesty aside, he was already well known for his college football broadcast work. Loeffler hopes his commentary is "mundane enough to speak to the average Joe but sophisticated enough to speak to the Bee audience, who speak the language and are really into it." Loeffler can explain the relevance of clues each speller requests, such as alternate pronunciations or patterns common to particular roots. He calibrates this against each speller's strengths and limitations. A lot of information is exchanged during a spelling bee turn, and one of his jobs is to translate for the audience. He does this with admirable speed and flourish during the live broadcast. As he put it, "It's a big responsibility to tell people at home what might be going on in a kid's head."

In a pre-televised-spelling-bee era, only newspapers announced the winner of the Bee and published their photos. Finalists and top spellers likely appeared in their regional sponsoring newspaper but had no national visibility. Some of this changed with the live telecast of the final, especially when it transitioned to prime time. Yet there was no afterlife for those who did not win and no public way that they could remain relevant even if they wanted to. ESPN began to provide that opportunity with features of spellers filmed in their hometowns and the ESPN studio, statistics and graphics on their performance, gripping shots of their family members watching them onstage, and announcers who know all about them.

Broadcast and social media like ESPN and Twitter transform spellers into spellebrities. As a result, their legacies continue on YouTube, Instagram, Facebook, and as prominent tweeters who comment on Bee competition. Camera-ready, media-savvy members of Generation Z find this confluence of competition and notoriety appealing and inviting.

According to ESPN copy editor Amy Goldstein, the best three days of the year to work at ESPN are the first two days of March Madness and the National Spelling Bee.

"Everybody in the office suddenly gets very hyped and excited about it." She added that the same is true for the Little League World Series, which ESPN also broadcasts. Goldstein drew on her 1998 fourth-place finish to write about the "secondary goal" of appearing in the television broadcast. Similar to other non-professional athletes being featured in a televised event, "for a young competitor who is unlikely to channel the activity into a profession, television coverage is rewarding," she writes.[1] ESPN believes that presenting young amateur participants is a major draw. It treats the Bee as any other major sporting event, with requisite emphasis on showcasing elite competitors and their progress. All the better if they are featured in ways that show off their personalities.

Scripps National Spelling Bee Executive Director Paige Kimble confirms how exciting the prospect of being on ESPN can be for kids. When Kimble walks around the Bee today, she never hears kids talking about winning prize money. "What I have heard a lot is 'I'll be happy if I just make it into the ESPN broadcast.' That lets us know that the recognition and cool factor is a significant reward for the kids," she told me when we spoke in 2018. She added that today, kids perform for the cameras more. Scripps worked with a market research firm doing focus groups of parents and spellers. "The number-one word we hear from people is confidence. They see this as the most influential value of spelling bee participation," Kimble told me. Many of them come to the Bee with experience in debate, public speaking, and other competition that helps them stay confident and focused.

The National Spelling Bee finals were first broadcast live for television in 1946 on NBC. They were not broadcast again until 1974, when PBS aired a taped prime-time special that year and again in 1977. From 1994 through 2005, ESPN offered a live daytime broadcast. Between 2006 and 2010, ESPN covered the daytime contest and ABC took over for the prime-time broadcast. When the Bee was first televised, participants were eliminated through misspelling onstage alone, making the competition lengthy and unpredictable. It could take days, or it could go very quickly. "An hour into the two-hour telecast, there were only four competitors left!" recalled Dave Miller about one poorly paced ABC broadcast. When we spoke in 2015, Miller then worked at ESPN and was in charge of content and production of the National Spelling Bee. During that ABC broadcast, the crew scrambled to fill the time and aired more features, but it still came in twenty minutes short. For a traditional network, this posed a major scheduling problem. Miller explained it would have been fine on ESPN, where they cover many events that can vary in length. While ESPN could easily join another live sporting event or cut to the studio, "ABC can't do that. The news only comes on at 11 p.m.," he explained.

The uncertainty of the action and the time frame of the competition posed challenges for ABC that ESPN could better manage. Ashley O'Connor, Miller's former colleague, asserted that ESPN showcases competition, so the Bee is a perfect fit. "People develop a personal relationship to it. The kids are amazing." O'Connor handles the programming aspects of ESPN's broadcast and has worked on the spelling bee since 2006. When we spoke on the phone in 2017, she told me that about 1 million people watch their broadcast of the Bee each year. She explained that size of the viewing audience of the National Spelling Bee prime-time finals varies depending on any competing sporting events on at the same time. For instance, in 2017 and 2018, Game 1 of the NBA Finals began within an hour of the Bee broadcast and siphoned off potential viewers.

Given all the viewing options, consideration of what makes for good television content is not to be underestimated. Miller highlighted this point when we spoke on the phone before the 2014 Bee and again in 2015. The second time, I met Miller in his sunny Bristol, Connecticut, office, a space filled with a tasteful amount of sports memorabilia. His enthusiasm for the Bee was rivaled only by his desire to continually improve ESPN's coverage of the event. "We are storytellers," Miller proclaimed, assuring me that he would deliver this message in several different ways over the course of our conversation. Covering "your famous stick-and-ball sports" and others like football and basketball will always be part of ESPN's focus, he said, but so is "covering competition" in whatever form it takes.

When the Bee moved to the Gaylord National Resort and Convention Center in 2011, Scripps built a bigger, more attractive set that changed color. They improved the lighting and the overall look of the production—more cameras, a set location for hosts, and other things they do for big events that culminate in a championship. The stage color corresponds now with the two-minute spelling bee clock, with the first seventy-five seconds in green, yellow for the next fifteen seconds, and red for the final thirty, when spellers can no longer ask questions. "It gets more ominous. We're not trying to scare anyone, but trying to signal, 'Hey, this is a big moment, let's build the drama,'" Miller explained.

ESPN also suggested that Scripps could let the spellers dress however they pleased. "They're not all on the same team, per se," Miller mused, pointing out a flaw in the logic of having kids all wear matching Scripps shirts. Letting kids dress themselves opened up the possibility to do more with individual personalities, and they went in that direction. This eventually gave rise to the speller features interspersed throughout the competition, but especially the semifinals and finals. Miller favored slowing down the pace in this way to showcase spellers' stories. He explained that if they show five features, "you're going to pick at least one of the people to root for, for one reason or another. Maybe they're in your home state or live near you, or it's the way they carry themselves." I understood this well, as this was precisely what drew me in when I had watched the 2012 broadcast.

Other modifications made the broadcast more audience-friendly. Initially, some viewers were confused that a bell was rung only when someone misspelled. They apparently thought the bell was a positive sign and were perplexed that nothing audible happened when a word was actually spelled correctly. On-stage, a speller could observe the judge's nod for a correct answer and headshake and bell ring for an incorrect one, but this was not visible to home audiences. ESPN requested the judge to say "correct" for a successful turn, therefore clearly designating the bell for a misspelling.

To further enhance the home viewing experience, ESPN added on-screen graphics to show the information spellers ask for, including parts of speech, derivation, and definition. As competitors spell, correct letters uttered light up in green within the word on-screen, and in red if a letter is incorrect. Miller elaborated, "We've advanced the graphic elements to show what the spellers are saying, to help the viewer understand the pressure and pace and drama." Also popular is the "Play-Along" version with multiple-choice spellings. This interface offers information about the word's etymology, definition, and other data, whether or not spellers request it onstage. Its creators were inspired by the graphic interface of the game show *Who Wants to Be a Millionaire*. ESPN senior coordinating producer Ed Placey, who manages the National Spelling Bee content, explains, "It allows the average or even poor spellers—like many of us—to play along just as easily as very good spellers."[2]

Whereas viewers a decade ago had nothing to watch but the speller, they may now focus on bits of grammar and etymology in hopes of spelling a word right themselves. ESPN believes that these enhancements keep viewers engaged more deeply in the competition, especially when the words become less common and exceedingly difficult. ESPN takes the competition seriously because, as Miller explained, "This is a very serious competition. But they're kids." Making the event fun for kids and conveying a sense of levity is an important counterpoint to the pressure that is also visible. "You're showcasing it all," said Miller. He hoped that ESPN is the "fun" part and spelling is the pressure part. Miller was very careful to convey his view on broadcasting child competitions: "You often have skeptics saying, 'You're taking advantage of these kids.'" He explained that the primary aim of the network's broadcast is to "tell their stories and showcase their excellence." Above all, ESPN goes to great lengths to make sure it's "not making fun of the kids. We're showing the emotion but not exploiting them. That's the key."

Miller also emphasized the importance of capturing the human emotion of young people. Even so, he acknowledged the toll of losing and the painful moment when a speller is eliminated. Some seem fine, but some are "truly heartbroken." In these cases, the network decides to forego an interview and instead gives them space, out of sensitivity for the kids. I witnessed this delicate balance after the 2014 semifinals, when the finalists for the evening's live competition were announced. When a favored speller did not advance to the finals, I saw one of the ESPN production assistants dashing around. I asked her what she was looking for, and she explained that the producers had asked her to find the family of that speller. "Sometimes we focus on kids when they don't make it. That can also be very dramatic," she told me candidly. As we scanned the room, we spotted the family surrounded by a huddle in the middle of the auditorium. They were visibly disappointed and trying to manage the attention during a moment they would have preferred to experience privately. From what I could tell, the producers respected the family's privacy and no footage of them was shown in that evening's broadcast.

Each year when ESPN plans for this event, they consider how they can increase its entertainment value and draw in more viewers. *Bigger* and *special*, words Miller used frequently in our conversation, are ones that the entire ESPN team seems to care about. I observed this in 2014, when I closely followed their development and production of the National Spelling Bee. During an ESPN production meeting in Bristol in late April, freelance producer Tim Weinkauf allowed me to phone in to his team briefing, and I listened to him guide the staff through the highlights of the broadcast production process. It was as much centered on showcasing the personalities of the kids as it was on filming the spelling competition itself. The Bee Week team introduced themselves; one of them, Jerry Vaillancourt, would be my contact person. Over the next month, he would dutifully share

Bee Week production documents with me so that I could better understand the network's process.

Production units would be dispatched to various places around the country to film elite spellers' features. By April, most of the regional bees have declared winners. Scripps collaborates with ESPN to identify a batch of spellers to contact for features filmed in their hometowns. From thirty top spellers, they choose about a dozen who have a good chance of progressing far into the competition. "It is surprising how predictable this is. This elite group of spellers keeps winning and coming back," Miller said. Later, in May, production managers, editors, assistants, content associates, and others arrive on Sunday of Bee Week to set up. Some would work inside the Gaylord while others would be stationed in "the truck," Weinkauf explained. I was unclear about what that was, but it seemed important.

During Bee Week, the production team works around the clock. Even when spelling is not in session, they are filming features, editing, interviewing spellers, and directing the auditorium audience. I had observed several hours of feature filming earlier that week and was interested in how all that video footage would be edited in time for the competition. Vaillancourt offered to give me a tour of the on-site production facilities. I met him by the ESPN staff room, one of several rooms with paper signs taped to them designating their use for Bee Week. It was adjacent to the media room, which I had frequented for coffee and a quiet place to write notes. Vaillancourt had an abundant head of smooth white hair combed straight back and a plush white beard to match. Friendly and talkative, he was an ideal tour guide.

My visit to the on-site recording and editing facilities illustrated the scale and scope of this broadcast. We started with the two editing rooms, which each housed a massive Avid editing station. ESPN catalogs the footage so that it is available at all of their editing stations. Vaillancourt introduced me to the two men responsible for editing the hours of feature footage shot every day. One showed me the ninety-second feature he had created from a Houston, Texas, visit to speller Shobha Dasari. From over eight hours of footage, he'd spliced together an engaging highlight reel of a fourteen-year-old's life. For a forty-five-second segment, they needed about an hour of footage—which is about how long each kid spent in the ESPN studio.

After several minutes of watching editing, Vaillancourt moved me along. I had spent the previous day in the studio watching speller features, so we skipped that room. "Have you seen the truck?" Vaillancourt asked me. Second mention of the truck. It sounded important, and intriguing. "No, but I'd like to!" I said, trying to not sound overly excited. Some preparation was necessary. We stopped in the ESPN staff room where Vaillancourt rustled through oversized sheets of paper and pulled out a blueprint. Warning me that the truck would be small, dark, and crowded, he quickly reviewed the layout of its features. I didn't quite understand what I was looking at but didn't have a chance to formulate any questions. "Let's go!" Vaillancourt said, signaling that I should follow him out of the room.

Vaillancourt took off down the main hallway and then turned onto another one. It was deserted. He then took a sharp turn into an unmarked opening in the wall. I hurried along to find him holding open a service door. White-haired Vaillancourt darting through secret doorways gave the tour a fantastic *Alice in Wonderland* quality. Suddenly we were in a cavernous kitchen, in what looked like a food prep area. Workers in white-and-gray uniforms moved about quietly, carrying vegetables and mixing bowls. It was here that the Bee Week staff meals were prepared, and the awards banquet dinner would be served through doors leading directly into the ballroom. The uniformed workers paid us no mind as we wound our way through the space. "Watch the wire!" Vaillancourt said, pointing at what was easily a mile of cable snaking around the room. It ran from the ballroom and the editing studios to the kitchen and under and around counters. It was partially encased in a yellow cover to deter people from stumbling over it, but it seemed just as easy to trip on that. It went on endlessly as we followed it through the bowels of the kitchen.

Finally, we were at a door to the outside, with metal stairs leading down from a loading dock. "Watch your step," Vaillancourt cautioned. The bright sunlight was blinding after hours of dim artificial light in the auditorium and production rooms. Vaillancourt, who made this journey multiple times a day, kindly paused and waited for my eyes to recalibrate. Once I could see again, he gestured grandly to two large trailers with satellite dishes parked atop them. We alit a narrow metal staircase outside them. He reached for the door and cautioned, "Now, you have to be very quiet. And it's really crowded so we can't stay long."

We entered a self-contained world of television monitors, computers, large databases, and other machines whose function was anyone's guess. It was an entire production studio in a portable truck. The feed came via actual wire cable from the auditorium cameras, and it was formatted, arranged, and beamed out to the world from that tiny control center. There were three or four people per row, seated facing a wall of screens, some wearing headsets that allowed them to communicate with associates in the auditorium. All of them were men, over a dozen from my quick count. The wall of monitors had so many displays I had no idea where to look. Weinkauf, who was in the truck, briefly explained to me what I was looking at.

Each screen handles a different aspect of the broadcast—the speller bio, the definition of the word, the "spell at home" version with the word projected as the contestant starts speaking letters. A clock graphic is added when a speller is in danger of exceeding the time limit. They format the speller name, age, hometown, and other graphics in real time, even though some of the text elements are prepared ahead of the broadcast. Given the top-secret nature of the word list, ESPN does not receive it in advance; they can only see which word is coming next. Scripps preformats the words for the television broadcast. Weinkauf explained that they needed to know the correct spelling to decide whether to cut to the "bell cam." It is positioned to capture close-up the judge's hand gliding through space to ring the bell. "If they've made a mistake, we're ready to get a shot of the bell—ding. But not every time," added Vaillancourt. The director decides so that it is not "overused."

The mood in the truck was upbeat and encouraging. ESPN staff cheered and clapped when a speller was correct and sighed and "awwed" when they were eliminated. One of the crew seated in the back of the space told me, "The scene in the truck would be much more hectic if we were covering an actual sporting event like *Monday Night Football*." For that, he explained, they would need to edit highlight reels throughout the game and for halftime, and retrieve information on players who made big plays. By contrast, the National Spelling Bee was far more predictable. There would be no injured players substituted with unknown replacements.

When Vaillancourt motioned that it was time to go, I followed him and the path of cable wire through the kitchen. We were soon back in the familiar hallway where we'd started our adventure. Vaillancourt invited me to observe their remaining production meetings and activities and explained how the filming for the rest of the Bee would unfold. On Wednesday, they would broadcast on ESPN3 but would not control the timing of the spellers and commercial breaks. On Thursday, the morning finals would be broadcast during the day on ESPN2 and the prime-time finals on ESPN. That day, ESPN would direct the competition, cue the spellers, and roll speller features and "bumps," or short segments leading in and out of commercial breaks.

During these broadcasts, production assistants cue the audience to applaud or stay silent and alert them when the broadcast will resume. Periodically, the action pauses and the broadcast cuts to the ESPN host desk in the back of the auditorium. Those in the ballroom cannot hear what they are saying so there is silence until the action resumes up front. Once the finals progress to the championship word list, production assistants turn on the confetti machines, which take several minutes to warm up.

Ten cameras in the auditorium aim to capture a broad spectrum of the action in ways that bring the home viewer as close to the activity as they can. When Miller showed me a map of the space and where each of the cameras was stationed, he remarked that the network had refined its coverage of previously untelevised competitions through innovative camera work.[3] For instance, they put cameras on boats to make viewers feel as though they are on the water, to make yachting interesting to watch. Likewise, the "hole cam" in poker allows the home viewer to see the cards the player is holding, letting us inside the player's mind albeit ruining the suspense. For the spelling bee, a few cameras are locked in place: one on the bell that signals a misspelling, one behind the spellers showing the audience, a third focused on Dr. Bailly from a speller's perspective. Others cover the commentators, backstage, or handhelds for interviews and wide-shot views of the room.

Another successful innovation is to place family members in assigned seats for the finals, so that the camera can easily find a speller's parent or sibling during the brief duration of their turn. "We get the parents up closer where there is better lighting, because we don't light the audience that well. With a full seating chart, you can get that family connection and family emotion," Miller explained. During later rounds of competition, production assistants consult a seating chart and scurry back and forth with a camera crew to film families. The split-screen coverage of the onstage action alongside the family creates heightened drama. Sometimes the previous turn finishes quickly and the cameras can't get to the next family in time. In most cases, they do and the parents are flashed on the auditorium screen. Some stare straight at the stage, some close their eyes or bite their nails. "They're doing all kinds of things!" Miller exclaimed.

In recent years, former and current spellers in the room have been seated in the front section of the auditorium. One year, I saw former spellers Amber Born and Kate Miller seated well ahead of the media section along with many of their friends. They told me that Scripps and ESPN like to place young people up there so that they can flash their faces on television. Kate added, "So that they can commercialize your emotions. Which I'm totally okay with."

No sporting broadcast would be complete without player interviews sprinkled throughout. The results are varied when an

ESPN host interviews a speller midcompetition. Sometimes they offer terse responses, eager to get back to their seat and keep their mind on spelling. Equally tricky are the post-elimination interviews. In 2014, finalist Grace Remmer's feature aired and she stepped up to the mic for her turn. She misspelled but took an additional moment at the mic to soak up the applause and cheering of a standing ovation. An ESPN host beckoned her over to do an interview. "What had you struggling with that word?" the host asked, inviting her to analyze her turn for a live viewing audience. Grace responded eloquently, stopping short of saying "I just didn't know it." It was her fourth bee, and she told the interviewer that all the time she had earmarked for spelling study would subsequently be redirected into violin and viola practice.

Sometimes a sibling steps in to help on camera. When Jairam Hathwar was eliminated in 2015, he and his brother, 2014 cochampion Sriram, were both pulled aside for an interview. Jairam looked understandably stunned and disappointed. Sriram, himself once camera shy, responded to the interviewer's questions, assuring her that his brother would work hard to compete again the following year. Not only did Jairam compete, but he was named a 2016 cochampion.

All these aspects of the broadcast help elevate this educational contest into an entertaining sporting event. The color commentary that hosts and interviewers add ties the program together and smoothly leads the viewer through it.

Paul Loeffler's insights bring depth to the competition, as he has been watching the National Spelling Bee closely for years. He has his eye on top spellers, but cautioned, "You could test as the best speller but get one word that trips you up and you're done." The key to success, Loeffler said, is to have a healthy perspective on this nearly inevitable outcome. When we spoke before the 2015 finals, he named Gokul Venkatachalam as having this advantage, as a speller who had competed for several consecutive years and remained "unfazed." He also named Vanya Shivashankar, believing her to be sincere in her statement that she would be fine with not winning. "It may be her greatest attribute to let her win," he predicted accurately. Equating her composure to that of her poised sister Kavya, the 2009 champion, he declared Vanya to be the most prepared for this championship. "But anything could happen! All it takes is one word, one letter, there's no margin for error." While Loeffler would never share such a prophecy with spellers, he was certainly onto something. The two spellers he pointed out to me as having the strongest chance of winning were the very two that became cochampions that evening.

Loeffler is wonderfully adept at coaxing quirky details from spellers in the hours before the live prime-time finals. He glides through conversations about their hobbies, favorite words, and most dreaded languages of origin. He interacts with siblings who may be in tow, asking spellers how they get along with them, how they spend time in their hometown, and anything else that could bring depth and character to their commentary. He agrees with Sage Steele, former ESPN host for the Bee, who commented, "Speaking to [spellers] and their parents is extremely helpful. It gives me a greater appreciation for how hard they've worked and how diverse their interests are. Contrary to popular belief, they are normal kids."[4] Loeffler builds on research that Scripps generates about top spellers, such as languages they have studied and how they handle challenging words. He has made an art out of thoughtfully peppering the information he elicits throughout the broadcast in order to keep audiences invested in the kids onstage. "I'll try to use that in the commentary to create context," he explained. More than anything, Loeffler likes to get a feel for the kid and convey a bit of that to the viewer.

Complementing these details are the speller features, which elevate individual spellers into spellebrities. Many features have a robust afterlife on YouTube, garnering comments and views long after the Bee has concluded. Speller talents that I've seen showcased include throat singing, pogo stick, archery, hula hoop, Indian classical dance, tuba, horseback riding, and skateboarding. Miller estimates they started doing the features about fifteen years ago, with steady improvement over the past several years. Initially they had competitors send in their own videos, but this resulted in poor-quality footage not suitable for HD broadcasts. ESPN decided to produce the features themselves not only to collect higher resolution footage, but also to show kids as unique personalities.

"We get pro athletes who can't be bothered with us, but kids will talk to us!" Miller cheerfully told me. "We're trying to find the most interesting story. Not just numbers and states, but what makes them unique and interesting—study methods, hobbies, other skills." From those "interesting stories," they further cull them to identify who will handle the camera attention well. "Someone who is a good talker, who has a personality, they warm up to the camera. Some people are magnetic on camera." Spellers are often chosen for a feature if they have made multiple appearances at the Bee or have an elite speller sibling. They rarely come across someone who is too nervous to speak, but they try to avoid causing additional stress to any truly camera-shy individuals.

In addition to filming in spellers' hometowns, feature tap-ings are scheduled throughout Bee Week. Spellers arrive at their scheduled times and do a brief intake session before entering the studio. At least one parent accompanies them, sometimes the whole family. The entourage is invited to watch quietly and can shoot video or photos on any device that does not deploy a flash or make sounds. Inside the studio, spellers are directed by the production crew, handed props, and asked to say various short lines into the camera. Sometimes they are asked to perform amusing acts, such as sitting on an oddly shaped chair or doing something fancy that showcases their hobbies and interests. The tapings are filled with cute gag items and kid-friendly sets. For instance, oversized Scrabble tiles are set up sideways like domi-noes for spellers to knock down. Kids are invited to spell a favor-ite word, a word they dislike, or their name. "Don't be afraid to really push them down," coaxed the cameraman during several of the tapings I watched that year. The crew is kind and encour-aging. They zoom in and out quickly to heighten the drama and take still photos as well.

When Joseph, a returning speller, was invited to sit in a large red swivel chair, he accepted the "bee glasses" he was handed. The spectacles had antennae and large googly eyes. He held up a pic-ture frame to box in his torso and introduced himself. "Have fun with it, dance around!" exclaimed the director. Joseph's mother quietly remarked that she did not want to "stifle his creativity" and slipped out to wait in the hallway. A production assistant reassuringly told Joseph that he was a great dancer. The sound engineer then cued up the song they had all the kids lip sync to that year: "Best Day of My Life" by American Authors. The producer asked Joseph to choose more props and dance in front of a silver bead curtain for the camera while the song's chorus played. Feather boas, hats, sunglasses, and other accessories were available. The team was very complimentary about Joseph's performance and suggested they shoot a segment of him ringing the dreaded bell. He loved the idea. As they parted, they reminded Joseph to have fun at the Bee. "Tell everyone how fun the interview room is!" added one enthusiastic PA.

Another returning speller, Neha, came in to film a somewhat more elaborate feature. It involved her hero, Paige Kimble. Palmistry is one of Neha's hobbies, and Kimble had sportingly agreed to have her palm read on camera. Neha's younger brother was invited to be in the feature as well and settled in next to her in front of a crystal ball. The crew activated a smoke machine to enhance the mystique of the scene. Neha and her brother got so enthusiastic while rehearsing their routine that they knocked the ball over. They both jumped to retrieve it, forgetting that they were wearing mics. Wires tethering them got yanked and they ended up in a giggling, tangled heap. They were detangled and ready for Kimble when she entered, and they filmed the palm reading. After Kimble left, Neha's parents told the crew about her myriad other talents, including singing. "You ready for the Bee?" one producer asked Neha. Her father jumped in before she could reply, saying, "She studied so hard! The whole family came." Neha added that she was definitely ready. When asked about their son, Neha's mother wryly replied, "He has a spelling allergy."

Spellers who have watched their older siblings for years are often the most excited to finally become a spellebrity. This was the case with Mary Horton, whose older brother and sister had both competed in the Bee. When she walked into the studio,

I recognized her mother as the parent who spoke to me at the opening assembly two nights earlier. Mary first came to the Bee as a spectator when she was four years old. She was very familiar with the slate of Bee Week activities. This was her second Bee appearance. Apart from spelling, Mary liked to take pictures of her plants and spend time with her cat, Patches. She reflected thoughtfully when asked what she would do if she won. "I'd be too stunned to do anything. But I wouldn't want to make my siblings feel bad." Mary's favorite word to spell was *catawampus*, which she defined as "a ferocious, wild beast." As a device to help her spell, she air typed on an imaginary keyboard. Knowing that the camera would focus in on her hands during her turn, she had her nails painted in a bee theme. She was very excited to show off her yellow nails with small black wings and other apiary markings. The cameraman moved in for a close-up and the still photographer took additional shots. Standing with her fingers splayed for the camera, Mary remarked that she met another speller who also had a bee-themed manicure. "Dueling nails!" her mother exclaimed.

Features are shown directly preceding a speller's turn, inviting viewers to root for them. Occasionally, the content on-screen has some confluence with the speller's turn. In 2013, before one of Arvind Mahankali's turns in the finals, the soon-to-be champion was featured wearing a silk smoking jacket and holding a pipe. He narrowed his eyes and exclaimed, "I have been cursed by the German language!" A montage of German words he had struggled with or misspelled in past Bees followed. The feature ended, and as if it were planned, Arvind received a German word. The audience erupted with laughter. When he spelled it correctly, the room exploded with applause.

A feature can air more than once if the speller keeps advancing. Miller noted that producers have no clear sense of whether the same viewers will tune into ESPN3 online for the early rounds, ESPN2 on television for the semifinals, and ESPN for the prime-time finals, so they are not concerned about repeating a speller feature. Without knowing which spellers will advance, ESPN hedges its bets by creating features for at least a dozen additional kids on-site. They invite them on an ongoing basis as the competition progresses, including at least a few unexpected finalists who need to be taped.

Additionally, other short segments are created from footage provided by regional media affiliates. For instance, 2014 included a "marathon bee" that went sixty-seven rounds in Kansas City, Missouri. Other content includes blooper reels, highlight reels, misspellings by professional sports stars, and small comedic bits performed by Bee Week officials. As with many sporting events, statistics and trends are a vital part of the broadcast. Graphics include semifinalists who have champion siblings, a speller's finishes from their past Bees, and word categories that are trending during that Bee. One year highlighted words appearing in the then-popular television series *Downton Abbey*, and another year dog breeds and science terms predominated. Notable spellers might have interesting facts next to their photo: hometown, sponsor, and hobbies. When Shourav Dasari came to the mic to spell in 2016, his 2015 South Asian Spelling Bee title was prominently featured on the screen. In 2017, ESPN aired a feature showcasing Indian American success at the Bee alongside individual features.

One short called "It's Cool to Be Smart" featured Gokul and Vanya, 2015 cochamps. In it, they tote their giant trophies and casually but earnestly tell their peers that being smart has cachet. This is because not only could kids earn hardware, but also could appear on ESPN. "ESPN! So make sure to study and practice and learn as much as you can, so you too can one day be that cool," Vanya encouraged. The next year, she appeared on *SportsCenter* during the Bee with anchor Kevin Negandhi.

Negandhi's interest in hosting the Bee was piqued by the South Asian winning streak, and he became an on-air host in 2016. I recognized him as an anchor for *SportsCenter* and was curious whether ESPN invited him to host because of his shared ethnic background with numerous past winners. During the 2017 Bee, I spotted him strolling in the hallway outside the auditorium with his wife and three young children. Negandhi has the camera-ready looks befitting a news anchor, with an ease and affinity for banter that also makes him likable. He cheerfully agreed to speak with me later that day.

As we began to exit the auditorium, he was stopped by security guards. "Hey, man," the first security guard said to Negandhi, moving close to him. A second guard appeared and excitedly asked, "Who do you think is going to win the NBA Finals?" It was a timely question. Game 1 was scheduled for the following night, in direct conflict with the National Spelling Bee. The first guard raised an eyebrow at his coworker, suggesting he could have played it cooler. He smoothly said to Negandhi, "Hey, man, I'm a fan. I watch you on *SportsCenter*." Negandhi warmly shook their hands and embarked on a brief but in-depth dissection of each team's strengths and weaknesses. The guards leaned eagerly in as he spoke in hushed tones, since the onstage competition had resumed. Negandhi picked the Warriors to win and they nodded expectantly. He shook their hands again and their faces broke into large grins that signaled they had met a true celebrity.

This interaction was not at all unusual, as Negandhi is well known for his analysis of the stick-and-ball sports ESPN is known for. His association with the spelling bee is more recent. When ESPN management learned that Negandhi had been following the Bee, they approached him as soon as a host opportunity arose. He recalled, "I immediately loved the idea and it worked out perfectly." Negandhi is not a former speller. "Math was my thing." His father is an accountant, but the aspect of math that interested him most was statistics. If he had not become a sports anchor, Negandhi suspects he would have been interested in sports salary caps and team rosters. "Like *Moneyball*?" I asked, referencing the Brad Pitt movie about baseball player salaries. "Exactly!" he exclaimed.

Negandhi elaborated on his role as an announcer, asserting, "I don't think it matters that I'm Indian American. People think, 'He's interested, and he's doing a good job at this.'" He continued, "I'm a fan. I wanted to be relatable to the audience, like I try to be for any athletes and competitors I cover. I want this to be treated in the same way. We are celebrating being at the top of your game, being intelligent." Negandhi believes the Bee has become a place that showcases talents of young people, the importance of self-presentation in the media, and a public portrayal of what it means to be Indian American without that being the only thing that matters. According to him, celebrating excellence in this way is about *disrupting* rather than reinforcing stereotypes. He told me, "I am very proud to break stereotypes and humanize *any* of these kids, not just the Indian American ones. None of these kids are robots. They are all well-rounded human beings."

Elite spellers who are elevated to spellebrity status are certainly well-rounded, but they have also worked exceedingly hard for their forty-five seconds of televised fame. The high production value of the features offers a glossy counterpoint to pejorative media coverage of spelling bee kids as "word nerds" who do nothing but study. Spellers know that the afterlife of their accomplishment will live on in social media and that their speller features will have a permanent home on YouTube. Some spellers are included in the broadcast just to ramp up the human-interest element. At the 2018 Bee, speller Phoebe Smith from Morton, Pennsylvania, and Melodie Loya from Oneonta, New York, were featured as new best friends. They'd met at the Bee the year before. In 2018, they decided to meet up before the Bee and arrived together wearing matching T-shirts, earrings, and bee-themed manicures. The cameras loved focusing on one when the other was spelling and showing both on a split screen.

Other spellers have star power based on their distinctive personalities. Amber Born welcomed the spotlight during her years of competition. As an aspiring stand-up comedian, she is remarkably at ease in front an audience. Of the many witty remarks spellers have made at the National Spelling Bee microphone, Amber's are easily the most memorable. Amber paid no mind to advice from Bee officials that making jokes could break focus and cause distraction. "There's a saying, 'Funny spellers don't win,' but it's not true. They're all funny offstage. For me, it doesn't break my concentration. If you know how to spell a word, you're still going to know how to spell it regardless of what you said before it." During a turn at the 2013 semifinals, before asking for the sentence, she inquired, "Is the sentence funny?"—jokingly implying that she didn't want to hear it if the answer was no.

Amber's love of comedy pairs well with her best friend Kate Miller's love of writing. Early in their friendship, they imagined the joys of being cochampions together and enjoying what they see as one of the biggest perks of winning—appearing on *Jimmy Kimmel Live!* Amber and Kate aspire to move to NYC to write a sitcom together, something in the style of *Seinfeld*, but of their time. *Schadenfreude*, taking pleasure in another's suffering, will be a running gag in their script. "It is real! It is a super German word and emotion," Amber stated confidently.

Amber's tweets about society and current events, as well as about the triumphs and absurdities of being a young person, are easily sitcom-worthy. As she took her position at the mic during a turn at the 2013 finals, the action paused and her speller feature was aired for the television audience and in the ballroom. It cheerfully showed Amber in the ESPN studio, speaking about her likes and aspirations, ensconced in set decorations and props. The musical overlay was especially upbeat and playful. It concluded and the spotlight returned to Amber, who, without missing a beat, quipped, "She seems nice." Roaring laughter and applause filled the ballroom, cementing her spellebrity status.

Chapter Nine

Professionalizing Childhoods

Time management is a skill that Sriram Hathwar acquired over the course of his spelling career. He balanced his day carefully, aware that it was important to play sports and to spend time with his brother and on homework and other things. About 50 percent of his free time was allotted to spelling. His mother confirmed his interest in things other than spelling, adding, "But spelling was his passion." Sriram plays the oboe and piano and enjoys chess, badminton, tennis, basketball, and ice skating. He likes reading and volunteers at his local library. He plays on his school's tennis team and is a member of his school's marching band, for which he plays flute. When we spoke at the end of his spelling career in 2014, he was learning four languages, including Sanskrit and Mandarin. Being multilingual has allowed him to develop a deeper appreciation of the English language.

Prior to becoming the 2014 National Spelling Bee cochampion, Sriram won the South Asian Spelling Bee in 2013, the NSF junior spelling bee in 2009, the NSF senior spelling bee in 2012, and the NSF intermediate vocabulary bee in 2013. Sriram's post-spelling-career goals include geography and math competitions and more international travel. Sriram has entrepreneurial aspirations as well. He and his friend from the Bee, Shreyas Parab, won the Diamond Challenge for small business in 2015 to develop a spelling bee training platform. By fifteen, Sriram had delivered two TEDx Talks about his experiences as an elite speller. He had the honor of meeting President Obama at the White House to be commended for his achievements.

For Sriram, the National Spelling Bee offered a chance to work on his self-presentation, which improved dramatically over the years. Giving a good public interview and speaking on live media are adult skills that Sriram mastered in middle school. He believes one of the greatest abilities honed from his spelling career is developing a strong work ethic and persevering through difficulties. Mrs. Hathwar noted that Sriram had become far more confident and independent over his years of competing. Helping coach his younger brother, Sriram quizzed Jairam and taught him Latin and Greek roots. "He might have a good chance," Sriram told me in 2014. I nodded.

Two years later, after Jairam was named cochampion as well, the Hathwar brothers published a book called *Words from the Champs*. In it, they describe their path to success in the spelling bee, talk about some of their post-win experiences, and recommend study words for national level contests—just several thousand that they think could be helpful. In addition to helping out with educational competitions in the United States, the brothers are involved with Spelling Bee of China, that country's national bee, attending as ambassadors.

Enterprising Gen Z kids like Sriram are exceptional, but they are not necessarily outliers. Sriram found a way to harness the work ethic and discipline he developed over years of studying for spelling bees and apply it toward other career-building pursuits. Being interviewed by media allowed him to develop public speaking skills, paving the way for bigger talks. Platforms like TEDx, among others, give kids a way to communicate sophisticated ideas as young people. These opportunities, once limited to adults, are now part of childhood for Generation Z. The well-established structure of the National Spelling Bee as well as the minor-league bees that some kids participate in offer opportunities for developing human capital. Elite spellers cultivate life skills through prolonged preparation and competition and in the potential to coach afterward.

In this chapter, I explore how kids undertake professional activities during childhood. The kinds of marketable skills they develop, as well as the very ideas of market value and success, have established themselves in elementary and middle school life. By high school, kids may be well along their way in a career path. Each year, more elite spellers who have aged out of competition go into coaching. Some work for established companies that offer them clients, while others do so as self-employed entrepreneurs. They establish themselves in the marketplace and make money at rates unheard of for previous generations of kids. While some spellers do not feel entirely comfortable monetizing their training, many find it a natural progression after their spelling career. Parents often encourage and assist their kids in coaching as well.

The path of elite spellers becoming coaches, either independently or via a coaching company, also offers early returns on this human capital investment. Raising kids with an emphasis on human capital is a debate I began to explore in Chapter 5 and continue to examine here. Parents pass on certain kinds of capital to their children through a process social scientists call "social reproduction," which includes assets, skills, social knowledge, and social networks. Bee Parents I observed commit themselves deeply to their children's human capital development. As highly educated immigrants in the early stages of establishing themselves in the United States, it is the kind of capital most accessible to them. Most come to this country to work and earn and likely don't have the kind of wealth accrued over generations that characterizes white middle-class social reproduction. The human capital they cultivate in their children is what they can pass along in lieu of trust funds and inheritances. Of course, white middle-class families also cultivate human capital in their children—this is a point I've emphasized in the stories of spellers like Kate Miller and Shayley Martin. White elite spellers have long benefitted from becoming coaches, and that continues.

What further differentiates social reproduction between these two groups is the public reaction to each, especially negative public responses to immigrants' visible display of human capital at the National Spelling Bee. While decades of white winners drew no racial comment, the overwhelming success of Indian Americans at the National Spelling Bee has been met with visible, vocal backlash. Racist outbursts suggest that their display of human capital is a threat to white dominance and that some resent this Asian immigrant group for embodying the ideals of the model minority stereotype.

Even though all the Indian American champions of the National Spelling Bee were raised in the United States—with most of them born there as well—their dominance over this iconic

American, English-language contest signals for some the loss of opportunity for white Americans. This is the double-edged sword of developing human capital through a spelling career in an activity as public as the National Spelling Bee.

The title of "young entrepreneur" once referred to people in their early twenties, newly graduated from college. That age has steadily decreased. *Fortune*'s "18 Under 18: Meet the Young Innovators Who Are Changing the World" introduces us to 2016's young innovators.[1] In it, we meet kids like Noa Mintz, who started her first business at age ten and later founded and now manages Nannies by Noa, hiring adults to run her company while she focuses on high school. One sixteen-year-old makes profits of over $2 million annually selling lacrosse equipment. The winner of *MasterChef Junior*'s second season, Logan Guleff, is a fourteen-year-old food entrepreneur. Some young people pride themselves on being social entrepreneurs who build businesses that donate a portion of the proceeds to noble causes. A lemonade company founded by eleven-year-old Mikaila Ulmer, Me & the Bees, uses local honey and donates to save honeybees. Similarly, *Business News Daily* reports on remarkable young entrepreneurs like Neha Gupta. She founded Empower Orphans when she was nine, and it has become a registered nonprofit that has raised more than $1.6 million for needy children.[2]

Becoming a social media influencer is also well within the reach of kids today, some of whom are striking it rich on Instagram and YouTube. One elementary-school-age toy reviewer raked in $11 million one year, the youngest on *Forbes*'s 2017 World's Highest Paid YouTube Stars list. While his over 10

million subscribers watch, the seven-year-old unboxes and reviews toys on his YouTube channel. His parents help but this
doesn't seem to matter, as his charisma and screen presence draw
in plenty of viewers. Other aspiring young YouTubers demonstrate crafts, experiments, and video games.

Teens find celebrities to idolize on YouTube and Instagram
like earlier generations did on television or film. These social media stars can have millions of followers and receive free promo-
tional items from manufacturers aiming to build publicity for
their products.[3] They can be famous for hit songs they recorded
themselves and released digitally, beauty tutorials, advice videos,
or just stream-of-consciousness talk. Some Gen Z kids use social
media to sell products such as skin care for girls, like ten-year-old
Amanda Steele's YouTube channel MakeupbyMandy24 that led
to her starting her own cosmetic line by fifteen. Others link their
online business with brick-and-mortar retailers. Cory Nieves of
Mr. Cory's Cookies founded his company at age six and by age
twelve had worked with J.Crew, Barneys, and Pottery Barn.[4]

These Gen Z kids live by mottos that reveal their self-directed
mindset, including "If you can think it, you can do it" and "If
someone tells you your idea is not going to work, make it your
mission to prove them wrong." "Don't dwell on the past. Learn
from your mistakes and move on" is the motto of eighteen-year-
old venture capitalist Aaron Easaw, who supports entrepreneurs
under thirty. Corporations have taken note of these super-young
upstarts, and some have refocused their approach to cater to what
kids nowadays need to succeed in the marketplace.[5]

Some are reboots of century-old programs, like Junior
Achievement, that have updated their approach to rely on

start-up models and crowdfunding. Others are K–12 programs staged through different parts of elementary, middle, and high school and emphasize the importance of adaptation and innovation for market success. Local businesses hold competitions for venture capital grants, in the style of the reality television show *Shark Tank*. Kids pitch and they fund, together building local communities and brands.

Gen Z kids seem to understand the value of having a side hustle. This term is used by Millennials to refer to the smaller, informal jobs they do to supplement their occupation. For kids, being in school is their day job, and they may also have an after-school job. They can additionally have several side hustles well before joining the job market full-time. Especially among Gen Z kids aware of the difficulties Millennials face in the job market, no amount of preparation for what lies ahead seems like too much. The value of becoming an expert is high, and kids see the importance of being "market ready" at a much younger age. Being market ready in middle and high school once held little value because there were few lucrative outlets for kids' skills—not legal ones, at least. Today, kids both avail themselves of market opportunities earlier and create them where they see a niche. Many adults do not have a skill that can fetch $100 per hour, which puts these teenagers in an elite class of their own.

Being amazing at spelling used to earn kids little more than a pat on the back and some local notoriety. At most they might have been able to do face-to-face tutoring for whatever local rates allowed. At the start of the 2017 Bee, the *Washington Post* published an article about how recently aged-out spellers were getting paid $200 or more per hour to coach aspiring spellers.[6] That rate is not surprising, as coaching companies have always been pricey. What is new is that first- and second-year high school kids are now the coaches, not just their parents.

Some of these kids work for established tutoring company Hexco or newer outfits like Brainsy. Enterprising kids make websites and market their coaching services. Aspiring competitors who have seen elite spellers on television can find many of them for hire on the Internet. Elite spellers coach via video conferencing platforms like Skype or FaceTime and collect fees electronically. It is a cashless, virtual economy.

One of the teenagers featured in the *Washington Post* article is Amber Born. Her rate is far lower than Hexco's. She says she coaches out of her love for spelling more than anything else. Gokul Venkatachalam is a coach for Hexco, but this is only one of several post-spelling careers. Gokul wants to study business and be an entrepreneur but isn't waiting until he gets the Ivy League degree he hopes to earn. He is already part of at least two start-up projects. Gokul learned how to launch a start-up through an incubator called Catapult and went on to collaborate on the website Threading Twine, which empowers kids worldwide to "be successful changemakers" through accessibility, creativity, and networking.[7] The website showcases media creations submitted by young people. He served as the COO of this start-up but subsequently left to develop a new start-up that "incorporates machine learning to foster a platform for intelligent and respectful political discussion." Meanwhile, coaching for Hexco offers income and work experience.

The coaching company Hexco is a household name for spellers who make it to the National Spelling Bee. Those headed to the competition receive marketing materials from this company about its coaching services and study guides. As I progressed through this project, I met spellers who had purchased these study materials, while others had employed their coaches. My curiosity about Hexco and how they recruit new coaches led to a pleasant back-and-forth email interview with cofounder Linda Tarrant in July 2017. Tarrant and her husband were working for IBM when their daughters began to compete in the National Spelling Bee.

Tarrant's oldest daughter got serious about spelling bees in 1981, and Hexco printed its first guide in 1982 and called it *Valerie's Spelling Bee Supplement*. This guide covered "off-list" words that could appear at regional bees but were not included on the list from Scripps. Valerie competed in the 1987 Bee, and the Tarrants' second daughter in the 1989 contest. That year, one of their customers, Scott Isaacs, became champion. It put the company on the map. Isaacs later established his own coaching service but still stays in touch with the Tarrants. The Tarrants' third daughter competed in 1992 and 1993. The company still prints an annual booklet with the Scripps study list in it, plus additional spelling words, and offers many more products for beginning through very advanced spellers. Hexco's coaching program has been in place for over a decade. The company also produces products for eighteen other academic competitions.

Over the years, Hexco has released multiple versions of products to keep up with the rising complexity of words appearing in the Bee. Millennial spellers I interviewed had used the company's *Nat's Notes*. Released in 1991, it contained more than twelve thousand words from prior Bees, plus advanced words from years of annual study books. Tarrant believes this was a turning point, when spellers started getting increasingly competitive.

The first Bee winner to use *Nat's Notes* was 1994 champion Ned Andrews, whose mother then went to work for Scripps as a word-list creator. Hexco also offered *Verbomania*, a guide with more than twelve thousand vocabulary-enriching words. Recently revised versions of these guides now also include an "eMentor" application to study online with recorded pronunciations plus the definition, etymology, alternate pronunciation, part of speech, and often a sentence. Despite an overall rise in difficulty, the words in the last few years in particular have been "very, very hard," Tarrant emphasized. "About twenty percent have never been used in any Bee and are not in any of our published lists." Tarrant believes that today, vocabulary gives spellers more trouble than spelling.

During busy times, Hexco has forty or so kids enrolled in coaching, working with over a dozen coaches. The company had a record number of coached students at the 2017 Bee, nearly thirty, and nine were in the semifinals, with three advancing to the finals. That year's champion, Ananya Vinay, had been in their coaching program on a weekly basis for a year and several months. Others were eighth graders who primarily took Hexco's "crash course" after winning their regional bee. Tarrant told me, "We have a large percentage of Indians. In part, they have a great Underground Railroad of exchanging information, so others learn about us when their spellers are young. Many of our spellers have parents who were born in India. I think they credit their own education for their ability to move to the US, and they want their children to be educated to the maximum."

Spellers who enroll in Hexco coaching receive an assignment from their coach to study for one to two weeks before meeting for a quiz session via Skype. Coaches maintain relationships and field questions via email. Assignments usually include studying various lists of common, esoteric, and even vintage words, reading or viewing a video on a language family and learning a list of 250 words from that family, and the like. The coach serves as a guide and curator of spelling training and preparation— something that many parents who took a DIY approach cited as the hardest part of their spelling journey.

In the last few years, kids who have used Hexco's services have shown an interest in being coaches themselves. Like those that the company recruits, only the mature ones become coaches and are held to professional standards. Tarrant elaborated that they are all trained by the head coach and are held accountable for keeping up with the "paperwork." This includes writing to the speller and parent after each quiz session to report how the speller is doing, assessing the speller's strengths and weaknesses and areas of focus, and giving encouragement and new assignments for the next quiz session. After a coach is assigned a speller, the head coach listens in on at least four and up to eight quiz sessions and debriefs with the coach after each. This kind of monitoring for quality assurance has become routine in adult customer-service transactions and is now a part of childhood careers as well.

"If you're coming to nationals, get a coach. It's a great recommendation," said Scott Isaacs, the 1989 champion who now works as a full-time coach. I spoke to him during the 2018 Bee, when his coaching business had been in operation for five years. Isaacs was working as a chiropractor when he got back into coaching unexpectedly. Reminiscing about his stint on the Bee Week college staff, he decided to return in 2011 to watch the competition and see friends. He thoroughly enjoyed being back. Soon after, he responded to a Craigslist ad for a spelling bee tutor. He coached his first speller, Frank Cahill, who won his state spelling bee for the first time and placed seventh overall. It was Cahill's first and only attempt at nationals, and the outcome encouraged Isaacs. "That is a tremendous achievement, you don't see that often. After that result, I thought I may have a knack for this sort of thing!"

Coaching meant reentering a world that had been transformed from the one he'd mastered in the late 1980s. Isaacs remarked that in addition to no Internet or online dictionary, even the available word lists were limited back then. Mostly he used printed lists from past champions, or newspapers and dictionaries. "I used *Valerie's* supplements, but Hexco didn't nearly have the resources they do now." Isaacs's uncle was a pharmaceuticals representative and passed along medical dictionaries he thought his nephew should study. Isaacs made it to the national finals in sixth, seventh, and eighth grade. He enjoyed the first two outings but got serious for the third. "I knew 1989 would be my last time. It really lit a fire under me. I redoubled and redoubled my time studying. I started imagining myself winning too. No one had said anything like that to me, but I decided to do it. My mom was my coach that year."

Over the years, Isaacs has seen a tremendous increase in the demand for coaching. When he started coaching, he and Hexco were the only two players. Hexco courted him for a while, and he considered working for them. Ultimately, he decided, "I'm a coach who likes his freedom. They have a tremendous infrastructure, but I like to cater my coaching to each student. Not every student is at the same level. Not everyone says 'I absolutely want to win the national bee and that is my be-all, end-all.' I have some students who may want that in a couple of years, but for now, they would really like to make it to the oral rounds of the state bee, so hopefully that happens." Isaacs charges $100 an hour. He began his coaching business in 2013 and by 2018 was working with as many as fifteen students per year. Some hire him year-round, while others approach him after they have qualified for nationals. In 2018, he had five spellers competing: two who had won their regional bees and three who were invited through RSVBee. One of his former students, Sylvie Lamontagne, went on to become a coach herself.

Sylvie is one of the more visible spellers-turned-coaches I observed at the Bee. She competed in the National Spelling Bee in 2015 and 2016. When she returned in 2017, she was charging $200 an hour as a coach. She was in ninth grade. We spoke at the 2018 Bee, when she attended to watch the progress of some of her protégés. By then she was a sophomore in high school. Sylvie told me about her flourishing business, as well as what she now charges. She clarified, "There is an article out there that claims that I charge $200 an hour. That's through the ECN, the Expert Calling Network for spelling coaches." Sylvie explained that she was required to charge this fixed rate for calls done through that service. When she started it was $200 but has since dropped to $100. Most of the coaching she does now is on her own and no longer through the ECN.

Sylvie became a coach because she really enjoyed spelling and wanted to stay involved once she aged out of competition. Moreover, she likes the speller-coach dynamic. "I worked with Dr.

Scott Isaacs when I was a speller. I absolutely would not have gotten nearly as far without his help. He was a good role model for me, and I wanted to become that person for other people." Isaacs started working with Sylvie when she was eleven, in fifth grade. Her training plan included a combination of learning language patterns and roots, memorizing certain words, and discovering how to study effectively. "It gave me an understanding of what needs to be done in order to be successful at this. Just spending the years that I did studying for the Bee intensely has transferred over well into coaching, because I know what I need to do to help these kids learn. I know what will help them be successful," she said. In 2018, Sylvie coached six spellers; five made it to nationals. Of those, three won their regionals and two were invited through RSVBee.

Like other Gen Z kids, Sylvie has another career as well. She is also a competitive dancer. Once she finished participating in bees, she joined a competitive dance team that performs in the Denver area. Her specializations include ballet, tap, jazz, lyrical, and hip-hop. But spelling remains a central focus in her life. "I coach on my own and I have my own business. My business is called Sylvie Lamontagne, Spelling Coach. Yeah. I don't have a snazzy business name. It's just kind of, like, there."

Sylvie turned down a spot with Hexco, for which she was offered $50 an hour, and opted instead for what she described as greater independence in her coaching. She also wanted to be sure that the kids she was already working with could continue to pay her rate, not what Hexco charges. Her rate in 2018 was $25 an hour, up from $15 the year before. Sylvie doesn't advertise but hopes her coaching service continues to grow. "At the moment I'm going to see how my business goes. I have a blog I write on every couple of weeks just because I have fun, and if people see it they can find me through that," she said.

Not everyone I met is a fan of professional coaching. One former champion who asked not to be named told me, "I don't feel it would be fair to serve as a coach that charges $200 an hour to study root words. The overt emphasis on money diminishes what the Bee is all about. The individual process of preparing is more valuable to a speller and to their family and to their network than what these coaches might be planning to provide." This person elaborated, "For me, it was more useful to have to figure out some things on my own." Put differently, part of their reservation was pedagogical, advocating that certain kinds of learning happen when spellers have to find their own way through challenging materials.

Other former elite spellers who acknowledge the growth of this field expressed stronger concerns, especially for those who cannot afford these services. Spellers like Sai Chandrasekhar, for instance, competed in the Bee for multiple years and had high test scores but never advanced past semifinals. She could not hire a coach for economic reasons and believes it put her at a disadvantage. She told me, "It's kind of sad; if you can't afford it, you don't have many options. You can read the dictionary, but it's not the easiest path to take. It's daunting that other kids have coaches and people dedicated to them." Sai added that only the very strongest spellers succeed as coaches and remarked, "If you win, your coaching career is made."

Despite these objections, many see the benefit of coaching. "For a lot of spellers who use coaches, it is a question of being familiar with the Bee and their processes, and maybe this is not something that they could ask beforehand. So that could be helpful," one speller remarked. For spellers without a solid spelling community, paid coaching might be the only option aside from trial and error.

At the 2018 Bee, former champion Balu Natarajan accompanied his son Atman, who was competing. Balu told me that Atman had been interviewed by his Chicago public media sponsor, WGN, and he'd told them he got up at 4 a.m. to study. "Well, that seems like a lot of work and doesn't seem worth it," the interviewer had remarked. Balu disagreed. Whether it is spelling bees or wanting to be a concert pianist or an MLB player, kids have to stick with it, he remarked. "Without that, now, you really can't achieve a lot in competition. Kids are *that specialized* in their competition." For Balu, the real goal is not to bring home another trophy, though that would be nice. "If nothing else happens, my son will walk away from this saying 'I worked hard for something, I achieved being able to get here, I bonded with my family, I learned a bunch of material. I showed respect to my coach.' Those are all life's huge lessons. To get that at twelve, and for my other son to see it at nine, those are all big deals. That's what we're counting our blessings about."

Balu believes that the human capital Atman is building is important, as is the realization that trying hard at an activity may not be enough to make him successful. Atman has two years of competition left. Balu remarked, "He'll probably need at least one. This is an impressive playing field. We'll see if he's onstage tomorrow morning." Atman did not advance to the finals the next day but holds out hope for 2019. Spelling is just one of Atman's activities; he also plays piano and community soccer and learns tae kwon do. Atman's younger brother channels his competitive energy into travel soccer. Balu commented, "Some of his friends have gotten cut from the team, so he's learned what effort it takes to be able to stay at that level. Atman's never tried to win on that level." Until now.

Gen Z kids are aware of and intensively involved in the activities available to them. When opportunities present themselves—far earlier in childhood than with other generations, it seems—young people are increasingly recognizing and taking advantage of those moments. Accumulating human capital as a child is a normalized aspect of many Gen Z childhoods, but this idea does not sit well with critics. One constituency is older Baby Boomers, whom I noted in earlier chapters as bemoaning how professionalized their Millennial children's childhoods were compared to their own.

For many white middle-class families, passing along economic security and social status from one generation to the next is expected. This may lead to a view that childhood should remain focused on play rather than skill building. There are notable exceptions, such as regions of the country like New York City with highly competitive public school systems that require admissions-based testing for middle and high school. These parents are no strangers to competition and instilling a way to manage it in their children is part of how kids are socialized. This may not be true in other areas of the country.

Increasingly, there is intense anxiety surrounding the family as a site for the formation and accumulation of human capital. Human capital is built through education, training, and emotional and mental work, all of which are valued in neoliberalism.[8] Asian American Studies scholar Susan Koshy asserts that a neoliberal project of child-rearing privatizes the growth and re-production of human capital. That is, rather than relying on schools and other institutions to build human capital, families take this on as a central focus of child-rearing. Thinking about human capital in the context of social reproduction can further illustrate what is at stake.

Social reproduction includes everything that adults aim to pass on to their children, ranging from social values and cultural beliefs to wealth and social status. French sociologist Pierre Bour-dieu wrote about social reproduction by defining different forms of capital through which intergenerational knowledge and wealth can be transferred. Bourdieu defines economic capital as finan-cial resources; social capital as networks and human resources; and cultural capital as knowledge about culture, language, tradi-tion and institutions, including formal and informal educational and professional credentials.

Social reproduction is helpful to take into account when considering who wins at an activity like spelling bees. While the ethos of the National Spelling Bee is that from a level playing field, the best will emerge, some have argued that the National Spelling Bee strongly favors kids with the economic capital to prepare for the competition with adult support and costly re-sources. Research shows that despite its egalitarian philosophy, the Bee is skewed toward highly educated kids. The racial dis-parities can also be formidable, with African Americans under-represented throughout the contest's history.[9] The social capital of South Asian American families allows them to use their net-works to learn from one another about how to prepare for spell-ing bees. The Bee Parents I met talked about "investing" in their children, making parenting focused on human capital building as much as it is about becoming an adept member of society and their community.

Ganesh Dasari, father of elite spellers Shobha and Shourav, explained that due to their high educational backgrounds, Bee Parents "think critically, rather than prepare passively." They regard their time spent on spelling as an investment, as building human capital. Mr. Dasari remarked, "Why does *this* community prepare so hard? What motivates them? The motivation probably comes from parents who grew up in a place where education can get you a lot." The Dasaris became so invested in spelling that they decided to continue after Shobha and Shourav aged out. With both kids competing at the National Spelling Bee multiple times, they found many aspiring spellers' families contacting them about how they studied.

In 2018, months after Shourav retired from elite spelling, the Dasaris founded a company called SpellPundit, funded in part by a Kickstarter campaign. The family hired a software developer to create interactive modules of all the content the Dasaris had developed for their own study, including spelling, vocabulary, homonyms, hyphenated and phrased words, and roots. Spellers can opt for a flash-card version or a testing version. "It's a faster way to learn words, and more efficient. Not as dry as reading from a book," Shobha told me in 2018, shortly after the company was launched.

SpellPundit competes with Bee Parent Vijay Reddy's company, GeoSpell, as well as Hexco. The Dasaris believe they stand out based on their online modules, which include content from the online dictionary that the Bee has increasingly included. Mrs.

Dasari reported that modules have been selling well. SpellPundit donates a portion of the online sales proceeds of these modules to the North South Foundation. By the 2018 Bee, it had already donated nearly $5,000, according to Mrs. Dasari.

Shobha, Shourav, and their mother also offer one-on-one coaching. They have students all over the United States and charge $40 per hour—significantly less than Hexco. These monies they keep. Coaching is not their primary objective, Shobha told me, but she does see great value in it. She elaborated, "I did Hexco for a year; they jump-started me. I figured out how I should be studying. After a year I felt good to go off on my own." With the National Spelling Bee welcoming nearly twice as many spellers as before, "there's a larger demand from the national spellers and aspiring ones that haven't made it to nationals yet."

While SpellPundit appears to be off to a solid start, the real takeaway from the spelling bee, according to the Dasaris, are the life skills that their children built. Shobha and Shourav have had a great deal of onstage time, and they have grown accustomed to the spotlight. Starting young and going to so many bees has helped them manage their nerves, even if they do not know the word they are given. The Dasari kids have become so practiced at this activity that they worry only about the words, not the lights, audience, media, and attention. "That's where the discipline comes in. Sacrifice and giving things up throughout the year," Mr. Dasari told me. As much as they love winning, their spellers have also learned to "make a graceful exit when they miss words and have to become runner-up," Mrs. Dasari said. Shobha shared this view, noting, "Maybe you watch someone predicted as a favorite to win go out and they don't show anything." Taking that as an example, she noted that elite spellers learn to manage their emotions publicly and maintain composure. Learning life skills applicable to the professional world is a major takeaway of their spelling careers.

Professionalizing childhood seems to come more naturally to some kids, with Bee Parents helping to drive this process. For instance, Shobha was content with limiting other activities so that she could prioritize spelling. She explained, "The thing is that everyone has a different life. I have friends who spend most of their time playing sports. I'm doing the same thing; the Bee is a mental sport." Yet her brother Shourav was less willing to adopt this mindset when he was younger. When we spoke in 2014, he admitted, "Sometimes I really want to play video games instead of doing spelling." That year, he also wanted to watch more of the World Cup than his spelling schedule permitted. When I realized I was keeping him from watching a game that was under way during our interview, I apologized. Mr. Dasari gently dismissed my apology, arguing that Shourav had to give up something to compete at the national level, like any elite athlete would.

Despite his conflicting interests, Shourav found resonance in his father's comparison of his journey to accomplished competitors like Peyton and Eli Manning, who prioritized their game over leisure. Mr. Dasari emphasized, "As a parent we say, 'We invested: time, resources, strategies, and methods in a limited amount of time.' All those people who are really invested, they will really work hard." Included here are he and his wife, who have built this activity into a long-term business for themselves and their children.

It is incomplete to consider these changes to the professionalization of childhood without explicit attention to racial privilege and racial prejudice. There is no question that the Indian American spelling bee families I feature here enjoy certain privileges. They are well-educated people who have been, by and large, fortunate to create comfortable lives for themselves in the United States. With their professional skills, they are well positioned to enjoy the higher income and stability of white-collar employment. While they represent only a portion of South Asian immigrants to the United States—the most educationally accomplished—they are also highly visible as winners of a nationally televised contest that is regarded as quintessentially American. As a result, they are not simply winners; they are seen as Indian American winners. And increasingly, they have been targeted as "un-American" because they are not white.

This response was most pronounced in 2014, when there had already been some negative response to the Indian American winning streak. No sooner had cochampions Sriram Hathwar and Ansun Sujoe been announced when Twitter erupted with racist vitriol. Cloaked in digital anonymity, these Twitter racists, or "twacists" as some called them, unleashed hate using all the coded language one would expect, such as there were no "real Americans" left in the contest and that "American parents need to step it up." They lamented the annual elimination of "Caucasians" and called for whites to take back the Bee.

In an effort to counter these responses, others defended the two Indian American winners as being as American as anyone else, saying that white is not the only color in America. One chastised the haters by saying that "the families of winners value and encourage learning and hard work. They don't spend their time blaming others for their problems."[10] Even the Anti-Defamation

League issued a press release condemning their labeling as "non-Americans," with the ADL director railing against those who had turned "a crowning achievement for two young stu dents into an opportunity to spread racism and hate."[11] One elite speller's mother summed up the racist-backlash thinking to me: "We want them to learn our language, but not too well." Regarding Sriram Hathwar, she queried, "Who is more American than someone born in New York? American in this sense clearly means Caucasian."

By 2015, this issue had been well examined by several major media outlets, most extensively by Joe Heim in the *Washington Post*. One of his headlines read: "Indian Americans Dominate the National Spelling Bee. Why Should They Take Abuse on Social Media for It?"[12] This abuse was also the tipping point that pushed Kimble to answer the question directly at the 2015 press conference. Indian Americans had won the Bee all but four of the previous fifteen years, and despite sidestepping the topic in the past, she addressed it in 2015. Kimble spoke out strongly against the racist backlash and offered her opinion on why Indian American kids kept winning. What differentiated them, she stated, is their multiyear commitment to studying spelling to pursue the championship title. Crediting the community's adherence to this goal over time, she suggested that they simply do not allow themselves to become deterred.

When we spoke in 2018, Kimble elaborated: "My position has always been they're Americans. When anyone asks what I think about Indians winning the spelling bee, often times its phrased just like that; 'American' is completely dropped out of it. Occasionally 'Indian American' is used. My response is that they are very proud of their heritage, but they probably want to be known as Americans. Framing the conversation that way is very important to do. People can go on social media and say hateful, thoughtless, racist, bigoted things. We know that that has happened with the spelling bee and some of our highest achievers, who are of Indian heritage. I feel a deep responsibility to speak up for them and the Bee."

Others in the spelling bee world responded in kind. Mr. Shivashankar—the BeeFather and parent of 2015 cochampion Vanya—told me that journalists that year had asked him about the racist responses. He'd responded that Vanya was born in Kansas and is American. She just isn't white. The struggle to place Indian Americans in the US racial order seems to play out every year after the spelling bee. In 2017, when CNN anchor Alisyn Camerota interviewed winner Ananya Vinay, she implied that many of the words would have been easy for Ananya to spell because she spoke Sanskrit. This remark left the thirteen-year-old champion speechless.

Like Latin, Sanskrit is not a spoken language. Yet the comment insinuated that her win came from skills she developed as someone foreign, that a true American would naturally not have. Camerota's racist assumption is a reminder that these kids have yet to be seen as American. Even when they win an iconic American contest, they still have to prove their belonging. An apt rebuttal here is comedian Hari Kondabolu's quip about the spelling bee: "Finally brown people get to say to white people, 'Hey, learn English!'"

The racist responses to Indian American champions are, in effect, a reaction to human capital building. This activity is heightened for Bee Parents, who strive for their children to become as skilled as they are. Their drive to cultivate human capital in their children is far more intense than Gen X stealth-fighter parents who emphasize high achievement, greater independence, and world readiness. Long-term preparation, ideas about sacrifice, and prioritizing spelling training over play and leisure is not only part of spelling bee success, but also a threat to white success.

This threat marks an important shift in the model minority stereotype over the past two decades. When this concept first emerged from popular press articles in 1966 about Asian Americans that appeared in the *New York Times* and *U.S. News and World Report*, it framed the self-sufficiency and law-abiding character of Chinese and Japanese Americans as a counterpoint to purportedly state-dependent and allegedly non-law-abiding African Americans. The stereotype pitted African Americans and Asian Americans against one another, a pernicious idea that persists in contemporary depictions.

If we consider the otherwise uplifting 2006 Hollywood feature film *Akeelah and the Bee*, the tension once again is between disenfranchised African Americans and overachieving Asian Americans. The Indian American spelling family is ruthless in their aggressive quest to win and is more than willing to take down underdog protagonist Akeelah in the process. The positioning of the immigrant Asian family against the impoverished African American family draws attention away from the real problem: a state that does not prioritize education enough such that it solicits skilled labor from abroad (the Indian family) while it fails to raise the standards for students in under-resourced schools (Akeelah).

This fictional account aside, the real issue with Indian Americans winning the spelling bee is the threat it poses to white educational advancement. Earlier generations of white Americans did not face such strong academic competition from children of immigrants. There were fewer of them in Generation X; by the time Millennial college admissions were in full swing, the number of second-generation immigrant college applications steadily rose. In recent years, with Gen Z applying to college, there has been vociferously negative responses to Asian American college admissions. Evident in the backlash to Asian Americans being overrepresented at top colleges, the fear of these students taking seats that were once occupied by white students has heightened the stakes of this human capital debate. It reveals a broader societal cost of human capital accumulation, the cornerstone of professionalizing childhood.

One of the most important things Gokul learned from his spelling career is to "not be afraid to speak up" about matters of political and social importance. The year Gokul won the Bee, he observed that there was far less social media racism expressed against him and cochampion Vanya than the year before. Gokul had steeled himself for a social media outburst, anticipating that it could be part and parcel of winning. He was relieved to experience less of it and credits this to Vanya and his firm rooting in American popular culture, especially sports. "I guess we seemed normal. I had on basketball shoes and people focused on that," he remarked.

Gokul was nonetheless disparaging about the tireless media focus on Indian Americans winning the spelling bee. A parallel can be drawn between this sentiment and that of Spike Lee, who prefers to be known as a filmmaker rather than a black filmmaker. Having his race qualify his filmmaking lessens his accomplishments, instead of letting them stand alone as a white filmmaker's would. Likewise, Gokul just wanted to be seen as a winner.

Other spellers were similarly frustrated with how the media focused on the race of spellers without saying anything meaningful about it. Amber and Kate thought that such portrayals downplay the hard work winners have invested in their sport. Moreover, it seems to be focused only on minorities. "Before, there were, like, fifty white people in a row and no one was like, 'Hmm, this is suspicious,'" Amber remarked. Kate additionally pointed out that before Nupur Lala won in 1999, boys had won for seven straight years. "No one wondered about that!" exclaimed Kate.

Enmeshed in these politics of human capital building, the complexities of professionalizing childhood are tied to a transformation of ideas about what childhood should be and what happens when racial minorities achieve visible success at a very young age. The reasons spelling bee kids professionalize early remain open-ended. Those whose parents have spent thousands of dollars and/or hours on coaching are happy to see their aged-out speller putting those finely honed skills to further use. Some do this for free, coaching at their schools or in their communities. Others opt to maximize their years of expertise and learn to be a thoughtful and responsive coach. In spelling bees, Indian Americans have transformed the competition and raised the stakes for all who participate.

For Generation Z more broadly, their parents' goal of increasing human capital in children is becoming a more commonplace familial project. Those raised by immigrants in the United States might know this as the only kind of parenting; anything else is too uncertain for those without an economic safety net. The overwhelming importance that Bee Parents place on investing in their kids puts their emphasis on professionalization in sharp relief.

Conclusion: Gen Z Futures

In 2018, I met Amber and Kate for coffee in the Gaylord's atrium. I arrived early to get an iced tea and a table. They arrived shortly thereafter, looking taller, more radiant, and grown-up than I remembered. I stood in line with them at the coffee kiosk, offering to buy them refreshments. They communicated with each other in the overlapping spurts that only close friends can decipher. After much discussion and deliberation, they chose to split a jelly donut, but at the last minute changed to a frosted vanilla cupcake with bright pink translucent sprinkles. A long line formed behind us while they finalized their drink choices. We eventually made our way to a table where we had sat several times before.

I first met Kate and Amber when they were fourteen and fifteen and have watched them grow up over the years. It was our fifth year of connecting at the Bee. This time, we spoke as adults. I heard about Amber's first year at Boston University, including a linguistics course that was the subject of numerous tweets. It ended up not being her favorite. Kate's big news was that she'd chosen to attend a small liberal arts college, Hamilton, located conveniently close to Amber. Despite only seeing each other once a year for a few or two action-packed days at the Bee, they remain best friends.

Kate and Amber reflected that in their day, the Bee used to be much smaller and more social. It still is social, they clarified, but there seem to be fewer groups of friends and more spellers who take an even more businesslike approach than they did. They waxed fondly over the Order of the Squushy Carrots and the multiple group chats they inhabited with their speller friends. They're not sure many of today's top spellers care about those things. The spellers seem much more focused and directed than even they were. Some competitors from their era stay connected to the Bee while others never seem to circle back to that world. Kate wonders what they are doing instead.

Kate still loves this world and is a counselor at North American Spelling Champion Challenge, which she describes as a spelling bee sleepaway camp. In its fourth year, half the camp's spellers come from the United States and half from China. It is, from what I can tell, one of the first opportunities for kids to do competitive spelling outside of Scripps or the South Asian American circuit. Numerous elite spellers show up in pictures tweeted by the camp, including Sriram Hathwar, Shobha and Shourav Dasari, and others. It is evidence that the spelling bee is growing and continuing to be a significant presence in the United States. This shows no sign of changing for younger members of Generation Z.

Over the course of this book, I have explored what spelling bees reveal about Generation Z kids and how we can better understand childhood success through the lens of spellers who compete at an elite level. In researching and writing it, I've also watched Gen Z take shape in real time through the kids in this book. Their spelling careers gave them an early start on how to manage the years that lie ahead. The skills and habits that Gen Z kids have developed through a number of intense competitive activities predispose them to further professionalized pursuits as young people. The grit it takes to be competitive at any major arena is built slowly over time, but also has numerous other applications.

Innovation and self-definition happen at a younger age for Gen Z kids. Those who have observed Millennials navigate increasingly competitive college and job markets especially understand the importance of being entrepreneurial and enterprising. According to one study, Generation Z members are "the least likely to believe that there is such a thing as the American Dream" because "Generation X, the most influential parents of Gen Z, demonstrates the least credence in the concept of the American Dream among adult generations."[1] Gen Zers seek out opportunities rather than expecting things to be handed to them. Digital fluency is highest among this group, as is the value placed on social and broadcast media as tools for networking and self-promotion. What else they decide to do with all that media power remains to be seen.

Gen Z kids who have worked their way up to elite levels of any field are usually raised by parents who have provided significant support consistently over several years. They have invested time in their children to cultivate human capital. Highly educated immigrant parents are raising the bar in certain areas and in what childhood can encompass overall. The shift from US-born Baby

Boomer helicopter parenting to Generation X stealth-fighter parenting has fostered greater self-reliance. The non-US-born Bee Parent style of highly skilled immigrants furthers this trend by advocating for human capital building from childhood. Parents today are raising their children against a backdrop of increasingly diverse and, for many, constantly evolving family forms. In other words, there will be many changes in what parenting and childhood mean, with influences coming from a variety of sources.

The total US population is projected to increase by 98.1 million between 2014 and 2060.[2] According to projections from Pew based on census data, immigrants and their US-born children are expected to drive growth in the US working-age population through at least 2035. This includes some Millennials but mostly Generation Z.[3] One Pew study on how Millennials have overtaken Baby Boomers as America's largest generation notes that the post-Millennial generation (Generation Z) numbered 69 million in 2014 and is projected to increase as updated statistics and immigration numbers are generated in the coming years.[4] It is entirely possible that Gen Z will grow to be the biggest generation of them all.

This is a complicated time to be part of an immigrant family. I have offered a view of Gen Z in which its core generational traits are shaped by immigrant kids and parents as much as they are by any other population segment. Immigrants draw public resentment not only when they are perceived to not learn English, but also when they learn it too well. Both of these critiques are leveled simultaneously at the non-US-born South Asians and their US-born children.

While American society does not take notice when white middle-class family wealth and stability is passed along between generations, the success of non-white groups draws notice. When people ask, "Why do Indian Americans keep winning the spelling bee?" they are also asking why white kids are no longer winning the Bee, as they had for decades prior. The simplest response is that they are the children of highly educated, recent immigrants who were solicited by the United States. From a social reproduction standpoint, it is not surprising that they would excel at brain sports and other endeavors. These young people will age into an America in which minorities will gradually outnumber white people.

These complex politics will surely color Gen Z's future for decades to come. From what is evident so far, there may not be a more qualified group of young people to take on these issues. Whatever Gen Z kids decide to do, they seem committed to creating opportunity in a world that does not guarantee them anything. Approaching their future with realism, elite spellers, bellwethers of their generation, have shown that they do not feel entitled to anything, but are nonetheless determined to succeed.

Acknowledgments

Funding for this research was generously provided by the National Science Foundation Cultural Anthropology Program (award #BCS-1323769) and the Wenner-Gren Foundation for Anthropological Research. Special thanks to National Science Foundation program officer Jeff Mantz for his ongoing support of this project.

I owe a debt to the individuals and institutions that granted me open access to spelling bees and their media coverage. At Scripps, Paige Kimble, Valerie Miller, Abi Evans, Corrie Loeffler, and Jacques Bailly. At ESPN, Tim Weinkauf, Amy Goldstein, Dave Miller, Jerry Vaillancourt, Paul Loeffler, and Kevin Negandhi. At the South Asian Spelling Bee, Rahul Walia, Daisy Walia, and Rupam Kavi. I am also grateful to Ratnam Chitturi at the North South Foundation. Special thanks to Peter Sokolowski at Merriam-Webster for several years of excellent conversation and friendship at the Bee.

Over the past six years, I've met hundreds of wonderful spellers and their families and am truly grateful to each of them for their time and interest in my project. Even those who only chatted briefly with me were helpful to get a fuller sense of this world. They include Alia Abiad; Amber Born; Sai and Vidhya Chandrasekhar; Shobha, Shourav, Usha, and Ganesh Dasari; Dev, Rani, and Mrs. Jaiswal; Sriram, Jairam, Roopa, and Jagdeesh Hathwar; Mr. and Mrs. Kalpande; Roshni and Mrs. Kainthan; Nupur Lala; Sanjana, Shravanth, and Mr. and Mrs. Malla; Shayley and Lydeana Martin; Kate Miller; Sameer Mishra; Shreyas Parab; Syamantak, Pramatha, and Sanjukta Payra; Rageshree Ramachandran; Aditya, Mohan, and Shaila Rao; Chethan and Vijay Reddy; Sukanya Roy; Kavya, Vanya, Sandhya, and Mirle Shivashankar; Ansun and Mrs. Sujoe; George Thampy; Anamika Veeramani; Gokul and Mr. and Mrs. Venkatachalam; and Akash and Krishna Vukoti. Additionally, I thank Scott Isaacs, Sylvie Lamontagne, and Linda Tarrant for speaking with me about coaching.

My agent, Doug Stewart, was an early believer in this book, and I appreciate his ongoing efforts to see it through to publication. Likewise, my editor at Basic Books, Leah Stecher, has offered close feedback throughout the editorial process. Minna Proctor and Janet Steen provided excellent editorial suggestions. Three saintly individuals read entire drafts of this manuscript and offered thoughtful, honest critiques: Ilana Gershon, Kurt Mueller, and Ravi Shankar. Numerous individuals gave me feedback on portions of the manuscript, and I truly appreciate their time and engagement: Jillian Cavanaugh, Graham Jones, Bambi Schieffelin, and David Valentine. For their ongoing interest and conversations, I also thank Scott Collard, Shilpa Dave, Pawan Dhingra, Dana Dillon, Tara Godvin, Ben Hallman, Mark Hauser, Matthew Johnson, Bill Leonard, Kalyani Menon, Priya Nelson, Sameer Pandya, Michael Silverstein, Stan Thangaraj, Aarti Thiagarajan, and Will Wiseman.

Aspects of this book took shape through op-eds I wrote under the mentorship of Michele Weldon and Holly Kearl in the Northwestern Public Voices OpEd Fellowship program. Their guidance and encouragement were invaluable. Ideas presented in this book were also shaped by questions and feedback from audiences at the Graduate Center, City University of New York; New York University; Northwestern University; Notre Dame University; Princeton University; Teachers College, Columbia University; University of Chicago; University of Toronto; and Yale University. I am deeply grateful to Kate Newbold, Madison Bondy, and Faith Kares for their excellent research assistance and Scott Spicer for his transcription work.

My family has been excited about this book since I first mentioned it, and they have remained steadfastly invested in its progress. My mother, Shyamala Shankar, first suggested that I try to write it for a broader audience and has cheered me on throughout this arduous process. My father, Ratnaswamy Shankar, has been a devoted and inquisitive supporter. I thank them for that, as well as for their tireless child-care and puppy-care help so that I could find extra time to write. My extended family has expressed ongoing enthusiasm for this project, for which I am very appreciative: G. Ambuja; G. Balachandran; Shekar Chandrasekar; Shekhar, Gita, Rohini and Vikram Chandrashekhar; Dan, Karen, and Linda Mueller; Malathi Subramanian; Mangala, Vivek, and

Ramani Venkatramani; and Shuba Vidhyasagar. I am also grateful to Julie Anne Alexander for her child care and Bev Aron for guidance and moral support.

Anyone who has lived with a writer has my sympathy, especially my dear children and husband, who stood by me through what was at times a very bumpy road to getting this book completed. My son, Roshan, asked smart questions along the way, while my daughter, Anisha, plied me with beautiful drawings, poems, and messages of support. Our dog, Fozzie, was outstanding company for many long, lonely days of writing. Finally, my dear husband, Kurt Mueller, has produced unending enthusiasm for this book, propping me up through so many low moments. I couldn't have finished it without him, and we are both so grateful that it is done.

Notes

Introduction

1. Throughout this book, the Scripps National Spelling Bee is also referred to as the "National Spelling Bee" or simply "the Bee." Interviewees may also refer to it as "Scripps" or "Scripps-Howard," the latter being an earlier name for the contest.

2. In 2018, the first-place winner received $40,000 and a trophy from Scripps, $2,500 and a reference library from Merriam-Webster, and other prizes. Cash prizes for second- through sixth-place winners ranged from $30,000 to $2,500, with gift cards for some lower finishers.

Chapter 1: Kids Today

1. Kat Kinsman, "The Agony and Ecstasy of the National Spelling Bee," CNN, May 27, 2014, http://www.cnn.com/2012/05/31/living/spelling-bee-experience/.

2. All definitions of spelling bee words are from Merriam-Webster's online dictionary, www.merriam-webster.com, unless otherwise noted.

3. Competition rules for 2018 state that spellers "must not have passed beyond the eighth grade on or before February 1, 2018" and "must not have reached the age of 15 on or before August 31, 2017."

4. Angela Duckworth, *Grit: The Power and Passion of Perseverance* (New York: Scribner, 2016).

5. Malcolm Gladwell, *Outliers: The Story of Success* (New York: Back Bay, 2011).

6. Carol Dweck, *Mindset: The New Psychology of Success* (New York: Ballantine, 2007).

7. "Cooper Komatsu and Jem Burch Win the National School Scrabble Championship!" *Scrabble TV Live* (blog), April 10, 2016, https://scrabbletvlive.com/2016/04/10/cooper-komatsu-and-jem-burch-win-the-national-school-scrabble-championship/.

8. Malcolm Harris, *Kids These Days: Human Capital and the Making of Millennials* (New York: Little, Brown, and Company, 2017).

9. Tamar Lewin, "The Bee, the New Celebrity Showcase," *New York Times*, June 4, 2006, https://www.nytimes.com/2006/06/04/weekinreview/04lewin.html.

10. Benoit Denizet-Lewis, "Why Are More American Teenagers Than Ever Suffering from Severe Anxiety?" *New York Times*, October 11, 2017, https://www.nytimes.com/2017/10/11/magazine/why-are-more-american-teenagers-than-ever-suffering-from-severe-anxiety.html?_r=0.

11. *Spellbound*, directed by Jeffrey Blitz, ThinkFilm, 2002.

12. *Breaking the Bee*, directed by Sam Rega, Exit Zero Productions, 2018.

13. Gen Z population range drawn from https://knoema.com/infographics/egyydzc/us-population-by-age-and-generation and https://www.reddit.com/r/dataisbeautiful/comments/68lmq4/us_population_by_generation_oc/.

14. Magid Generational Strategies, *The First Generation of the Twenty-First Century: An Introduction to the Pluralist Generation* (2014), p. 6.

15. Gretchen Livingston, "More Than a Million Millennials are Becoming Moms Each Year," Pew Research Center, May 4, 2018, http://www.pewresearch.org/fact-tank/2018/05/04/more-than-a-million-millennials-are-becoming-moms-each-year/.

Chapter 2: Brain Sports and Kid Competitions

1. Hilary Friedman, *Playing to Win: Raising Children in a Competitive Culture* (Berkeley and Los Angeles: University of California Press, 2013).

2. Shalini Shankar, "'Brain Sports' Are Gaining Momentum," *Boston Globe*, May 18, 2015, https://www.bostonglobe.com/opinion/2015/05/17/brain-sports-are-gaining-momentum/4C4KN7hCA7LZxvP5fzDP1H/story.html.

3. Stuart N. Omdal and M.R.E. Richards, "Academic Competitions," in *Critical Issues and Practices in Gifted Education: What the Research Says*, ed. Jonathan A. Plucker and Carolyn M. Callahan (Waco, TX: Prufrock Press, 2014), 5–13.

4. Tammy V. Abernathy and Richard N. Vineyard, "Academic Competitions in Science: What Are the Rewards for Students?" *Clearing House* 74, no. 5 (2001): 269–276.

5. Ibid.

6. James B. Schreiber and Elisha A. Chambers, "After-School Pursuits, Ethnicity, and Achievement for 8th- and 10th-Grade Students," *Journal of Educational Research* 96, no. 2 (2002): 90–100.

7. Mehmet A. Ozturk and Charles Debelak, "Affective Benefits from Academic Competitions for Middle School Gifted Students," *Gifted Child Today* 31, no. 2 (2008): 48–53.

8. Judy Dutton, *Science Fair Season: Twelve Kids, a Robot Named Scorch…and What It Takes to Win* (New York: Hachette, 2011).

9. Hana Schank, "Science Fairs Aren't So Fair," *Atlantic*, March 12, 2015, https://www.theatlantic.com/education/archive/2015/03/why-science-fairs-arent-so-fair/387547/.

10. Karin Calvert, "Patterns of Childrearing in America," in *Beyond the Century of the Child: Cultural History and Developmental Psychology*, ed. Willem Koops and Michael Zuckerman (Philadelphia: University of Pennsylvania Press, 2003), 62–81.

11. Peter Stearns, "Historical Perspectives on Twentieth-Century American Childhood," in *Beyond the Century of the Child: Cultural History and Developmental Psychology*, ed. Willem Koops and Michael Zuckerman (Philadelphia: University of Pennsylvania Press, 2003), 96–111.

12. Bernard Mergen, "The Discovery of Children's Play," *American Quarterly* 27, no. 4 (1975): 399–420.

13. Helen B. Schwartzman, "The Anthropological Study of Children's Play," *Annual Review of Anthropology* 5 (1976): 289–328.

14. Giovanni B. Sgritta, "Childhood: Normalization and Project," *International Journal of Sociology* 17, no. 3 (1987): 38–57.

15. Patricia A. Adler and Peter Adler, "Social Reproduction and the Corporate Other: The Institutionalization of Afterschool Activities," *Sociological Quarterly* 35, no. 2 (1994): 309–328.

16. Lewin, "The Bee, the New Celebrity Showcase."

17. Michèle Lamont, Jason Kaufman, and Michael Moody, "The Best of the Brightest: Definitions of the Ideal Self Among Prize-Winning Students," *Sociological Forum* 15, no. 2 (2000): 187–224.

18. Harris, *Kids These Days*.

19. Malcolm Harris, "Competition Is Ruining Childhood: The Kids Should Fight Back," *New York Times*, November 6, 2017, https://www.nytimes.com/2017/11/06/opinion/students-competition-unions-bargaining.html.

20. Friedman, *Playing to Win*.

Chapter 3: Spelling Bees

1. This booklet had words classified by difficulty levels, versus another that followed called "Paideia," which was arranged by theme.

This was eventually replaced by "Spell It!" that is still distributed to spellers who win their school spelling bees.

2. Personal correspondence with Valerie Miller, Corrie Loeffler, and Paige Kimble, Scripps National Spelling Bee, September 28, 2018.

3. Rachel McArthur, "Out of Many, One: Spelling Bees and the United States National Spelling Bee," *English Languages: History, Diaspora, Culture* 2 (2011): 1–22.

4. For further insight on Merriam-Webster's dictionary-making process, see Kory Stamper, *Word by Word: The Secret Life of Dictionaries* (New York: Pantheon, 2017).

5. Sarah B. Benor, "*Mensch, Bentsh,* and *Balagan*: Variation in the American Jewish Linguistic Repertoire," *Language and Communication* 31 (2011): 141–154.

6. Bambi Schieffelin, Kathryn Woolard, and Paul Kroskrity, eds., *Language Ideologies: Theory and Practice* (New York: Oxford University Press, 1998).

7. Suzanne Romaine, "Signs of Identity, Signs of Discord: Glottal Goofs and the Green Grocer's Glottal in Debates on Hawaiian Orthography," *Journal of Linguistic Anthropology* 12, no. 2 (2002): 189–224.

8. Mark Sebba, *Spelling and Society: The Culture and Politics of Orthography Around the World* (Cambridge, UK: Cambridge University Press, 2007).

9. Alexandra Jaffe, "The Second Annual Corsican Spelling Contest: Orthography and Ideology," *American Ethnologist* 23, no. 4 (1996): 816–835.

10. McArthur, "Out of Many, One."

11. Sam Whitsitt, "The Spelling Bee: What Makes It an American Institution?" *Journal of Popular Culture* 43, no. 4 (2010): 881–897.

12. Allen Walker Read, "The Spelling Bee: A Linguistic Institution of the American Folk," *PMLA* 56, no. 2 (1941): 495–512.

13. James Maguire, *American Bee: The National Spelling Bee and the Culture of Word Nerds* (New York: Rodale, 2006), 68.

14. Paul Sullivan, "Beyond Soccer Moms: Relocating for a Child's Sport," *New York Times*, April 6, 2018, https://www.nytimes.com/2018 /04/06/your-money/children-sports-relocation.html.

15. William Grimes, "Test of Wits and Sobriety," *New York Times*, August 1, 2013, https://www.nytimes.com/2013/08/02/arts/petes -candy-store-hosts-a-spelling-bee-for-adults.html.

16. Zachary M. Seward, "Why ESPN Is So Good at Televising Spelling Bees, Poker, Yachting, and Other Non-Sports," Quartz, May 30, 2013, http://qz.com/89499/espn-coverage-of-scripps-national-spelling-bee/.

17. *Akeelah and the Bee*, directed by Doug Atchinson, Lionsgate Films, 2006.

18. *Bee Nation*, directed by Lana Šlezić, Idle Hunch Ltd., 2018.

19. US Census Bureau, "American FactFinder, Community Facts." US Census Bureau News, US Department of Commerce, https://fact finder.census.gov/faces/nav/jsf/pages/index.xhtml (accessed April 27, 2017).

20. Moni Basu, "Why Indian-Americans Win Spelling Bees: P-R-A-C-T-I-C-E," CNN, May 29, 2015, http://www.cnn.com/2015 /05/29/us/spelling-bee-south-asians/index.html.

21. Vauhini Vara, "Bee-Brained: Inside the Competitive Indian-American Spelling Community," *Harper's*, May 2017, https://harpers .org/archive/2017/05/bee-brained/.

22. *Breaking the Bee* website, http://www.breakingthebee.com.

Chapter 4: Gen Z Kids

1. "2 Sisters, 2 Spectacular Spellers: Championship Spelling Runs in Shivashankar Family," KMBC News, June 2, 2010, https://www .kmbc.com/article/2-sisters-2-spectacular-spellers/3660256.

2. "Behind the Bee Day 3: Being a 'Legacy,'" YouTube video, 2:37, posted by *Kansas City Star*, May 28, 2015, https://www.youtube.com /watch?v=dQ3U-oGbHY4.

3. For further discussion, see Jennie Bristow, *The Sociology of Generations: New Directions and Challenges* (London: Palgrave Macmillan, 2016).

4. David Costanza, "Can We Please Stop Talking About Generations as If They Are a Thing?" Slate, April 13, 2018, https://slate.com /technology/2018/04/the-evidence-behind-generations-is-lacking.html.

5. For example, see June Edmunds and Bryan S. Turner, "Global Generations: Social Change in the Twentieth Century," *British Journal of Sociology* 56, no. 4 (2005): 559–577, or Mark McCrindle and Emily Wolfinger, *The ABCs of XYZ: Understanding the Global Generations* (Kensington, Australia: University of New South Wales Press, 2010).

6. Richard Fry, "Millennials Projected to Overtake Baby Boomers as America's Largest Generation," Pew Research Center, March 1, 2018, http://www.pewresearch.org/fact-tank/2018/03/01/millennials -overtake-baby-boomers/.

7. Jeffrey S. Passel and D'Vera Cohn, "Immigration Projected to Drive Growth in U.S. Working-Age Population Through at Least 2035," Pew Research Center, March 8, 2017, http://www.pewresearch .org/fact-tank/2017/03/08/immigration-projected-to-drive-growth -in-u-s-working-age-population-through-at-least-2035/.

8. In March 2018, Pew changed the cutoff year from 1997 to 1996. See Michael Dimock, "Defining Generations: Where Millennials End and Post-Millennials Begin," Pew Research Center, March 1, 2018, http://www.pewrescarch.org/fact-tank/2018/03/01/defining -generations-where-millennials-end-and-post-millennials-begin/.

9. "The Whys and Hows of Generations Research," Pew Research Center, September 3, 2015, http://www.people-press.org/2015/09/03 /the-whys-and-hows-of-generations-research.

10. Neil Howe, "Introducing the Homeland Generation," *Forbes*, October 27, 2014, https://www.forbes.com/sites/neilhowe/2014/10/27 /introducing-the-homeland-generation-part-1-of-2/#7a42e0342bd6.

11. Stephen Dupont, "Move Over Millennials, Here Comes Generation Z: Understanding the 'New Realists' Who Are Building the Future," Public Relations Tactics, Public Relations Society of America, May 1, 2015, http://apps.prsa.org/Intelligence/Tactics/Articles/view/11057/1110 /Move_Over_Millennials_Here_Comes_Generation_Z_Unde#.

WMwdABD6dyU; Bruce Horovitz, "After Gen X, Millennials, What Should Next Generation Be?", *USA Today*, May 4, 2012, http://usatoday30.usatoday.com/money/advertising/story/2012-05-03/naming-the-next-generation/54737518/1; and Cheryl Russell and New Strategist Press editors, *American Generations: Who They Are and How They Live*, 8th ed. (New York: New Strategist Press, 2013).

12. John Palfrey and Urs Gasser, *Born Digital: Understanding the First Generation of Digital Natives* (New York: Basic Books, 2009).

13. Kathryn Dill, "7 Things Employers Should Know About the Gen Z Workforce," *Forbes*, November 6, 2015, https://www.forbes.com/sites/kathryndill/2015/11/06/7-things-employers-should-know-about-the-gen-z-workforce/#5eceffe9fad7.

14. Sonia Livingstone, *Children and the Internet: Great Expectations, Challenging Realities* (Cambridge, UK: Polity, 2009).

15. Nikhil Vimal, "An 18-Year-Old Who Just Graduated High School Explains Which Apps Gen Z Is Currently Obsessed With," *Business Insider*, August 12, 2017, https://www.businessinsider.com/an-18-year-old-explains-which-apps-gen-z-loves-2017-8; Sparks & Honey, "Meet Generation Z: Forget Everything You Learned About Millennials," PowerPoint published on LinkedIn, June 17, 2014, https://www.slideshare.net/sparksandhoney/generation-z-final-june-17/5-A_generation_with_disposable_income5Gen.

16. *Childtasticbooks: Great Books for Great Readers*, http://childtasticbooks.wordpress.com.

17. *Hagan's World of Awesome*, http://hagansworldofawesome.blogspot.com/.

18. Amanda Hess, "The New Bedtime Story Is a Podcast," *New York Times*, March 10, 2017, https://www.nytimes.com/2017/10/03/arts/kids-podcast-panoply-pinna.html.

19. Grace Masback, "5 Ways That Gen Z Is Changing the World," *Huffington Post*, March 26, 2017, https://www.huffingtonpost.com/grace-masback-/5-ways-that-gen-z-is-changing-the-world_b_9547374.html.

20. Neil Howe and William Strauss, *Millennials Rising: The Next Great Generation* (New York: Vintage, 2000).

21. Fry, "Millennials Projected to Overtake."

22. Jean Twenge, *Generation Me: Why Today's Young Americans Are More Confident, Assertive, Entitled—and More Miserable Than Ever Before*, revised and updated edition (New York: Atria, 2014) 97.

23. Paul Taylor and the Pew Research Center, *The Next America: Boomers, Millennials, and the Looming Generational Showdown* (New York: PublicAffairs, 2016).

24. Neil Howe and William Strauss, *Millennials Go to College: Strategies for a New Generation on Campus*, 2nd ed. (Great Falls, VA: LifeCourse Associates, 2007).

25. Pew Research Center, "Millennials in Adulthood: Detached from Institutions, Networked with Friends," March 7, 2014, http://www.pewsocialtrends.org/2014/03/07/millennials-in-adulthood.

26. Taylor, *The Next America*.

27. Robin Marantz Henig, "What Is It About 20-Somethings?" *New York Times Magazine*, August 18, 2010, http://www.nytimes.com/2010/08/22/magazine/22Adulthood-t.html?pagewanted=all&_r=0.

28. Peter Kelly, "Generation Y: Flexible Capitalism and New Work Ethics," in *Handbook of Youth and Young Adulthood: New Perspectives and Agendas*, edited by A. Furlong (London: Routledge, 2009), 399–405.

29. Malcolm Harris, *Kids These Days: Human Capital and the Making of Millennials* (New York: Little, Brown and Company, 2017).

30. Fifty-six million Millennials were represented in the labor force, compared with 53 million Xers. Richard Fry, "Millennials Are the Largest Generation in the U.S. Labor Force," Pew Research Center, April 11, 2018, http://www.pewresearch.org/fact-tank/2018/04/11/millennials-largest-generation-us-labor-force/.

31. Magid Generational Strategies, *The First Generation*; Sparks & Honey, "Meet Generation Z."

32. Masback, "5 Ways That Gen Z."

33. Alex Williams, "Move Over, Millennials, Here Comes Generation Z," *New York Times*, September 18, 2015, https://www.nytimes.com/2015/09/20/fashion/move-over-millennials-here-comes-generation-z.html.

34. Dupont, "Move Over Millennials."

35. Masback, "5 Ways That Gen Z."

Chapter 5: Parents of Gen Z Kids

1. Neil Howe, "Meet Mr. and Mrs. Gen X: A New Parent Generation," AASA: The School Superintendents' Association, http://www.aasa.org/SchoolAdministratorArticle.aspx?id=11122.

2. Amy Chua, *Battle Hymn of the Tiger Mother* (New York: Penguin Press, 2011).

3. Robert Klara, "5 Reasons Marketers Have Largely Overlooked Generation X," *Adweek,* April 4, 2016, http://www.adweek.com/brand-marketing/5-reasons-marketers-have-largely-overlooked-generation-x-170539/.

4. William Strauss and Neil Howe, *13th Gen: Abort, Retry, Ignore, Fail?* (New York: Vintage, 1993) 59–61.

5. Paul Taylor and George Gao, "Generation X: America's Neglected 'Middle Child,'" Pew Research Center, June 5, 2014, http://www.pewresearch.org/fact-tank/2014/06/05/generation-x-americas-neglected-middle-child.

6. Margot Hornblower, "Great Xpectations of So-Called Slackers," *Time*, June 9, 1997, http://content.time.com/time/magazine/article/0,9171,986481,00.html.

7. Stanford News Service, "Generation X Not So Special: Malaise, Cynicism on the Rise for All Age Groups," news release, based on research presented by Eric Rice and David Grusky at the meeting of the American Sociological Association, 1998, http://news.stanford.edu/pr/98/980821genx.html.

8. Abby Ellin, "Preludes: A Generation of Freelancers," *New York Times*, August 15, 1999, http://www.nytimes.com/1999/08/15/business/preludes-a-generation-of-freelancers.html.

9. Sandra L. Colby and Jennifer M. Ortman, "Projections of the Size and Composition of the US Population: 2014 to 2060, Population Estimates and Projections," US Census Bureau, Current Population Reports, March 2015, p. 2, https://www.census.gov/content/dam/Census/library/publications/2015/demo/p25-1143.pdf.

10. Judith Treas and Christopher Steven Marcum, "Diversity and Family Relations in an Aging Society," in *Handbook of Sociology of Aging*, ed. R. A. Settersten Jr. and J. L. Angel (New York: Springer, 2011), 132.

11. Steve Gillon, *Boomer Nation: The Largest and Richest Generation Ever and How It Changed America* (New York: Free Press, 2004), 5.

12. Daniel Belgrad, *The Culture of Spontaneity: Improvisation and the Arts in Postwar America* (Chicago: University of Chicago Press, 1998), 224.

13. Twenge, *Generation Me*.

14. This will be the case in all three older age group categories (ages 65 and older, ages 85 and older, and ages 100 and older): while native-born older adults in these three age groups are projected to increase by 57 percent, 123 percent, and 163 percent, respectively, the corresponding increases for foreign-born older adults in these age groups are 173 percent, 200 percent, and 200 percent, respectively. James H. Johnson Jr. and Allan M. Parnell, "The Challenges and Opportunities of the American Demographic Shift," *Generations: Journal of the American Society on Aging* 40, no. 4 (2016): 9–15.

15. "A Demographic Snapshot of South Asians in the United States," South Asian Americans Leading Together (SAALT), December 2015, http://saalt.org/wp-content/uploads/2016/01/Demographic-Snapshot-updated_Dec-2015.pdf.

16. Daya S. Sandhu and Jayamala Madathil, "South Asian Americans," in *Culturally Alert Counseling: A Comprehensive Introduction*, vol. 1 (Thousand Oaks, CA: Sage Publications, 2007), 357.

17. Zaynah Rahman and Susan J. Paik, "South Asian Immigration and Education in the U.S.: Historical and Social Contexts," *Social and Education History* 6, no. 1 (2017): 36.

18. Min Zhou, Anthony C. Ocampo, and J. V. Gatewood, "Contemporary Asian America: Immigration, Demographic Transformation, and Ethnic Formation," in *Contemporary Asian America: A Multidisciplinary Reader*, 3rd ed., ed. Min Zhou and Anthony C. Ocampo (New York: New York University Press, 2016), 101–128.

19. Tamara M. Valentine, "Asian Indian Immigrants," in *Encyclopedia of American Immigration*, vol. 1, ed. Carl L. Bankston, III (Pasadena, CA: Salem Press, 2010), 79.

20. A 2013 Pew Research Center report notes that Asian countries are now the source of about three-quarters of these temporary visas as of 2011. In that year, India accounted for 72,438 of the 129,134 H-1B visas granted, or 56 percent. "The Rise of Asian Americans," Pew Research Center, April 4, 2013, http://www.pewsocialtrends .org/2012/06/19/the-rise-of-asian-americans/.

21. Rahman and Paik, "South Asian Immigration," 31.

22. "A Demographic Snapshot of South Asians in the United States."

23. Asian Indian: 3,982,398 (+/-41,908); Pakistani: 518,769 (+/-22,240); Bangladeshi: 187,816 (+/-16,352); Nepalese: 140,319 (+/-10,332); Sri Lankan: 59,946 (+/-7,293); Bhutanese: 23,882 (+/-5,668). Source: US Census Bureau, 2015 American Community Survey 1-Year Estimates, Asian Alone or in Any Combination by Selected Groups, https://www .census.gov/history/pdf/acs15yr-korean62017.pdf.

24. Margaret Mead and Rhoda Bubendey Métraux, *Margaret Mead: Some Personal Views* (London: Angus and Robertson, 1979) 107.

25. Michael Thompson and Teresa Barker, *The Pressured Child: Freeing Our Kids from Performance Overdrive and Helping Them Find Success in School and Life* (New York: Random House, 2005).

26. Wendy S. Grolnick and Kathy Seal, *Pressured Parents, Stressed-Out Kids: Dealing with Competition While Raising a Successful Child* (Amherst, NY: Prometheus Books, 2008).

27. Madeline Levine, *The Price of Privilege: How Parental Pressure and Material Advantage Are Creating a Generation of Disconnected and Unhappy Kids* (New York: HarperCollins, 2008).

28. Madeline Levine, *Teach Your Children Well: Why Values and Coping Skills Matter More Than Grades, Trophies, or "Fat Envelopes"* (New York: HarperCollins, 2012).

29. Alice Iorio, *Champion Parenting: Giving Your Child a Competitive Edge* (Bloomington, IN: Westbow/Thomas Nelson, 2010).

30. Emma Parry, ed., *Generational Diversity at Work: New Research Perspectives* (New York: Routledge, 2014), 2.

31. Marilyn S. Wesner and Tammy Miller, "Boomers and Millennials Have Much in Common," *Organization Development Journal* 26, no. 3 (2008): 89–96.

32. Corey Seemiller and Meghan Grace, *Generation Z Goes to College* (San Francisco: Jossey-Bass, 2016), 4.

33. Neil Howe, "Revisiting the Homeland Generation," LinkedIn, July 31, 2015, https://www.linkedin.com/pulse/revisiting-homeland-generation-part-1-2-neil-howe.

34. GeoSpell Academy website, www.geospell.com.

35. Ibid., 5.

36. Ibid., 231–236.

37. Caroline Cunningham, "Q&A with 'Tiger Mom' Amy Chua," *Washingtonian*, February 11, 2015, https://www.washingtonian.com/2015/02/11/qa-with-tiger-mom-amy-chua/.

38. Chua, *Battle Hymn*, 236.

39. Cunningham, "Q&A with 'Tiger Mom' Amy Chua."

40. Anna S. Lau and Joey Fung, "Commentary: On Better Footing to Understand Parenting and Family Process in Asian American Families," *Asian American Journal of Psychology* 4, no. 1 (2013): 71–75.

41. Minkyeong Shin and Y. Joel Wong, "Beyond the Tiger Mom: Asian American Parenting and Parent-Child Relationships," in *Parenting: Challenges Practices and Cultural Influences*, ed. Peter Barberis and Stelios Petrakis (New York: Nova, 2013), 103–122.

42. Grace H. C. Huang and Mary Gove, "Asian Parenting Styles and Academic Achievement: Views from Eastern and Western Perspectives," *Education* 135, no. 3 (2015): 389–397.

43. Ibid., 393–394.

Chapter 6: Bee Week

1. W. Hampton Sides, "Killer Bees," *Washington Post*, May 30, 1993, https://www.washingtonpost.com/archive/lifestyle/magazine/1993/05/30/killer-bees/d905871d-d9d4-4ca4-8b6c-4d8423f3c56d/?utm_term=.a11c0e2953a6.

2. Noor Al-Sibai, "Here's How Many Ties There Have Been in the History of the Scripps National Spelling Bee," *Bustle*, May 27, 2016, https://www.bustle.com/articles/163498-heres-how-many-ties-there-have-been-in-the-history-of-the-scripps-national-spelling-bee.

3. Lewin, "The Bee, the New Celebrity Showcase."

Chapter 7: Becoming Elite

1. Anders Ericsson, *Peak: Secrets from the New Science of Expertise* (New York: Eamon Dolan/Houghton Mifflin Harcourt, 2016).

2. Shana Lebowitz, "A Top Psychologist Says There's Only One Way to Become the Best in Your Field—but Not Everyone Agrees," *Business Insider*, February 14, 2018, https://www.businessinsider.com/anders-ericsson-how-to-become-an-expert-at-anything-2016-6.

3. Allan Wigfield and Jenna Cambria, "Students' Achievement Values, Goal Orientations, and Interest: Definitions, Development, and Relations to Achievement Outcomes," *Developmental Review* 30 (2010): 1–35.

4. Angela Lee Duckworth et al., "Deliberate Practice Spells Success: Why Grittier Competitors Triumph at the National Spelling Bee," *Social Psychology and Personality Science* 2, no. 2 (2011): 174–181.

5. Aige Guo, "Competition Preparation and Deliberate Practice: A Study of the 2005 National Spelling Bee Finalists" (dissertation, University of Toledo, 2006).

6. Geoff Nunberg, "What's a Thamakau? Spelling Bee Is More About Entertainment Than English," NPR, June 11, 2015, http://www.npr.org/2015/06/11/413645991/whats-a-thamakau-spelling-bee-is-more-aboutentertainment-than-english.

7. Adam Gopnik, "How to Raise a Prodigy: Can Achievement Be Engineered?" *New Yorker*, January 29, 2018, https://www.newyorker.com/magazine/2018/01/29/how-to-raise-a-prodigy.

8. Lizzie Fiedelson, "Inside the High-Drama World of Youth Competition Dance," *New York Times*, December 21, 2017, https://www.nytimes.com/2017/12/21/magazine/inside-the-high-drama-world-of-youth-competition-dance.html.

9. John Leland, "The Littlest Chess Champions," *New York Times*, April 22, 2016, https://www.nytimes.com/2016/04/24/nyregion/the-littlest-chess-champions.html.

10. Isabel Fattal, "How to Parent an Olympic Athlete," *Atlantic*, February 8, 2018, https://www.theatlantic.com/family/archive/2018/02/how-to-parent-an-olympic-athlete/552743/.

11. Gopnik, "How to Raise a Prodigy."

12. Maria Castro et al., "Parental Involvement on Student Academic Achievement: A Meta-analysis," *Educational Research Review* 14 (2015): 33–46.

13. Yoko Yamamoto and Susan D. Holloway, "Parental Expectations and Children's Academic Performance in Sociocultural Context," *Educational Psychology Review* 22, no. 3 (2010): 189–214.

Chapter 8: Making Spellebrities

1. Amy Goldstein, "The National Spelling Bee's Moment," ESPN, June 2, 2011, http://sports.espn.go.com/espn/commentary/news/story?id=6615595.

2. Mac Nwulu, "Viewers Can Test Their Skills with Enhanced ESPN3, Watch ESPN Coverage of Spelling Bee," ESPN Front Row, May 26, 2015, http://www.espnfrontrow.com/2015/05/viewers-can-test -their-skills-with-enhanced-espn3-watchespn-coverage-of-spelling-bee/.

3. Seward, "Why ESPN Is So Good."

4. Quoted in Mac Nwulu, "Scripps National Spelling Bee: Spellbinding Drama on ESPN2, ESPN3," ESPN Front Row, May 29, 2012, http://www.espnfrontrow.com/2012/05/scripps-national-spelling-bee -spellbinding-drama-on-espn2-espn3/.

Chapter 9: Professionalizing Childhoods

1. Polina Marinova, "18 Under 18: Meet the Young Innovators Who Are Changing the World," *Fortune*, September 15, 2016, http:// fortune.com/2016/09/15/18-entrepreneurs-under-18-teen-business/.

2. Jennifer Post, "9 Companies Founded by Amazing Young Entrepreneurs," *Business News Daily*, December 29, 2016, https://www .businessnewsdaily.com/5051-young-entrepreneurs.html.

3. Jillian D'Onfro and Tess Danielson, "Ranked: The 20 Most Influential Vine and YouTube Stars Under 21," *Business Insider*, December 11, 2015, //www.businessinsider.com/the-20-most-viral-social -media-stars-under-21-2015-12.

4. Post, "9 Companies."

5. Tom Foster, "These Nine Organizations Are Turning Kids into Entrepreneurs," *Inc.*, February 27, 2017, https://www.inc.com/tom-foster /how-kids-become-entrepreneurs.html.

6. Ian Shapira, "The National Spelling Bee's New Normal: $200-an-Hour Teen Spelling Coaches," *Washington Post*, May 30, 2017, https://www.washingtonpost.com/local/the-national-spelling-bees -new-normal-200-an-hour-teen-spelling-coaches/2017/05/30/cc8 eb8de-4228-11e7-adba-394ee67a7582_story.html.

7. Threading Twine website, http://www.threadingtwine.org /#home.

8. Susan Koshy, "Neoliberal Family Matters," *American Literary History* 25, no. 2 (2013): 344–380.

9. Corinne Kirchner, "The Word is Egalitarian," *Contexts* 7, no. 1 (2008): 61–63.

10. Quoted in "Indian-Americans' Spelling Bee Win Draws Racial Remarks," *Times of India*, May 30, 2014, http://timesofindia .indiatimes.com/nri/us-canada-news/Indian-Americans-spelling-bee -win-draws-racial-remarks/articleshow/35794405.cms.

11. "ADL Condemns Hateful Messages Labeling National Spelling Bee Winners 'Non-Americans,'" ADL, May 30, 2014, http://www .adl.org/press-center/press-releases/discrimination-racism-bigotry/adl -condemns-hateful-messages-labeling-spelling-bee-winners.html# .U5zpQKhU0tw.

12. Joe Heim, "Indian Americans Dominate the National Spelling Bee: Why Should They Take Abuse on Social Media for It?" *Washington Post*, May 25, 2015, http://www.washingtonpost.com/ local/indian-americans-dominate-national-spelling-bee-then -slurred-on-internet/2015/05/25/8ec01098-f414-11e4-bcc4-e8141e5eb0c9 _story.html.

Conclusion: Gen Z Futures

1. Magid Generational Strategies, *The First Generation*, 10.

2. Colby and Ortman, "Projections of the Size," 1–13.

3. Passel and Cohn, "Immigration Expected to Drive."

4. Fry, "Millennials Projected to Overtake."

Index

Credit: Kholood Eid

Shalini Shankar is professor of Anthropology and Asian American Studies at Northwestern University. A Guggenheim fellow and National Science Foundation grant recipient, she is the mother of two Gen Z children. Shankar splits her time between Evanston, Illinois, and Brooklyn, New York.